A HISTORICAL GUIDE TO
Ralph Ellison

HISTORICAL GUIDES
TO AMERICAN AUTHORS

A Historical Guide to Ernest Hemingway
Edited by Linda Wagner-Martin

A Historical Guide to Walt Whitman
Edited by David S. Reynolds

A Historical Guide to Ralph Waldo Emerson
Edited by Joel Myerson

A Historical Guide to Nathaniel Hawthorne
Edited by Larry Reynolds

A Historical Guide to Edgar Allan Poe
Edited by J. Gerald Kennedy

A Historical Guide to Henry David Thoreau
Edited by William E. Cain

A Historical Guide to Mark Twain
Edited by Shelley Fisher Fishkin

A Historical Guide to Edith Wharton
Edited by Carol J. Singley

A Historical Guide to Langston Hughes
Edited by Steven C. Tracy

A Historical Guide to Emily Dickinson
Edited by Vivian R. Pollak

A Historical Guide to Ralph Ellison
Edited by Steven C. Tracy

A
Historical Guide
to Ralph Ellison

EDITED BY
STEVEN C. TRACY

OXFORD
UNIVERSITY PRESS

2004

OXFORD

UNIVERSITY PRESS

Oxford   New York

Auckland   Bangkok   Buenos Aires   Cape Town   Chennai
Dar es Salaam   Delhi   Hong Kong   Istanbul   Karachi   Kolkata
Kuala Lumpur   Madrid   Melbourne   Mexico City   Mumbai   Nairobi
São Paulo   Shanghai   Taipei   Tokyo   Toronto

Copyright © 2004 by Oxford University Press, Inc.

Published by Oxford University Press, Inc.
198 Madison Avenue, New York, New York 10016

www.oup.com

Oxford is a registered trademark of Oxford University Press

Library of Congress Cataloging-in-Publication Data
A historical guide to Ralph Ellison / edited by Steven C. Tracy.
p. cm.— (Historical guides to American authors)
Includes bibliographical references and index.
ISBN 0-19-515250-6; 0-19-515251-4 (pbk.)
1. Ellison, Ralph—Criticism and interpretation.   2. African Americans
in literature   I. Tracy, Steven C. (Steven Carl), 1954–   II. Series.
PS3555.L625 Z73 2004
813'.54—dc22   2003015965

1 3 5 7 9 8 6 4 2
Printed in the United States of America
on acid-free paper

For Cathy, Michelle, and Michael

Acknowledgments

The contributors to this volume are all scholars for whom I have the greatest admiration and people who have made major contributions to the study of African-American literature. As we continue to study Ralph Ellison, as we continue to grapple with the social, political, and aesthetic issues that Ellison raised in his work, it is comforting to know that these scholars will be among the grapplers and among those who will be teaching the future scholars who will study Ellison's work. To Robert Butler, Maryemma Graham and Jeffery Mack, Lawrence Jackson, William Maxwell, Alan Nadel, and James Smethurst, I extend my sincerest thanks for their participation in this project.

Those of us who study the work of Ralph Ellison owe a debt of gratitude to the scholars who preceded us or who are working alongside us in the field. The work of such scholars as Houston Baker, Kimberly Benston, Robert Bone, Mark Busby, Ron Gottesman, John Hersey, George Kent, Kerry McSweeney, Robert G. O'Meally, Berndt Ostendorf, Susan Resneck Parr, John M. Reilly, Eric Sundquist, Joseph Trimmer, and many others continues to inspire with the richness and nuance of insight these scholars bring to their work. We would be remiss without acknowledging the valuable work of John Callahan, Ellison's literary executor, who continues to edit and discuss Ellison's work with a careful and discerning critical sensibility.

My job as a critic has been made much easier through the support and critical acumen of my colleagues in the Department of Afro-American Studies at the University of Massachusetts, Amherst. My discussions with James Smethurst, Esther Terry, and Michael Thelwell regarding issues related to Ellison's work have been infinitely enlightening. Ernest Allen has been a much-needed advisor and helper with computer issues related to generating this text, for which he has my utmost gratitude. Finally, a good bit of the work that went into the editing of this manuscript was accomplished while I was on sabbatical from the University of Massachusetts, Amherst. I extend my appreciation to Dean Lee Edwards and the university for the opportunity to have the sabbatical time to work on the manuscript.

Special thanks go to Elissa Morris and Jeremy Lewis at Oxford University Press for guiding me carefully and sympathetically through the maze of the publishing world. Linda Seidman and William Thompson assisted me with researching photos from the Special Collections and Archives at the University of Massachusetts, Amherst, W. E. B. Du Bois Library.

The first several times I read *Invisible Man*, it was with the guidance of Angelene Jamison-Hall, Arlene A. Elder, and Wayne C. Miller, each of whom guided me through the material in significant ways. Edgar Slotkin, whose courses in folklore and other subjects always galvanized me, helped provide context for me to understand the folkloric elements of the text. I offer thanks to these teachers for their passion, guidance, and support.

I would also like to express my appreciation to Arnold Rampersad. His support and answers to a variety of queries have made work on this project easier. Ellison scholars look forward to his forthcoming work on Ellison.

Finally, all honor to Ralph Ellison, whose insight and artistry continue to amaze and delight with each rereading of his works. By approaching the lives of African Americans and the calling of creative writing with a broad understanding, an earnest commitment to humanity and to American ideals, and a pursuit of an adequate craft and skill to produce his body of work, he helped ensure that serious consideration of important issues concerning race and democracy would not recede from the American radar screen. I hope this volume helps ensure that his work does not fade from consideration as well.

Contents

Abbreviations

CE   *The Collected Essays of Ralph Ellison*. New York: Modern Library, 1995.

FH   *Flying Home and Other Stories*. New York: Random House, 1996.

GT   *Going to the Territory*. New York: Random House, 1986.

IM   *Invisible Man*. 1952. Reprint. New York: Vintage, 1989.

J   *Juneteenth*. New York: Random House, 1999.

SA   *Shadow and Act*. New York: Random House, 1964.

TT   *Trading Twelves: The Selected Letters of Ralph Ellison and Albert Murray*. New York: Modern Library, 2000.

A HISTORICAL GUIDE TO
Ralph Ellison

Introduction

Steven C. Tracy

I

In the year 1913, Harriet Tubman died. For more than six decades of her more than ninety years, she was so connected to the tribulations of nineteenth-century slavery and freedom that many people today are surprised to learn that she lived into the twentieth century. She may have seemed almost anachronistic to some by that time, this fearless Black Moses so symbolic of the indomitable human will to live unfettered. Tubman, the willful, flesh-and-blood woman of the fields, was a tender of human souls. She helped build and operate a railroad, not of steel and wood, not on the backs of immigrant workers, but of love and compassion and on behalf of the poor and downtrodden. Can the anti-Semitic Henry Ford, who asserted, "Anything which is economically right is morally right" (Martin 180), and who established his automotive assembly-line production technique in 1913, say the same? And what would Tubman, the conductor of souls on the underground railroad, make of Niels Bohr's 1913 theory of atomic structure, which explored the scientific and technical explanation of the nature of existence, as she struggled with more immediate human concerns of compassion and decency? Tubman, who led human beings safely out of bondage, whose life was the art of humanity—what would she have made of the primitivistic and mechanistic art of Stravinsky's 1913 *Le Sacre du Printemps* or the cubist and postimpressionist art of the 1913 Armory Show in New York, especially in light of the contemporary characterizations of Africans and African Americans as primitive "others" themselves? And how would she have responded to the celebrated generosity of the Rockefeller Institute, established in 1913, when the philanthropy was funded by a "robber baron" trust king who was for some synonymous with unscrupulous rapacity, exploitation, and greed (though he was known to provide copious funds for the education of African Americans)? Harriet Tubman bore witness to the continuing dilemma facing Americans regarding the unresolved race issues brought about by slavery, proof that these issues of humanity and brotherhood and personal sacrifice had not simply gone away, and were not simply irrelevant, in an age when Ford was asserting that "there is something sacred about big business" (Martin 180).

Fifty-one African Americans were lynched in that same year, 1913, the year Ralph Ellison was born.[1] The lyrics of an old blues song go, "One of these days, I'm gonna build me a railroad of my own." Harriet Tubman had built a railroad of her own, and would have built another, or perhaps simply laid some new track on her time-tested original, in response to the events described above. The twentieth century needed another humanitarian effort in order for Tubman to be able to attempt to control her own fate and allow others to control theirs by having the opportunity to create their own avenues of mobility. Harriet Tubman, the blues lyric, and manifestations of the train-as-spiritual-deliverer motif in spirituals and gospel music—all are part of the inspiration for Ralph Ellison's own literary journey, one which expanded the horizons of literary taste and aesthetic appreciation by traveling through the canonical terrain in a unique, insightful, eye-opening way that emphasized African-American creativity and humanity in the face of dehumanizing circumstances. It was part of the historical continuity of African-American experience that Ellison reflects in his work, as were the industrial, scientific, artistic, and philanthropic issues he confronted from his own African-American humanistic perspective in the stories, novels, essays, and interviews that make up his compact but weighty output.

2

> I'm gon get up in the mornin, I
> believe I'll dust my broom.

On 5 August 1951, Elmore James recorded those words for Trumpet Records in Jackson, Mississippi. He had gotten the words and distinctive boogie guitar figure from the Mississippi blues tradition via fellow musician Robert Johnson, who recorded the piece in 1936. But Elmore had now identified the song with his personal fingerprints, pointing toward a new generation of broomdusters who would imitate and, if they were good, make James's song their own. It is an interesting element of dusting one's broom that, however fresh a start we intend by making the proverbial clean sweep of things, we are still carrying that old broom and our habitual style of sweeping with us. There are continuities even in the cleanest breaks.

Exactly a year and a week later, Random House published Ralph Ellison's *Invisible Man*. In the novel, Ellison was recounting the story of the South-to-North migration of an intelligent but naïve young African American in a racist and duplicitous landscape, from a perspective in the post–World War II era that would vault unavoidably into the national consciousness through school desegregation court cases, bus boycotts, lunchroom counter sit-ins, and civil rights marches within a few years after release of the book. Certainly, it was a story that had been told before, in language that had been used before, with a cultural context that had been portrayed before. But Ellison made the story his own, taking the tradition but modifying it with his individual talent, as Eliot's essay described it, to bring Frederick Douglass, Herman Melville, Booker T. Washington, Fyodor Dostoevski, W. E. B. Du Bois, Marcus Garvey, leftist politics, Langston Hughes, Richard Wright, André Malraux, spirituals, jazz, blues, and a host of other elements into his own particular focus and style, making the African American an undeniable part of the national identity. He was aided by a prodigious technique and discipline—two elements he would emphasize in his critical pronouncements on art—but above all by probing intelligence, fertile imagination, and a vision of American ideals and possibilities that allowed him to unify a diverse array of materials and experiences into an unsettling but coherent whole.

Over a half century later, readers are still being unsettled by and seeking coherence in Ellison's work—a mark of Ellison's continued relevance and enduring artistry. Ellison, of course, neither began nor ended his career with his novel *Invisible Man*, yet it has continued to be the focal point of readers and critics from the time of its publication in 1952, through publication of his collections of essays *Shadow and Act* (1964) and *Going to the Territory* (1986), the appearance of various Hickman stories from his projected second novel over a period of fifteen years, and the posthumous appearance of his *Collected Essays* (1995), short story collection *Flying Home and Other Stories* (1996), the much-anticipated second novel assembled by John Callahan, *Juneteenth* (1999), and *Trading Twelves: The Selected Letters of Ralph Ellison and Albert Murray* (2000). Ellison, never lacking for critics in his own lifetime given his early leftist radicalism, high-profile intellectualism, and acknowledgment of Euro-American influences; the remarkable sensation created by *Invisible Man*; and his refusal to walk in lockstep with critics and artists of the Black Arts movement and beyond, has nonetheless weathered all of the criticism, both negative and positive, and found his place as a canonical writer who forced alteration of the canon to accommodate his own syncretistic brand of artistic brilliance. If *Invisible Man* is his pièce de résistance—not just his most important work but his refusal to capitulate to the visions of others regarding his work—his essays, stories, and letters, as well as his ill-fated novel *Juneteenth*, are all of a piece with that piece. They merit our attention, not just for how they illuminate *Invisible Man*, but for how they illuminate, in their own right, the world as Ellison saw it, and the world as we continue to see it today.

Just how can we account for the conflicting responses to Ellison's work? On the one hand, *Book Week* in 1965 and *Wilson Quarterly* in 1978 named *Invisible Man* the best American novel published since World War II, and the Modern Library list of the best twentieth-century novels put *Invisible Man* at number nineteen. On the other, John O. Killens's 1952 review vilified the book as a "vicious distortion of Negro life" (Butler xxii), and a 1968 *Negro Digest* poll found many young black writers (dis)regarding Ellison either negatively or as of marginal importance. Indeed, Ernest Kaiser dubbed Ellison an "Uncle Tom" in a 1967 essay (Reilly 11), and Ellison experienced quite a bit of heckling in the 1960s when he appeared at literary conferences. Jerry Gafio Watts's *Heroism and the Black Intellectual* (1994) is the most recent major manifestation of such negative assessments, and, in his comments for the PBS American Masters series, Amiri Baraka's praise for Ellison's abilities is qualified by his criticism of Ellison's "backward thinking" with regard to his social and political ideas. The answer does not play out simply in black and white. Irving Howe, for example, was a prominent white Ellison detractor, while Larry Neal turned an about-face and praised and defended Ellison's work in his famous essay "Ellison's Zoot Suit."

The key seems to be in the sociopolitical postures of the critics, translated into positive or negative literary judgments about how Ellison portrays elements of African-American life, identified by Neal as being based in a "specific body of Marxian and Black Neo-Marxist thought" (31). Given the political climate in the forty years following publication of the novel, it is not surprising to find Ellison's stock rising and falling in the gradual or sudden gusting of social change. From the anticommunism of the McCarthy era, the postwar emergence of the Civil Rights era, the upheaval of assassinations, the rise of the Black Power movement, the disillusionment of the Watergate era, the championing of multiculturalism as a positive American value, and the trickle-down conservatism of the Reagan years, historical events have both reflected and created turmoil that caused different segments of the public to view Ellison's works from different and shifting perspectives. For example, while for some, Ellison's anticommunist stance seemed a major issue when *Invisible Man* was published, in a world that has seen the fall of communism in

Eastern Europe and the dismantling of the Berlin Wall, it seems to some readers in some ways less relevant. The Brotherhood in *Invisible Man* has become, rather, merely a temporal stand-in for any self-interested, cynicism-inducing, manmade sociopolitical movement, though the historical realities of Ellison's experience and stance are, of course, significant. Furthermore, Ellison's words written for a 1944 issue of *Antioch Review* (not published)— seeking "the creation of a democracy in which the Negro will be free to define himself for what he is and, within the larger frame-work of that democracy, for what he desires to be" (*SA* 304)— seem rather obvious now to the American public at large, whereas at the time they would have shocked or angered many. On the other hand, the notion of working within and accepting the framework of the values of American democracy is far from palatable to others in a world where global relativism has cast a jaundiced eye on American imperialism and McDonaldism.

Ultimately, Ellison has been subject to the same responsibili-ties (and burdens) that all other African-American writers have shouldered, including a kind of sociopolitical responsibility to advance the cause of African Americans in all that he writes. Of course, just how one does that—and whether one should have to—has been a topic of debate and continues to factor into the reputations of African-American writers as a canon has been es-tablished. It has also resulted in the welcome revisitation of a number of neglected writers, among them Jessie Fauset and Nella Larsen, who suffered charges of middle-class gentility until critics emerged who read their works with a keener eye. How-ever, as African-American writers and their works have become more high profile since the 1960s, Ellison has been joined in his lofty status by a variety of novelists—Zora Neale Hurston, Alice Walker, and especially Nobel Laureate Toni Morrison among them—each of whom has taught readers to be sensitive to feminist/womanist issues in works by both men and women. Thus the emergence of African-American women novelists has caused us to examine again Ellison's work for his portrayals of the lives of women. And, as historical times change, we will find newer perspectives from which to examine the work, just as the cubists in the Armory Show in the year of Ellison's birth sought various perspectives from which to examine and portray their world.

3

In 1993, the year before Ralph Ellison died, Toni Morrison won the Nobel Prize for literature. She was the first African American to win the prize, honored for the six novels, a play, and the literary and social criticism that she had generated up to that time. Her most recent novel prior to the Nobel Prize, *Jazz* (1992), is a Harlem Renaissance–era story of violence, death, and reconciliation that casts a characteristic interdisciplinary net with its mixture of a blues and jazz "soundtrack," jazzlike improvisatory ambience, and Faulknerian concern with point of view and the impingement of historical events and their interpretations upon the present. That year, Morrison also published *Playing in the Dark: Whiteness and the Literary Imagination*, which brilliantly examines how white canonical American literary texts situate themselves in relation to blackness, continuing her concern with the ways in which perspective influences our subjective understanding and portrayal of history. In her output, Morrison demonstrates a remarkable breadth, as a creative artist, literary critic, and historical, social, and cultural commentator whose work reveals both timely contemporary and timeless aesthetic dimensions.

It is not difficult to see the concerns and achievements of Ralph Ellison's career as preparing the way for Morrison's achievements and recognition, though he is not, of course, her sole literary ancestor. Ellison, too, dealt with the violence, death, and reconciliation, personal, social, and political, so much a part of African-American and American—human—existence. The practical and spiritual uses of African-American vernacular cultural traditions, especially folklore and music, most especially jazz, were central to his subjects and aesthetic concerns, highlighting an interdisciplinary cross-pollination that is reflected in his work. Joseph T. Skerrett, Jr., for example, sees an explicit connection between Ellison's Peter Wheatstraw and Morrison's character Pilate in *Song of Solomon*, both nurturing but enigmatic repositories of communal folk wisdom (199). Ellison had an abiding interest in considering a broader context for his work and the lives of African Americans. In particular, Ellison explored how he, as an African American, was both portrayed and influenced by those who were not born African Americans, and what that reflected about American cultural and political ideals and actualities nearly two centuries after the Declaration of Independence and the Constitution set the bar at a level not yet vaulted, and perhaps never to be, though we can, as Ellison urges, always hope. Certainly his critical commentary on Mark Twain, Stephen Crane, T. S. Eliot, Ernest Hemingway, William Faulkner, and others, in such essays as "Twentieth-Century Fiction and the Mask of Humanity," "Change the Joke and Slip the Yoke," "Stephen Crane and the Mainstream of American Fiction," and "What America Would Be Like without Blacks," written from the 1950s to the 1970s, has resonated and provoked discussion and debate over the years, and finds a counterpart in Morrison's *Playing in the Dark*. Just as Ellison had endeavored to assert the absolute centrality of African Americans to the definitions of whiteness, America, and freedom—and an "American aesthetic"—through the Liberty Paints episode in *Invisible Man*, where black drops give the paint its crucial, core whiteness, Morrison reexamines those issues in the arguments of her critical work in the 1990s. Ellison's own dialogue with Faulkner is carried out in the technique, language, and subject matter of both *Invisible Man*, as explored by Michael Allen, Alan Nadel in this volume, and others, and in the posthumously published *Juneteenth*, which was, of course begun in 1954 and occupied his attention for the next forty years. And he maintained a commitment to the highest standards of his craft as a writer that is clearly evident in Morrison's work. Ellison's sense of purpose, broad and vigorous intellect and critical acumen, passionate commitment to craft, sense of aesthetics growing from his individual take on the high standards of the African-American creative community, honoring of sustaining and healing traditions, and ardent belief in humanity in the wake of horrific inhumanity are all characteristic of Morrison's work as well. Although these elements are not exclusively Ellisonian, his towering reputation and high visibility in the American literary canon mark him as a figure with whom subsequent authors must reckon.

In response to a question put to him by Robert Stepto in 1977 regarding Leon Forrest's comment that Forrest, James McPherson, Toni Morrison, Albert Murray, and Ellison may have belonged to a literary "crowd," Ellison responded that he may have shared "ideas and certain goals" with several of those writers, but added, "I don't know Miss Morrison personally," and he did not comment specifically on their artistic affinities (Butler 10). Other critics have sensed a connection between Ellison's work and that of Morrison, from Trudier Harris's assertion that Morrison's Stamp Paid in *Beloved* created an alternative reality "that Ralph Ellison identified with the ingenuity that shaped black folk tradition" (330), to Valerie Smith's that Morrison's characters, "like Ralph Ellison's Invisible Man, inhabit a world where inhospitable social assumptions obtain," though without the option of living underground (274), to Michael Awkward's feeling that Morrison's output represents a feminist revision of such precursors as Ellison and Baldwin (177, 180–81). Reviewer Brooke Allen compared the style of Morrison's *Paradise* to the work of Ellison and Eugene O'Neill in her 1998 review of that novel (6). Morrison herself posited Ellison as an "elder" in "Rootedness: The Ancestor as Foundation" (343), commented to Charles Ruas that she admired Ellison's work "enormously" (96), and in conversation with Gail Caldwell specifically mentioned Ellison and Zora Neale Hurston as writers who "went before" (244). In 1999, five years after Ellison's death, Morrison weighed in on the publication of *Juneteenth* in praise of Ellison's "generosity, humor, and nimble language," but most especially his "vigorous intellect" and "majestic narrative concept." Not only that, but her spirited reading of a section from the newly published novel on 18 June 1999, a portion of which is included in the Ralph Ellison American Masters biography from PBS, demonstrates her warm appreciation of Ellison's distinctive voice, intellect, and vision in this much-anticipated, posthumously assembled and published work. It is the appreciation of a Nobel Laureate for an author whose output, perhaps too small to attract Nobel recognition, is nonetheless among the most influential literary bodies of work in the twentieth century. Ellison's work is influential by virtue of those qualities that Morrison praises in *Juneteenth*; by virtue of its experimentation; by virtue of its engagement with important social, political, and aesthetic issues in a way that connects the individual to the various groups to which he or she belongs in a symbiotic relationship; and by virtue of the fact that it is a multifaceted reading experience—by turns elegant, bawdy, playful, and deathly serious, steeped reverentially in both vernacular and high culture. And always so brimming with a pastiche of varied human ideas, attitudes, and passions that it seems to breathe—sometimes yearningly, sometimes fitfully, sometimes excitedly, sometimes wearily, and, yes, even sometimes a bit long-windedly—on its own.

4

The essays written for this volume all attempt to place Ralph Ellison in the context of the turbulent times in which he lived, marking how he was both shaped by and helped shape his world. Ellison was particularly attuned to the forces of history and their effects on African Americans as they sought to overcome the historical limitations of their existence in social, political, and economic terms, while bringing with them the art forms that had helped them survive and transcend through a simultaneously communal and individualistic aesthetic that had already affected an unwitting America. At the same time, Ellison embraced what he found useful and beautiful about cultures other than African American, placing himself in a historical and aesthetic context that was as broad as his ability to read, feel, and confront. Understanding Ellison in these terms—in his present, embracing his past, and imagining his future, all the while trying to rewrite and overcome the imposed and imposing present, past, and future—is central to Ellison's own endeavor, as it is to ours in this volume.

In "'Creative and Cultural Lag': The Radical Education of Ralph Ellison," William J. Maxwell examines the origin and nature of Ellison's education as a "black radical." Maxwell roots

Ellison's leftist interests in his impoverished youth and young adulthood in the midst of America's worst depression as well as in his Harlem associations with writers Langston Hughes, Richard Wright, and Angelo Herndon, and links his political education to his aesthetic roots in African-American music. After a lengthy association with communism, during which Ellison built up an impressive corpus of work (later "buried" after the release of *Invisible Man*), Ellison made a turn toward anticommunism but remained influenced by the education the party gave him "in the intimate dialectic of belatedness and vanguardism" that informed the structure of *Invisible Man* and Ellison's activities in Harlem. Thus, Maxwell asserts, Ellison's novel is not sharply divided between communist and anticommunist periods, but informed in the ruminations about history by this dialogue initiated for Ellison in his period of communist involvement.

A high school and college musician and music major with dreams of composing Wagnerian scores, Ellison made it apparent in numerous essays, stories, letters, and his novels that African-American vernacular music was central to his life and work. Though he didn't believe that a thorough knowledge of folklore, for example, was essential to understanding his work as long as the work was approached without preconception, clearly Ellison's very personal connections to the music make a thorough knowledge of the music and Ellison's perceptions of it extremely useful in helping the reader appreciate much more deeply Ellison's craft with regard to the choices he made for his work. "A Delicate Ear, a Retentive Memory, and the Power to Weld the Fragments" focuses on how Ellison employs both classical and vernacular music aesthetically and sociopolitically in his work, set in the context of attitudes toward the music and musicians at the time. By employing both "sacred" and "secular" vernacular music with great frequency in his work, Ellison underscores the importance of both to the community and to his art and emphasizes the power of the music to move and instruct in ways that many did not dream were possible in vernacular music at the time.

James Smethurst's "'Something Warmly, Infuriatingly Feminine': Gender, Sexuality, and the Work of Ralph Ellison" considers how the work of previous critics dealing with these issues in Ellison's work sometimes seems at odds over Ellison's portrayals of women and gender roles. However, their seemingly contradictory conclusions regarding these issues are not in fact incompatible. After examining the gender politics of Ellison's essays, Smethurst turns to the intersections of race and gender in the novel, finding that Ellison's neomodernist and postmodernist strategies for examining the workings of gender and sexuality in *Invisible Man*, considered within the feminist, Marxist, and Cold War contexts for the novel, support the conclusion that while there are virtually no positive portrayals of women in Ellison's novel, they are crucial to its artistic and ideological meaning.

Alan Nadel's "The Integrated Literary Tradition" identifies Ellison as a modernist committed in his work to the vision and practice of integration, both in the American literary tradition and as a moral imperative in American life. Ellison's explorations and applications of his realist, naturalist, and modernist forebears are informed by his realization that the presence of Africans in America implicitly and explicitly challenged America's lofty self-definition. For Ellison, America's greatest canonical writers struggled at some point with this moral dilemma in their own work, as Ellison did in his. From the vantage point of contemporary 1940s interpretations of works by Melville and Twain, Nadel explores how Ellison uses these literary ancestors in his own work. Nadel's considerations of autobiographies by Frederick Douglass, Booker T. Washington, and W. E. B. Du Bois, and fiction by James Weldon Johnson, Richard Wright, Fyodor Dostoevski, and particularly William Faulkner examine how Ellison emulates and revises both black and white writers from the integrated American literary tradition. Finally, Nadel sees Faulkner as "Ellison's white artistic counterpart . . . working to create an American literary identity reflective of its multiracial legacy commensurate with the American historical and regional identity that provided Faulkner's driving impetus."

Ellison biographer Lawrence P. Jackson offers an interesting take on Ellison's attention to his literary reputation in his lifetime in "Ralph Ellison's Politics of Integration." Ellison, through his critical essays and professional activities, helped transform the nature of the response to *Invisible Man* and his position in the American literary canon in relation to social, political, and literary pressures facing him as an embattled African-American artist whose success in canonical terms created an artistic burden that affected his work in the 1950s and 1960s. In the essay, Jackson explores how Ellison responded to the attacks by African-American writers and critics whose negative responses, countered by his success in the white literary community, served in many ways to separate Ellison artistically from his African-American contemporaries. Ellison's willingness to embrace notions of the importance of "artistic standards" over ideological expression, defense of the relevance of the novel as an artistic form, individual theory of American cultural life, and applicability to the New Critical enterprise effectively elevated his literary profile and made him a voice of "moderation" in a politically volatile time. However, because Ellison "insisted on the value of the artistic achievement residing in the representational relationship of art to a true empirical reality, an ideal mimesis, and, on another level, the existence of that ideal outside the mediation of critical discourse," his failure to produce a larger fictional body of work and his increasing publication of criticism provides an ironic twist to his career. Along the way, Jackson touches on issues confronting African-American authors in relation to mainstream acceptance through his exploration of ideological versus New Critical responses to Ellison's achievement, the relation of racial identity to national identity, Ellison's desire to create, perhaps, a universal comment on human identity in the closing line of the novel, and a shift in the interpretation of the final thrust of the novel's ideological and aesthetic consciousness by diverting attention away from the celebratory notion of limitless possibilities in African-American culture and toward the sense that individual values are what will ultimately produce success. Of course, not everyone will agree that Ellison was so consciously manipulative of his legacy, but the issues with which Jackson deals place Ellison squarely in the midst of some of the contentious issues of his time, and they continue to demand our attention today.

Though Ellison reminisced about his early years in a variety of essays and interviews, more specific details concerning his life are just beginning to emerge as scholars begin to focus on biographical information in our quest to understand how he arrived at his mature vision. With Lawrence Jackson's biographical treatment of Ellison up to the release of *Invisible Man* and Arnold Rampersad's authorized biography in the works, scholars will have a much better grasp of the forces operating in Ellison's life. Maryemma Graham and Jeffery Dwayne Mack offer in their biographical essay a sense of Ellison's world from his origins in Oklahoma to his prominence on the international literary stage. Robert J. Butler's bibliographic essay, "Probing the Lower Frequencies: Fifty Years of Ellison Criticism," examines the critical responses to Ellison's work over the years as they have reflected sociopolitical and aesthetic tastes influenced by historical events. As Butler notes, much work remains to be done not only on *Invisible Man*, but also on those works that are now being collected and disseminated—the stories, uncollected essays, *Juneteenth*—so that Ellison's complete achievement and legacy can be explored and understood.

NOTE

1. In his recent biography, Lawrence P. Jackson points out that, although Ellison's birthday is traditionally given as 1 March 1914, the absence of a birth certificate leaves room for doubt. The source of the 1914 birth date is an affidavit signed by a family friend in 1943 used by Ellison to enter the Merchant Marine. However, all formal records before that time, including the 1920 Census of Oklahoma, Douglass School Transcript, Tuskegee Application and Transcript, and 1938 Connecticut Certificate of Marriage, indicate a birth date of 1913. As such, the 1913 date will be used throughout this text, including places where Ellison's age is given, such as the celebration of his eighty-first (not eightieth) birthday.

WORKS CITED

Allen, Brooke. "The Promised Land." *New York Times*, 11 June 1998, 6.

Allen, Michael. "Some Examples of Faulknerian Rhetoric in Ellison's *Invisible Man*." In *The Black American Writer*. Vol. 1, edited by C. W. E. Bigsby. Baltimore, Md.: Penguin, 1971.

American Masters series. "Ralph Ellison: An American Journey." PBS, 2002.

Awkward, Michael. "'The Evil of Fulfillment': Scapegoating and Narration in *The Bluest Eye*." In *Toni Morrison: Critical Essays Past and Present*, edited by Henry Louis Gates, Jr., and K. A. Appiah, 175–209. New York: Amistad, 1993. 175–209.

Butler, Robert. *The Critical Response to Ralph Ellison*. Westport, Conn.: Greenwood, 2000.

Caldwell, Gail. "Author Toni Morrison Discusses Her Latest Novel, *Beloved*." In *Conversations with Toni Morrison*, edited by Danille Taylor-Guthrie, 239–45. Jackson: University Press of Mississippi, 1994.

Harris, Trudier. "Escaping Slavery but Not Its Images." In *Toni Morrison: Critical Essays Past and Present*, edited by Henry Louis Gates, Jr., and K. A. Appiah, 330–41. New York: Amistad, 1993.

Martin, Jay. *Nathaniel West: The Art of His Life*. 1970. Reprint. New York: Carroll and Graf, 1984.

Morrison, Toni. "Rootedness: The Ancestor as Foundation." In *Black Women Writers: 1950–1980*, edited by Mari Evans, 339–45. New York: Doubleday, 1984.

Neal, Larry. "Ellison's Zoot Suit." *Black World* 20, no. 2 (Dec. 1970): 31–50.

Reilly, John M., ed. *Twentieth-Century Interpretations of* Invisible Man. Englewood Cliffs, N.J.: Prentice Hall, 1970.

Ruas, Charles. "Toni Morrison." In *Conversations with Toni Morrison*, edited by Danille Taylor-Guthrie, 93–118. Jackson: University Press of Mississippi, 1994.

Skerrett, Joseph T., Jr. "Recitation to the Griot: Storytelling and Learning in Toni Morrison's *Song of Solomon*." In *Conjuring: Black Women, Fiction, and Literary Tradition*, edited by Marjorie Pryse and Hortense J. Spillers, 192–202. Bloomington: Indiana University Press, 1985.

Smith, Valerie. "*Song of Solomon*: Continuities of Community." In *Toni Morrison: Critical Essays Past and Present*, edited by Henry Louis Gates, Jr., and K. A. Appiah, 274–83. New York: Amistad, 1993.

Stepto, Robert B., and Michael Harper. "Study and Experience: An Interview with Ralph Ellison." In *The Critical Response to Ralph Ellison*, edited by Robert J. Butler, 3–16. Westport, Conn.: Greenwood, 2000.

Ralph Ellison, 1913–1994

A Brief Biography

Maryemma Graham and Jeffery Dwayne Mack

When one thinks of the African-American writers who began writing in the period just before the flowering of the Civil Rights movement in the mid-1950s, one most often thinks of Richard Wright, Ralph Ellison, and James Baldwin. Of the three, it was Ellison who found through language a way of encompassing the strange and the familiar and who inspired a new confidence in the infinite possibilities of black folk expression. Although he could trace his lineage, like Wright, to the black belt South, he was decidedly not one of its products. Neither was he descended, like Baldwin, from the great mass of African Americans who headed north during the Great Migration. Ralph Ellison, with the telltale middle name of Waldo, was a midwesterner, a lineage he very proudly claimed, one that by his own admission gave new and by no means unproblematic meaning to the categories "black" and "American." A staunch advocate of the rugged individualism he inherited from his Oklahoma childhood, Ellison brought a unique perspective to the literature he began to create in the 1930s. It was a perspective he honed while living in Harlem, the place that took him in when he had to leave a southern black college penniless, forsaking his degree. He remained true to Harlem, living most of his life there, refusing many opportunities to repatriate for greater freedom abroad.

Ralph Ellison is best known for his novel, *Invisible Man*, which appeared two years before the 1954 *Brown v. Board of Education* decision, the event marking the advent of the Civil Rights movement. The book, like its author, had taken America by storm. But Ellison would spend the next forty years working on a second novel that would match his first. In his own mind, he had failed; in the eyes of much of the world, he would always be the author of one of the greatest books of all times, a modern classic, one by which much of contemporary black *and* white American writing continues to be judged. Who was this writer whose sensibility was so different, who forced us to challenge fixed notions of race and race writing in America? How did he become one of our most revered writers? Not surprisingly, the man that Ellison was is not always consistent with the legend that he became. Whether man or legend, however, Ellison was nothing if not one of America's most troubled literary icons. Keenly aware of the paradoxical nature of race relations in America, he earned his reputation honestly, but he remained forever uncomfortable with it. By the time he died on 16 April 1994, of pancreatic cancer, he had spent a lifetime engaging this paradox, giving expression to the various registers of blackness, allowing art and the imagination to invent a new synergy.

Ellison had learned early to trust the soundness of art and to recognize the registers of blackness. The man who came to occupy such a central place in America's literary culture was born on 1 March 1913, the first of two children, to Lewis and Ida Millsap Ellison, transplants to Oklahoma City from the South. Lewis and Ida were a proud, ambitious couple, who had tried one place, then another, before joining the migration of Exodusters to Oklahoma and Kansas. The move was a declaration of independence, for the Ellisons had grown up in the shadow of slavery, and Lewis especially had inherited his father's strong beliefs. Interestingly, it is his grandfather, rather than his father, that Ellison evokes in the opening scene in *Invisible Man*. We recall the narrator's quandary upon hearing his grandfather's "advice" uttered from the deathbed, words that maintain a haunting presence throughout the novel: "Live with your head in the lion's mouth. I want you to overcome 'em with yeses, undermine 'em with grins, agree 'em to death and destruction, let 'em swaller you till they vomit or bust wide open" (*IM* 16). Like so many other episodes in the novel, this one hardly seems real, an untranslatable gibberish that foregrounds the novel's ironic tone.

Ellison never saw his grandfather Alfred, but his affinity for such a man in his own family does not seem surprising. Two generations earlier, Alfred Ellison, who was born and lived his early life as a slave, knew well the meaning and heavy cost of freedom. Alfred was illiterate, but he used his early connections to powerful white allies to earn him political positions in Abbeville, South Carolina, during Reconstruction. Freed early by his master's widow, Mary Ann Ellison, Alfred became a constable, marshal, and magistrate (Jackson 3). When the sudden end of Reconstruction curtailed his political career, Alfred returned to driving a dray and chopping cotton while his wife, Harriet, worked as a washerwoman. Alfred's political defeats did not diminish his assertive spirit, defiance, and strong sense of his own place in society, qualities that his son and his grandson would claim as their own.

Lewis, Ellison's father, had been a soldier in Cuba, the Philippines, and China. But his career was cut short as well. In 1901, he was found guilty of insubordination and was remanded to the stockades of Presidio de Manila for two years. He received the charge because he refused to perform drills carrying a full backpack, giving the reason that he was recovering from malaria. The explanation was deemed unacceptable, and he was given a dishonorable discharge from the army (Jackson 9). Still not discouraged, he moved to Chattanooga, Tennessee, where he joined the westward movement. Three years before their first son was born, Lewis and his young wife, Ida Millsap, moved to Oklahoma. Within a short time, Lewis's enterprising spirit had paid off. He was his own boss in a business selling ice and coal.

As if anticipating their son's own desire for individuality, if not his future fame, his parents chose the names Ralph Waldo, thinking, of course, of Emerson, the noted American writer. Life for young Ellison was turbulent at first. Blacks who moved to the

West went primarily because of the promise of a future life devoid of racial discrimination. They would have to fight hard for their freedoms, and Ida Ellison did so through the platform of the Socialist party. This fighting spirit and the promise of possibility contributed to Oklahoma's frontierlike atmosphere, fostering a sense of freedom and the realization of human potential, two themes that would permeate Ellison's work. His experiences in Oklahoma allowed him to create his own heroes who embodied self-determination.

When their second son, Herbert, was born, the Ellisons became even more dedicated to providing their children with an enriched life. Unfortunately, malpractice and an accident cost Lewis his life. He died of an abscess of the liver in 1916. Ellison was only three years old, and his mother, now widowed, soon became destitute. Ida moved her two sons to the Avery Chapel African Methodist Episcopal church parsonage, where she lived in as a domestic. This did not prevent her from cultivating her oldest son's artistic side by bringing home records, books, and magazines. When he was four, Ellison went with his brother to South Carolina to visit his grandparents. The experiences of the Deep South, like those in Oklahoma, encouraged Ellison to look at his own family's life and that of his extended family as sacred, filled with wonderful memories of places, persons, sounds, and textures, all of which would provide the raw materials for his work.

The cross-cultural interaction among blacks, whites, and Native Americans was relatively commonplace in Oklahoma City. Ellison could identify with an array of people, including the heroes in the stories he heard while working in J. D. Randolph's pharmacy on Deep Second Street, in the heart of Oklahoma City's black community. These stories reinforced some of the frontier tales, which gave him heroic models, such as "gamblers and scholars, jazz musicians and scientists, Negro cowboys and soldiers from the Spanish-American and First World Wars, movie stars and stunt men, figures from the Italian Renaissance and literature" (SA xv–xvi).

He also interacted with actors like Richard B. Harrison. Whenever the Bunting Repertory Company came to town, Miss

Clark, the maid to the English actress Emma Bunting, stayed with the Ellisons. Through Miss Clark, Ellison met Harrison, who had made the role of De Lawd in *Green Pastures*. Ellison's fascination with the arts, especially music, was made apparent early. In 1919, he entered the Frederick Douglass School, where he was able to develop his passion for music. His exposure to music theory with Mrs. Zelia N. Breaux, music supervisor for Oklahoma City's Negro schools, gave him the foundational training that he needed. Although he studied the soprano saxophone, the trumpet, and other brass instruments, it was his proficiency as a trumpeter that garnered him invitations to play for religious, social, and school functions throughout the city and for special productions at Oklahoma City's Aldridge Theater.

Ellison admired the elegance, artistic discipline, and infinite capacity for self-expression that were for him the hallmarks of the jazz musicians. These men and women were the heroes and heroines of Oklahoma City's Second Street, the "Deep Deuce." At the Aldridge Theater and at Slaughter's (a public dance hall), Ellison heard Ma Rainey, Ida Cox, King Oliver, the Blue Devils (later the Count Basie Band), Walter Page, Oran "Hot Lips" Page, Eddie Durham, and Jimmy Rushing. In 1933, his accomplishments as a trumpeter earned him a state scholarship to Tuskegee Institute. He left for Tuskegee to study military and classical music with the hope of becoming a more versatile musician and a symphonic composer. He dreamed of writing a symphony encompassing his varied experiences: as a poor black boy who never felt inferior to anyone because of race or class, as a frontier boy with a certain city slickness, and as a classically trained musician who, steeped in blues and jazz, wanted to capture their rocking power in classical form (Busby 6).

At Tuskegee, he gained two music mentors: noted composer William L. Dawson, dean of the music school, and Hazel Harrison, head of the music department. Harrison introduced him to Alain Locke, professor of philosophy at Howard University. Locke, a leading figure in the Harlem Renaissance, visited the college in 1936. Later, he would be instrumental in introducing Ellison to Langston Hughes. Hughes, in turn, would introduce Ellison to Richard Wright. But until then, Ellison studied music, playing first chair in the trumpet section and occasionally serving as the band's director at Tuskegee.

His exposure to the arts did not stop with music, however. He played a leading role in a campus play, and he experimented with painting, photography, and sculpture. His sophomore English instructor, Morteza Drexel Sprague, head of the English department, guided his reading, but he discovered, on his own, T. S. Eliot's *The Waste Land*. Eliot's poem would be a powerful influence, partly because of its elusiveness and depth of feeling. Ellison described it as being "caught up in a piece of poetry which moved me but which I couldn't reduce to a logical system" (*GT* 39). He could relate to Eliot because he saw him as both a poet and a jazz musician. For these artists to be effective, they had to have a thorough understanding of their background and a willingness to improvise upon it (*GT* 40). The encounter with Eliot marked the beginning of his literary career. "It was . . . my transformation (or shall we say, metamorphosis) from a would-be composer into some sort of novelist" (*GT* 40), Ellison would later recall.

He was changing and learning a lot in the South and at Tuskegee. Of his experiences there, Ellison noted that the environment encouraged movement away from individuality and toward commonality. The youth of the South, he observed, were conditioned not to reach beyond certain limits: "Much of the education that I received at Tuskegee (now, this isn't quite true of Oklahoma City) was an education *away* from the uses of the imagination, *away* from the attitudes of aggression and courage" (*GT* 65). These limitations seemed to come from within the black community. Individualism had to be discarded as a matter of survival. When an entire community could be punished for the actions of individuals, blacks in the South learned a method of survival that at the same time compromised their creativity, Ellison felt.

Facing expulsion from school for lack of funding—due to some confusion over his scholarship, he was unable to pay the $40 tuition or room and board—and frustrated with the South's racist and anti-intellectual attitudes, Ellison left for New York in his third year. A poem by Richard Wright in the *New Masses* in-

spired him to go in search of the author and perhaps to save
enough money for school. In the summer of 1936, Ellison moved
to New York, looking for what he thought would be summer
employment to earn enough money to return to Tuskegee in the
fall. Summer turned into one year, then another, and he tried a
variety of things, including one year of studying sculpture with
Augusta Savage and Richmond Barthé.

Ellison arrived in Harlem on 4 July 1936. To him, Harlem
was a magical place filled with wonderful music and style. For
most of his first year there, Ellison worked behind the food bar
of the Harlem Annex of the YMCA, where he roomed. At
that time, he still had plans to return to Tuskegee. Like many
struggling artists, he took a series of odd jobs to support himself
while he worked on his craft. One such job was a temporary
receptionist/file clerk position for Harry Stack Sullivan, a psycho-
analyst. Although his employment lasted only for a few months,
what he read in the patient files inspired him to look at dreams
and at ways they could be used in fiction. In Harlem, however, no
one looked at him as if he were going out of his mind. If anything, he was surrounded by people like himself, fellow artists
and writers. But twelve years later, Ellison would describe life in
Harlem as living in the "bowels of the city," a "ruin, . . . over-
crowded and exploited politically and economically" (SA 295–96).
The city was a place replete with contradictions and chaos, and
his fiction developed under the influence of these observations.
Ellison had come to realize that the social limitations present in
the South were also in the North. Ellison thought of himself as
"having to enact, touch-and-go, the archetypal American role of
pioneer" (GT 148), in that he had to discover, for himself, the social restrictions present in the North. The only difference in the
South was the overt segregation that made it easier for a young
African American to navigate the terrain. In the North, those
forms of segregation and restriction were much less explicit.

By the late 1930s, he had given up the trumpet and had begun
to focus more on writing. It was not the first time he had heard
the call, Ellison would later write. The real beginning had been
in high school:

It must've been around the eleventh grade, I had a very bad cold that just clung to me. The school nurse, Miss Waller, saw me on the street one day—I was still coughing—and she made me go to a lung clinic at one of the hospitals. I had to wait in a reception room with all these obviously ill people. I was rather horrified and I began to try to describe what was going on to some of the people who were around me. I was doing it in the style, I thought, of O. O. McIntyre, who was a syndicated columnist who used to appear in the Oklahoma City papers. I remember that as a first doodling with writing. The next thing I did was to set to verse a thing on the swamp country by the Southern writer Albion Tourgée. I took this to the American literature teacher and he looked at me as though I had gone out of my mind, because I hadn't shown too much interest in the class itself. It was nothing that I did consciously or with any intensity, but those were the beginnings. (Graham and Singh 89)

Although Ellison would insist later that Richard Wright was "no spiritual father," he was one of his major influences. Ellison met Alain Locke again while residing at the Harlem YMCA. Locke was a familiar face among the writers and artists, and Ellison was soon to be among them as well. With Langston Hughes, Ellison shared an appreciation for African-American vernacular culture; with Richard Wright, he shared the southern experience. Ellison considered that he and Wright were both intellectuals struggling to create art during the Great Depression; a close friendship quickly formed between them.

Ellison began shaping his own stories and essays in response to Wright. The relationship was mutually beneficial. Ellison was a momentary reprieve from the turbulent working environment Wright experienced at the Harlem bureau of the *Daily Worker*, the communist newspaper. For Ellison, on the other hand, Wright was an encouraging teacher, mentoring an apt pupil's work, seeing to it that Ellison landed his first publication opportunity. Almost immediately, Ellison began reading Wright's works before publication. With Wright's encouragement, Ellison published a book review of Waters Edward Turpin's *These Low Grounds*. The review appeared in the fall 1937 issue of *New Challenge*, a Marxist literary magazine edited by Wright and Dorothy West. Ellison's first short story, titled "Hymie's Bull," which drew upon his experience as a hobo, was to be included in the winter 1937 issue of the magazine. Unfortunately, the short story ended up being replaced by a collection of Margaret Walker's poems. But problems among the editors led to the cancellation of the issue. When the two other editors, Dorothy West and Marion Minus, were unable to resolve the conflict, publication was suspended. Eventually the magazine ceased publication altogether.

On 16 October 1937, after falling off a porch and being misdiagnosed with arthritis, Ellison's mother died of tuberculosis of the hip, the day after Ellison's arrival in Dayton, where his mother had moved with Ellison's stepfather, John Bell, and brother in 1936. Ellison remained in Dayton with his brother, Herbert, and for seven months immersed himself in reading Dostoevski, James Joyce, Gertrude Stein, and Ernest Hemingway. Since he had little money, he and Herbert supported themselves by hunting quail, eating some and selling others. He emerged from that tumultuous period with a new purpose: to write a novel. By the time he returned to New York in late April 1938, Ellison found that the depression had all but depleted opportunities for the patronage of the Harlem Renaissance. With Wright's assistance, Ellison was hired to research and collect facts and folklore for books on "Negro culture" for the Federal Writers Project, where he was employed from 1938 to 1942. While working with the FWP, Ellison struggled with questions of identity, cultural connectedness, and the influence of the past on present culture. Much of what he experienced while working on the project would eventually influence the writing of *Invisible Man*. Because of his careful examination of language, what he learned about folklore and the relationship between identity and the past helped him find his voice. He resigned from the Federal Writers Project in 1942 to edit the *Negro Quarterly*, a leading publication that reviewed black life and culture.

Ellison wrote book reviews for numerous radical periodicals until 1944, including *New Challenge, Direction, Negro Quarterly*, and *New Masses*. Partly because of his own experiences with segregation and poverty, and his mother's involvement in the Socialist party, Ellison was drawn to political writings that encouraged the participation of intellectuals in the redemption of an immoral world ravaged by war and depression. His readings in Marxist thought influenced his work and his political commentary during this period. In his book reviews, he often described black Americans as a nation within a nation, one in which blacks needed some form of united identity, a collective consciousness. This collective consciousness could be nurtured through a national literature, instilling in the black reader not only a race consciousness, but also an awareness of class, thus rallying the working class, of all nationalities, against the bourgeoisie, black and white. Ellison was drawing upon the "black belt thesis," one of the platforms proposed by the Communist party as it worked among national minorities. For Ellison, the responsibility of the black writer was to overcome the restrictions placed on him by a race- and class-conscious society and to teach his readership to do the same. Toward this goal, Ellison's first review, of Turpin's *These Low Grounds* (1937), had been a call for heightened awareness of literary technique and tradition among black writers, focusing on the use of black folklore in writing.

In 1940, Ellison published "Stormy Weather" and in 1941 "Recent Negro Fiction." Both of these essays called for the examination of folklore as a basis for evaluating black literature, which he illustrated in his review of Hughes's *The Big Sea*. He wrote that Hughes's autobiography illustrated the connectedness to one's past that was necessary in order for there to be any semblance of individuality for black writers, separate from white writers. Although he identified Hughes as one of only a few individuals in the New Negro movement who avoided imitating whites and mined the resources of the black vernacular, overall Ellison felt that Hughes's writing was not radical or realistic enough for the black American audience. Ellison felt that Hughes's style and charming simplicity could be viewed as a mask, which put the author at risk for being misunderstood:

> Many *New Masses* readers will question whether [understatement] is a style suitable for the autobiography of a Negro writer of Hughes's importance. In the style of *The Big Sea* too

much attention is apt to be given to the [a]esthetic aspects of experience at the expense of its deeper meanings. To be effective the Negro writer must be explicit; thus realistic; thus dramatic. (Ellison, "Stormy Weather," 20)

Ellison remained somewhat skeptical of "understatement" in fiction. He felt that proper autobiography makes the author responsible for showing the process through which he acquired his artistic consciousness. The objective of the black writer was to recognize that his "consciousness" was attached to the people about whom he wrote. Such recognition would enable them to construct a new way of living in the United States. Thus, the black writer was a constructor of a conscious hero. For example, in 1942, Ellison wrote a review of William Attaway's *Blood on the Forge*, arguing that although Attaway grasped the destruction of folk culture, he did not see the rebirth of the new consciousness necessary to meet the needs of the new environment. Frustrated by this lack of "consciousness" on the part of black leaders, Ellison wrote an unsigned editorial that same year for the *Negro Quarterly*, criticizing the Communist party and urging black leaders to focus more on the needs of the black community.

Although many black intellectuals of the period had been deeply attracted to Marxist ideology and the communist movement because of its promise of equality, in the 1940s Ellison, like others, began to question the party's commitment to the black community. By 1944, Ellison had begun to distance himself from the American Communist party, believing, like many black intellectuals, that they were being reduced to mere pamphleteers. The country was preparing for war; the Great Depression had ended; but the situation for blacks had changed little. The party presented what Ellison called a "shamefaced support" for the armed forces, and many blacks argued that the war against fascism needed to be fought in the United States as well as abroad. Ellison felt that the party emphasized foreign policy over the needs of black Americans, which would eventually lead to their exploitation. Blacks might fight against fascism abroad but were forced to defend a segregated America. Ellison argued that blacks needed to centralize their power, which could be accomplished through the analysis and the utilization of black folklore and language and the heritage, myths, and symbols of the people.

When Ellison joined the U.S. Merchant Marines in 1943, he was responding to this call for centralized power. To avoid being drafted into service in the army, he used his contacts in communist-influenced union circles to gain an appointment on board a merchant marine ship as a second cook and baker. From 1943 to 1945, Ellison remained a cook; he had hit the glass ceiling, finding efforts to move up impossible. He was not accepted into the U.S. Navy band, and he refused to be part of the segregated U.S. Army.

While in the service, he applied for and received a Rosenwald Fellowship to begin his first novel. He outlined a wartime story where a black pilot is shot down, captured by Nazis, and placed in a detention camp where he finds himself the highest-ranking officer and pitted against the white soldiers. Ellison said the purpose of this novel was to explore "what type of democratic relationships are necessary for a highly conscious Negro to function with white men and at the same time exercise the fullest potentialities of his personality" (Busby 15). Except for "Flying Home," the section that critiques American racism, it was never published.

The years between 1939 and 1944 are considered Ellison's fiction-writing apprentice period, according to Mark Busby (22). The eight published short stories—"Flying Home," "Slick Gonna Learn," "The Birthmark," "Afternoon," "Mister Toussan," "That I Had the Wings," "In a Strange Country," and "King of the Bingo Game"—show an evolving aesthetic. Although he acknowledged that his first two stories, "Slick Gonna Learn" and "The Birthmark," were persuasive and propagandistic, he vehemently argued that his "fiction was always trying to be something else; something different even from Wright's fiction" (GT 294). The next three stories, "Afternoon," "Mister Toussan," and "That I Had the Wings," revolve around Buster and Riley, two young boys from the Southwest. These stories, which build on the southwestern experience and black American folklore, represent the hope, promise, and possibility of the black frontiersman that Ellison experienced as a child. Inspired by the frontier myth of freedom, the boys find themselves at odds with their desire to transcend their environment and the restrictions placed on them by a racially charged system and by older blacks who suffer from a postslavery mentality. Through his use of black dialect and folklore, Ellison deepens the texture of black life in America by showing that the Negro is not merely a reflection of white culture but a valuable part of the diverse American experience.

In "Afternoon," first published in *American Writing 1940*, Ellison presents the dual conflict between the boys, Buster and Riley, and the white world in which they live and the restrictions placed on them by other blacks. The story opens on a lazy summer afternoon as the boys are walking down an alley, hitting an apple for a baseball, referencing the hum of the high voltage line, and talking about some bootleggers who had to pour their hooch down the toilet during a police raid. When they finally arrive at Buster's house, Buster is confronted for not helping his mother with the wash. Buster attributes her anger to white folks, thinking, "She was like this whenever something went wrong with her and white folks" (*FH* 42). Riley tries to console Buster by telling him that he should be glad he does not have a mean father like his, one who is mean because of the treatment he received from whites. They fantasize about being like Jack Johnson, the black heavyweight boxer, when they grow up. Finally, they sit, think of Johnson, and watch a wasp glide inside its "grey, honeycomb-like nest" (*FH* 44).

Published in *New Masses* in 1941, "Mister Toussan," Ellison's second Buster-and-Riley piece, emphasizes the boys' imaginative power as well as the dual conflict seen in "Afternoon." In this story, Buster and Riley tell their version of the Haitian hero Toussaint L'Ouverture, who led the slave revolt against Napoleon. As the story opens, Buster and Riley are being chastised by Mr. Rogan for trying to steal cherries from his cherry tree. Later, at Riley's home, the boys sit and hear Riley's mother singing an old Negro spiritual of which Riley had always been contemptuous. Observing a butterfly pass and wishing they had wings to fly away, the boys converse on life elsewhere. Buster says that he would go north, where he could be free. Then Buster begins to talk about Africa and Africans, whom he thinks are "the most lazy folks in the whole world . . . just black and lazy!" (*FH* 25). Riley challenges his stereotypical descriptions, causing Buster to recall the story of "Toussan," the African from "Hayti" who taught the "pecker-woods" a lesson. Their exchange mirrors the call-and-response pattern of a black religious service, and they are empowered by the story of a black man who overcame the oppression of whites, sparking a new assault on Mr. Rogan's cherries.

"That I Had the Wings," the third installation in the Buster-and-Riley selections, first appeared in *Common Ground* in 1943. In this story, Riley watches a mother robin teach her fledgling to fly. After the young robin hesitates, the mother flies to another tree, and the young one tries again, without the mother's encouragement. Riley sees in his own circumstances similarities with the fledgling. He is grounded, like the baby robin, because he had climbed atop the church roof the day before to catch pigeons; he had fallen and was grounded by his aunt as a result. Buster is bored staying in the yard and gets up to leave while Riley sings an improvisation of an old rhyme that calls the Lord's name in vain and sings of being president. His aunt hears him, admonishing accordingly, "Whut yuh think would happen to yo po ma if the white folks wuz to hear she wuz raisin' up a black chile whut's got no better sense than to talk 'bout bein' President?" (*FH* 47). Instead, she advises, they should sing some of the Lord's songs. Riley concludes that his aunt is too old to understand their attitudes. Feeling restricted, the boys begin to discuss the chickens in the yard, specifically Ole Bill, the rooster, whom Riley wants to be like. They give him heroic attributes and compare him to Louis Armstrong and then to Joe Louis. They decide to try to get Ole Bill to fly, but opt to parachute baby chicks from the garage roof instead. The plan is for Buster to drop the chicks from the roof, and Riley is to catch them before they fall to the ground. However, Aunt Kate catches them and shouts at Riley, effectively immobilizing him, which results in the chicks falling to the ground to their deaths. Aunt Kate says, "The Lawd's gonna punish yuh in hellfire for that," and Riley thinks that he's been hexed (61). Shortly afterward, while on his way back to the pen, Ole Bill jumps up on Riley and spurs him.

The final three stories were all published in 1944, and they reflect Ellison's improved, mature writing abilities. In these stories—"In a Strange Country" and "King of the Bingo Game," first published in *Tomorrow*, and "Flying Home" in *Cross Section*—Ellison focuses on themes of racial identity and alienation. His use of irony, symbolism, and African-American folk materials illustrates a difference in the development of character. The focus is no longer on boys but young men, and the characters are more complex, combining realism, myth, folklore, and surrealism, reminiscent of *Invisible Man*.

"Flying Home" is perhaps Ellison's most successful short story. It incorporates many themes, including isolation, racial strife, initiation, and identity. Its particular use of myth and folklore helped to set Ellison apart from the other modernists T. S. Eliot and Ezra Pound, whom he admired greatly. For them, myth had to be elevated to a place of universality and timelessness. Ellison preferred to combine myth with black folklore to historicize his work (Busby 35). In this story, Todd, a black trainee in Alabama, flies too high and strikes a buzzard (Jim Crow); then, he crash lands on the property of a white landowner and breaks his ankle in the process. When he regains consciousness, he is asked by Jefferson, the old black sharecropper on the farm, why he wanted to fly; he is warned that he could be mistaken and shot for a buzzard. Jefferson tells Todd two folktales. One is about seeing two buzzards rising out of a horse's carcass. The second is the 1919 tale of the "Colored Man in Heaven." In it a black man in heaven is given only one wing with which to fly. Although he learns to fly quite well with the one wing, he is eventually expelled from heaven for flying too fast and for disregarding the rules. But while he is there, "[he] was the flyin'est son-of-a-bitch what ever hit heaven!" (*FH* 160). Todd is offended by the story because he suspects that Jefferson is mocking him. When Dabney Graves, the landowner, arrives, he has Todd put in a straitjacket because "you all know you caint let the nigguh git up that high without his going crazy" (171). In the story, Todd struggles with his connection to the poor sharecropper and the racial assumptions that bind them together. Also, the story is a metaphor of the African American's restricted place in American society, and it paved the way for many of the stylistic techniques Ellison used in *Invisible Man*.

Ellison's final short story before he began work full time on *Invisible Man* was "King of the Bingo Game." In this story, the main character discovers a world based on chance and luck. The protagonist is unemployed and desperate for money to pay his wife's medical bills. He cannot get a job because he has no birth certificate, and he laments over the lack of community among the blacks: "But up here it was different. Ask somebody for something, and they'd think you were crazy" (*FH* 124). He enters a bingo game sales promotion at a local movie theater to win the prize money. On stage with the bingo king, the protagonist's luck literally runs out, and he realizes that his struggle for freedom and identity must be waged against history and fate, not individuals and groups. He sees himself as a pawn, a naïve individual who easily accepts the judgments presented to him by other forces, in this case, an indifferent bingo wheel. He sees the harshness of a society that has worked to shape his personality. So, with the spinning of the wheel, the protagonist finds his own identity and is reborn.

In "Flying Home" and "King of the Bingo Game," Ellison began to shift his writing away from protest to self-determinism, in keeping with his new thinking. In both stories, he presents conscious heroes who recognize the relationship between themselves and their environment in order to make sound judgments about culture and self and to better navigate the ever-changing modern world. Ellison had begun to question whether protest fiction could reveal the complexity of black life in America, rejecting the simple cause and effect of protest fiction. Instead his characters would be self-examining, trying to take control of their situations in order to change their fates. This concept of the "conscious hero" foreshadowed the eventual break with many of his literary and political colleagues.

One of the most important of these was Richard Wright. Ellison had praised Wright for being an illustration of the potential of the black community. In "Richard Wright's Blues" (1945), a review of Wright's autobiographical *Black Boy*, Ellison paid homage to Wright by lamenting the absence in America of any "social or political action based on the solid realities of Negro life as depicted in *Black Boy*" (*SA* 94). Likewise, in the review "Recent

Negro Fiction," he praised Wright's *Native Son* (1940) as the first philosophical novel by an American Negro because it possessed an artistry and emotional power that placed it in the front rank of American fiction. Despite the admiration Ellison held for his mentor, by the mid-1940s, the friendship was severely handicapped by what Ellison could only describe as the "anxiety of influence." However, it was not until his critical essays of the 1960s that Ellison made explicit his philosophical and aesthetic differences with Wright. Focusing on *Native Son*, Ellison saw Bigger Thomas as a despairing black figure, whose existence, as limited as it was, was solely determined by the oppression of whites. Ellison acknowledged that Bigger was "designed to shock whites out of their apathy," but he could not accept Bigger as an accurate depiction of black America (*SA* 114). To him, the characterization of Bigger was afflicted by social determinist thinking and Marxist rhetoric. Ellison was concerned that Wright's novel, and ultimately his career, would only perpetuate the myth about black criminality, that Bigger Thomas was the embodiment of what happens to socially victimized black Americans. Ellison had come to reject Wright's theory of naturalism as well as his Marxist ideology. Instead, he turned toward a reality opposite to Wright's, one where social determinism was not the focus. His work would include conscious, self-examining characters unencumbered by the limitations of social determinism.

In 1945, Ellison went to a friend's farm in Waitsfield, Vermont, after having taken a sick leave from the merchant marines because of a kidney infection. He had been working on the war novel but was having trouble finding an appropriate literary form flexible enough to speak to the wide array of American cultural backgrounds. Early one morning in the summer of 1945, he wrote the words "I am an invisible man," echoing the plight of the black American. Initially, he wanted to reject the concept, but he was intrigued by it. It quickly became the conceptual outline of a novel.

Back in New York and now married to Fanny McConnell, whom he had met while in the military, he continued work on the new novel. He worked steadily for five years, while freelancing as a writer, photographer, and electronics technician and taking only one year off to work on another novel. In 1947 the opening chapter of the novel was published as a short story in the British journal *Horizon*, and Ellison finally completed the first draft of the novel while he was staying at the home of Stanley Edgar Hyman and Shirley Jackson in 1951. *Invisible Man* was published to wide acclaim in 1952, heralded as a masterpiece in many quarters. In 1953 it became a bestseller, gained the attention of the literary establishment, and won the National Book Award. The appeal of *Invisible Man* derived from Ellison's use of sophisticated modernist literary techniques in exploring the universal theme of human complexity. Critics praised the novel for its use of folklore, myth, symbol, irony, double entendre, and ambiguity.

One of the book's major themes is the unnamed protagonist's search for identity. The protagonist hopes to become like the residents of the Men's House, who carry the *Wall Street Journal* in one neatly manicured and gloved hand while whipping a tightly rolled umbrella back and forth with the other. The unnamed narrator's association with the Brotherhood toward the end of the novel makes him aware of his double consciousness, viewing himself as an "old self" and a "new self" competing for control. In addition, the plot structure of the novel illustrates Ellison's ability to connect the formal literary strategies within the novel with the larger social question of blackness. The plot recapitulates various stages of the African-American struggle for survival in America, from slavery, to Reconstruction and accommodationism, to the migration north.

Near the beginning of the novel, the young protagonist dreams that the following message is engraved on a document presented to him at his high school graduation: "To Whom It May Concern: Keep This Nigger-Boy Running" (*IM* 26). Throughout the novel, the narrator continues to run, from his term at a southern college to his flight north and the dizzying sequence of events accompanying various brands of political and racial rhetoric in Harlem. The novel presents an array of remarkable characters and circumstances, expressed through different narrative styles, against which the protagonist attempts to define himself. The entire book is narrated from a "hole" in which the protagonist resides and where he thinks about the great black jazz player Louis Armstrong, whom the narrator believes has made poetry out of his invisibility.

As the chronological action of the novel begins, the protagonist witnesses the death of his grandfather, who instructs his son to teach the children how to live a double life, suggesting that their survival depends on it. The protagonist overhears his grandfather's words, but does not understand how they apply to the art of survival. Later, the protagonist is invited to give his graduation speech at an annual smoker held by the town's dignitaries. Before he can give his speech, however, he has to participate in the battle royal, where all the young black boys in attendance are blindfolded and forced to fight one another. By the night's end, the physically, verbally, and psychologically battered protagonist gives his speech, is awarded a calfskin briefcase, and receives a scholarship to the Negro State College.

Once in college, the narrator is dismissed for showing Mr. Norton, a white philanthropist, what the school president, Dr. Bledsoe, considers to be the unsavory elements of the town and the community. Then, in New York, he has a surreal experience at Liberty Paints, where he is involved in a boiler room accident, landing in the factory hospital. There, he receives electric shock treatment. After the doctors make sure he has forgotten his name and family background, he is declared "cured" and released. He is asked to join a group of white radicals called the Brotherhood, where he becomes the group's "new Booker T. Washington," is given a new name and a place to live, and is reminded that he was "hired to talk" but not "to think" (*IM* 307). Ultimately, the narrator realizes that the Brotherhood is just as chaotic, manipulative, and power hungry as all the other groups of people he has met both in the North and in the South. He leaves feeling thoroughly disillusioned and falls down a manhole into an abandoned, bricked-up cellar. There, he examines the contents of his briefcase, which includes not only his diploma but now other mementos from his journey. He realizes how much he has been betrayed by those claiming to support him, suddenly seeing the truth: when a person is associated with either an ethnic group or a social organization, he becomes a person with no identity and, therefore, invisible. He starts to understand the significance of his grandfather's last words. And, at the end of the novel, the narrator creeps into a dark empty cellar to indulge in his reflections.

Despite its wide acclaim, the novel was not without its attackers. Some black readers and those closely connected to left-wing activism were among the loudest critics of the novel. Generally, they felt that the novel failed to affirm humanity. Instead, they felt it focused on trivial aspects of human existence, unlike the characters in Ellison's previous short stories. Critics like Irving Howe, who had celebrated Ellison's earlier characters' fight for individuality, now questioned the Invisible Man's potential to affirm his self-worth. Some critics felt that Ellison was alienated from the African-American community and was using his distorted vision of the black aesthetic as his vehicle to pander to the white elite. Unfortunately, Ellison and Albert Erskine, his editor, had deleted many references that might have spurred revolutionary action or assured black readers of Ellison's progressive politics. These references were eliminated from the final draft for the purpose of gaining greater accessibility to a white audience. However, the momentum of *Invisible Man* greatly outweighed any negative criticism the novel may have received. And Ellison continued to garner national and international acclaim that would solidify his place among the great American writers.

Ellison's life appears to fit conveniently into two parts: before and after *Invisible Man*. The difficulty with this assertion is that although he did not publish another novel during his lifetime, Ellison made more appearances in print after 1952 than before. Eight excerpts from the new work in progress appeared, at least every two years, and two major collections of essays, *Shadow and Act* and *Going to the Territory*, came to be almost as highly revered as the novel. *Invisible Man* may have been the work of a thirty-eight-year-old writer who had intentions of writing more fiction than he did, but Ellison was anything but silent for the remainder of his life.

The year *Invisible Man* won the National Book Award, Ellison published his essay "Twentieth-Century Fiction and the Black Mask of Humanity" (1953), where he criticized the stereotypical depictions of African Americans in American literature. In 1954, he published the short story "Did You Ever Dream Lucky?" and that same year he received the Rockefeller Foundation Award. He was, in addition, enjoying enormous fame and financial success because of *Invisible Man*. Ellison won the Prix de Rome Fellowship awarded by the American Academy of Arts and Letters in 1955 and used the prize money to live in Italy for two years. While in Rome, he began work on the second novel and continued to publish short fiction and essays, including "Society, Morality, and the Novel." But by 1957, he was eager to return to the United States and especially to Harlem. "Living here is the only living that I could do as a novelist," he told Richard Kostelanetz in a 1965 interview:

> I have to hear the language. My medium is language and . . . I have to hear that sounding in my ears, I have to. A place like Harlem . . . has an expressiveness about it which is almost Elizabethan. . . . the language is always feeding back to the past; it's throwing up wisdom, it's throwing up patterns and I never know but when I'm going to hear something . . . which is going to be the making of some piece of fiction that I'm trying to write. (Graham and Singh 91–92)

Ellison was clear; the one and only place for him to write was Harlem. That belief paid off. Dismissing the temptation to remain in Europe, like James Baldwin, Richard Wright, and a host of other established writers, Ellison returned home and made substantial progress on his second novel and was greeted by numerous awards and invitations to teach, lecture, and serve as writer-in-residence at some of the country's most prestigious institutions. But he was especially pleased to be able to become an advocate for the arts.

In 1957, he became vice president of the National Institute of Arts and Letters. He also accepted a teaching appointment at Bard College, where he worked from 1958 to 1961. The year he started at Bard, he published "Change the Joke and Slip the Yoke," a response to Stanley Edgar Hyman's reading of *Invisible Man*. Ellison and Hyman were friends, and it disappointed Ellison that his friend, whom Ellison felt he had properly educated on the plight of African Americans in the United States, would adopt such a distorted reading of Ellison's work. Hyman's reading compelled Ellison to revisit and expound upon the image of blackness in the minds of white America.

Eight years after the appearance of his first novel, Ellison began publishing excerpts of his new novel in progress. In 1960 came the first two installments: "And Hickman Arrives" (*Noble Savage*) and "The Roof, the Steeple and the People" (*Quarterly Review of Literature*). The Hickman piece was his title story, bearing the principal character's name. Critics saw these "sneak previews" as evidence that Ellison was still at the top of his game, and the literary community eagerly awaited the release of his second novel.

Meanwhile, he continued his round of academic appointments: in the winter of 1962, he was the Alexander White Visiting Professor at the University of Chicago; from 1962 to 1964, he was visiting professor at Rutgers; in 1964, he began a stint as a visiting fellow of American studies at Yale. During this period, he also held brief lectureships at Harvard, Columbia, Princeton, and other institutions in the United States and abroad. Other pieces of short fiction, both from his upcoming novel and his past work, appeared during this time. In 1963, he published "It Always Breaks Out" in *Partisan Review*, the third installment of the new novel, and a revision of a story that had once been part of *Invisible Man*, "Out of the Hospital and under the Bar." He was awarded the Russwurm National Newspaper Publishers Award (1963) and honored with an honorary doctorate of humane letters from Tuskegee Institute (1963), from which he had never graduated. Additionally, that same year, a poll of two hundred critics of the *New York Herald Tribune Book Week* chose *Invisible Man* as the most distinguished novel since World War II. A year later, he became vice president of the American P.E.N.

Despite all of this positive attention, for Ellison, the 1960s marked a darker period in his life on many levels. He became increasingly resentful of the way in which *Invisible Man* was being interpreted as "race writing." Although his writing had not slowed down, his social/political views placed him outside the political agenda of the mainstream black community. He was attacked for his moderate views on race. The 1960s were a turbulent time, and an African-centered nationalism quickly replaced the integrationist ethos of a decade earlier. Ellison was denigrated and his work deemed irrelevant to the more activist designs of the period. Ellison's devotion to his craft seemed to make him a target. Generally, his detractors argued that he revered his craft and focused on the complexity of the human experience in America simply to avoid taking a stand against oppression. They felt that he used his art to shield himself from his social obligation to protest. Figures like Amiri Baraka (LeRoi Jones) and Haki Madhubuti (Don L. Lee) challenged Ellison for his lack of involvement in the highly visible Black Power movement and for his seeming disconnection from the concerns of the black community. Baraka went as far as to accuse Ellison of fiddling away his talent by teaching at a college. Ellison's critics could not comprehend the vision of a writer who had evolved as he had. In response to their charges, Ellison went on the offensive by asserting that he was not a separatist, calling himself "unashamedly an American integrationist." Then, white critic Irving Howe published "Black Boys and Native Sons" (1963), praising Richard Wright for writing "protest" works like *Native Son*, and criticizing Ellison's and James Baldwin's work for their lack of the same. Ellison responded to Howe's criticism in his famous "The World and the Jug," in two separate pieces. The first section of the essay bears the title and is the actual response to Howe's article, first appearing in 1963 in *Dissent*, which Howe edited. The second section, originally titled "A Rejoinder," was first published in the *New Leader* in 1964, only after Howe consented to write a reply to Ellison's attack. Both sections were combined and later preserved in *Shadow and Act* (1964), a collection of essays dedicated to Morteza Sprague, the English teacher at Tuskegee who exposed him to modern literature.

It was now twelve years after he had published his major work, and Ellison was still working through his own place as a writer. In the introduction to *Shadow and Act*, Ellison writes that the significance of the collection is to emphasize the writer's need to relate to and understand both his own past history and the present (*SA* xix). The collection draws from interviews, reviews, and Ellison's own experiences from 1942 to 1964. The pieces allow the reader to see the movement of his ideas from the Marxism of the 1930s to the 1960s repudiation of Marxism as well as any philosophy that circumscribes the writer or limits the definitions of African-American life. *Shadow and Act* is "concerned with three general themes: Literature and folklore; Negro musical expression—especially jazz and the blues; and the complex relationship between the Negro American subculture and North American culture as a whole," and it marked Ellison's deliberate attempt at defining the black American experience (*SA* xviii). In these essays, Ellison's broad sweeping approach to interpreting the black experience launches him "full flight into the dark" (*SA* xi), allowing him to illustrate black life through social, political, and cultural lenses. In the introduction, Ellison describes himself as a "frontiersman" in a territory filled with limitless possibilities and freedoms. He explains how he and his friends adopted their renaissance ideal and discusses the importance of jazz in the Southwest. Most important, he describes himself as a writer who entered into the craft only after going through a variety of experiences. The second theme emphasizes the fullness of African-American culture. He denigrates "the notion currently projected by certain specialists in the Negro Problem which characterizes the Negro American as self-hating and defensive" (*SA* xviii). In *Shadow and Act*, and later in *Going to the Territory* (1986), Ellison solidified his views on the complex relationships between race, art, class, and American culture. For example, in "The Art of Fiction," Ellison rejects the purely racial view of art and proposes one that emphasizes the importance of style and form. The initial appeal of the collection was that it offered a glimpse into the hidden Ellison, his autobiography, if you will. The introduction and "Hidden Name and Complex Fate" are largely autobiographical, and other selections highlight his emergence as an individual and as a writer, as does *Going to the Territory*.

In many ways, *Shadow and Act* is a defense of Ellison's social/political position, particularly the charges levied against him by some black nationalist leaders. In his defense, Ellison writes that "protest is an element of all art, though it does not necessarily take the form of speaking for a political or social program" (*SA* 137). He insists that the novelist is a "manipulator and depicter of moral problems." Thus, he does not have to try to escape the reality of black pain. He reminds the reader that he knows well the pain and anger that come with being black, for he experienced it firsthand—his mother had been arrested violating Jim Crow housing laws and he survived the segregationist policies of the South. He merely transformed these experiences into art; these essays are his "attempt to transform some of the themes, the problems, the enigmas, the contradictions of character and culture native to my predicament . . . into 'conscious thought,' " Ellison wrote (*SA* xix).

Ellison admitted to being troubled by the terms in which the success of *Invisible Man*—and his own career as well—had been defined. He was known to have referred to the novel as largely a failure, expressing his hope that *Invisible Man* be read simply as a novel rather than as a statement about the American Negro. In the aftermath of the heated exchange between Ellison and Howe leading up to the publication of *Shadow and Act*, and later the controversy surrounding his disappointment in the social expectations of *Invisible Man*, Ellison published "Tell It Like It Is, Baby" (*CE* 27–46), a 1965 essay that articulates his sense of loss over his father's death and his own "pursuit of eloquence" as a writer. By the time Ellison published "Juneteenth," his fourth installment of his second novel, in the *Quarterly Review of Literature* that same year, he was publicly announcing that, with some 368 pages of manuscript, he was nearing the novel's completion. During 1965, Ellison continued his staunch support of the arts by accepting more leadership roles as an advocate of the arts. He became a charter member of the National Council of the Arts and a year later was named to the Carnegie Commission of Educational Television (later, PBS), a position he held for nine years.

With even more honorary degrees from institutions, including Michigan, Rutgers, William and Mary, and Wesleyan, and his continuous publication, Ellison seemed to be enjoying the limelight. However, in 1967, there was a fire at his summer home in the Berkshires, near Pittsfield, Massachusetts. Not only was a large portion of the near-complete manuscript destroyed, but a major disruption in his method of work had also occurred. Ellison had now been working on the second novel since 1958, and he was profoundly affected by the loss. Unable to bring order to the multiple revisions or to reconstruct his evolving conception of the book, he retreated further and further from public discussion of what he had been calling *And Hickman Arrives*. Even as he published four more installments—"Night Talk," in the *Quarterly Review of Literature* (1969); "A Song of Innocence," in *Iowa Review* (1970); "Cadillac Flambé," in *American Review* (1973), which was part of the manuscript lost in the 1967 fire; and finally "Backwacking: A Plea to the Senators," in *Massachusetts Review* (1977)— the loss magnified the difficulties he was already having with the novel. The eight published excerpts constitute approximately 150 pages of the more than 300 he had written, a nearly complete manuscript, and they suggest that this second novel was to be a complex work revolving around themes Ellison continually examines in *Invisible Man*: "the spiral of history as the past boomerangs into the present, identity, resurrection, showmanship, amalgamation, and the positive and negative power of language and narrative to transform" (Busby 138).

One month before the fire, another event served to signal a deepening personal crisis and a change in public opinion regarding him and his work. At a reception following the awarding of an honorary doctorate by Grinnell College, Ellison was confronted by a student who disagreed with the ending of *Invisible Man*. The student, an uninvited guest to the reception, argued that the novel needed a more revolutionary ending, that the protagonist should have confronted his oppressors instead of retreating to his hole, as he does at the novel's end. Ellison calmly defended his ending to the student to which the student responded by pointing his finger at Ellison and calling him an "Uncle Tom." Shocked, Ellison stood silent for a moment; then, he became emotionally unglued. As Henry Wingate remembered it in a video about Ellison's life, Ellison was visibly shaken and then began to weep, repeating as he stood with his head on his friend's shoulder, "I am not an Uncle Tom. Wingate, you tell him. I am not an Uncle Tom" (Kirkland). Similarly, while delivering a speech at Oberlin College in April 1969, Ellison received a cold reception from black students who felt that his speech advocated black immersion into white culture. One student retorted, "Your book doesn't mean anything, because in it you're shooting down Ras the Destroyer, a rebel leader of black people." Then the student called Ellison a "tool of the oppressor." To this, Ellison responded that his book was written a long time ago and that he would not apologize for anything presented in it. "That just proves you're an Uncle Tom," the student continued (quoted in Busby 19). That Ellison had fallen out of favor was clear when, according to a *Negro Digest* survey in 1968, he was ranked fourth among important African-American writers. Wright was first.

Few knew his radical history or his advocacy work on behalf of blacks during the 1930s. Neither did it help that Ellison, who claimed a close kinship with fellow southwesterner Lyndon Baines Johnson, voiced full support of Johnson's domestic agenda and the Vietnam War. When, in 1969, the president bestowed upon him the Medal of Freedom, the event was accompanied by considerable criticism. To protect himself from further humiliation, Ellison kept to himself, granting fewer and fewer interviews. Young black artists and intellectuals found Ellison an easy target, interpreting his silence as alienation, and feeling, as Irving Howe did, that he was evading his responsibility as a black writer in America.

By the early 1970s, attitudes toward Ellison had begun to change again. In 1970, French novelist and historian André Malraux, who was minister of cultural affairs at the time, awarded him the Chevalier de l'Ordre des Artes et Lettres. Accepting a position at New York University as the Albert Schweitzer Professor of Humanities in 1970 gave Ellison access to a new and grateful audience. In 1972, in a survey of leading American critics, *Invisible Man* was listed among two dozen novels judged "the most likely to endure" (Graham and Singh xx). In December 1973, Ellison gave a speech at Harvard championing Alain Locke's notion of American pluralism. In his speech, Ellison commented that blacks are not an African people, but rather an American people. After a slightly nervous hesitation from the audience, there was thunderous applause. The following year, Harvard awarded Ellison an honorary doctorate (1974). That same year, he was made an honorary fellow of the Modern Language Association. The next year, he was inducted into the American Academy of Arts and Letters (1975).

By 1977, he had made the decision not to publish more sections of the second novel because he did not want the impact of the total work to be eclipsed by the individual sections. Also at this time, he refused to speculate about the completion date of the novel, citing that in the past he had been wrong in offering a completion date. By the time Ellison retired from NYU, becoming an emeritus professor in 1979, he had enjoyed nearly ten fulfilling years as a public intellectual and an engaging teacher with a highly distinguished record.

The 1980s saw Ellison's reemergence as a forerunner of American literature. Ellison was praised for his depiction of the affirming power of American life, and not the victimization of a race. He would look back on the turbulent times of the 1960s and 1970s and wonder in amazement how he survived it all. By the mid-1980s, Ellison had begun to transcribe the second novel on a word processor, working on it every day. He received another distinguished honor, the National Medal of Arts, in 1985, and in the following year published his third major work, *Going to the Territory* (1986). This collection of essays, lectures, personal reminiscences, and interviews, this time ranging from 1957 to 1985, including some that were left out of *Shadow and Act*, takes its title from Mark Twain and a Bessie Smith song. Viewed as a continuation of *Shadow and Act*, it illuminates Ellison the man more than Ellison the author through the use of similar themes: the craft of fiction, a problematic American identity, the complex relationship between black folklore and fiction, and Richard Wright's status as a writer. But this collection, according to Busby, lacks the structural unity of *Shadow and Act* (133). Through selections such as "The Little Man at Chehaw Station," Ellison offers readers a glimpse at the process and diligence of his craft. In "The Art of Romare Bearden," he exposes readers to the style of the Harlem Renaissance artist and the relationship between Bearden's art and jazz. In "What America Would Be Like without Blacks," Ellison argues that his purpose as a novelist is to reinforce African-

American presence in American culture. And, in "Society, Morality, and the Novel," one of Ellison's most celebrated essays, he examines cultural unity further as he explores the role of the novel in establishing American identity. Generally, these essays allowed Ellison to provide further insight into the forces that helped to shape his life. Besides the convenience of having his thoughts compiled into a single volume, the book provides few new insights into the direction of Ellison's work. Like *Shadow and Act*, *Going to the Territory* uses blues and jazz as vital metaphors. Through them, Ellison uses "language that dances with the inventive energy of a Duke Ellington composition. Ellison makes his case that it is above all on the level of vernacular culture that the possibility of America being a true 'melting pot' was actually fulfilled" (O'Meally 211).

As a writer, Ellison often examined the role of the novel; he stated that American fiction must regain the moral resolve that America's best nineteenth-century writers—Herman Melville, Mark Twain, and Henry James—demonstrated in their work as they attempted to use the novel to promote democracy. These writers understood the significance of slavery in the American experience and portrayed African Americans as representative of the most meaningful aspects of democracy. Ellison believed in an American culture. And, he felt that it is through African-American culture—folklore, art, music, dance—that young blacks would discover what is intrinsically valuable about being an American.

After the publication of *Going to the Territory*, there was a noticeable decline in frequency in Ellison's published work. There were few, if any, interviews granted. One can only speculate that this period marks his unofficial retirement due to his waning health. At the time of his death, the manuscript of the second novel was nearly 2,000 pages, and Ellison was still expanding it in other directions, envisioning a grand, perhaps multivolume, story cycle. Always, in Ellison's mind, the character Hickman and the story of Sunraider's life from birth to death were the dramatic hearts of the narrative. And, through this narrative, Ellison tried to grasp an American identity by exploring it through the lens of race. His work in progress was his attempt to examine

America, to see it whole, for what it is and for what it always has been. Unfortunately, Ellison never witnessed the birth of his second novel. Shortly after his eighty-first birthday, Ellison was hospitalized. He died at his home in New York on 16 April 1994, of pancreatic cancer.

The literary journal *Callaloo* produced a special issue titled "Remembering Ralph Ellison" in the spring of 1995. Leon Forrest and John Callahan were among the many contributors whose remembrances of Ellison were included. In his reflections, Forrest described Ellison as a "healer of the soul" who celebrated black consciousness through his "illuminating imagination," "intellectual gifts and a powerful sense of the absurdity of life" which allowed him to reveal the striking contradictions of American society with the stunning accuracy of a "literary surgeon" (Forrest 280). Forrest understood that the same resolve a skilled surgeon brings to his profession, a writer brings to his craft. As an artist, Ellison helped to save the life of the nation by giving it something to live for, and by challenging readers to fight racism and other contradictions that were destroying American value systems. Forrest hailed *Invisible Man* as an "ever-consuming and challenging work of fiction" whose author's "riveting power" and "narrative drive" makes it an engaging read (280). For Forrest, Ellison incorporated nearly every aspect of black consciousness into his work: music, slave heritage, preacher tradition, dance, and the relationship between North and South. With his hearty balance of artistic arrogance, ego, and humility, Ellison brought to the novel form a willingness to reshape its structure through jazz, allowing his work to sing like a grieving tenor saxophone, "screaming our American failures and projecting the new consciousness in a spirit that combined Coleman Hawkins, at one end of the stage, and Charlie Parker, at the other" (281). Ellison brought this poetic lyricism to his fiction, offering to "reflect upon the American possibility of art out of chaos" (282). Thus, Ellison was devoted to removing stereotypical black images from his work, noting that African Americans had been "set up by racist forces" (282). A prodigiously well-read perfectionist, Forrest wrote, Ellison, in his art, masterfully illustrated how best to incorporate the denied history of African Americans into the literary canon by handling "the furious fire of his literary vocabulary with harpooning, Hemingway-like precision" (282).

Not all contributors to the *Callaloo* special edition were as complimentary. Richard Stern described his meeting Ellison in 1957 (this actually may have taken place in 1961). Ellison sought a position at the University of Chicago, and Stern felt that inviting Ellison to give a round of powerful lectures as part of the university's Alexander White Lectureship would help secure his appointment. In 1961, when Ellison came to the lecture series, to his surprise, Stern wrote, Ellison arrived unprepared. He had nothing written on paper. Ellison said he did this so that his talk would have the influence of jazz, improvisational and true. Stern writes that the lectures were a disaster. Ellison stumbled repeatedly and went off onto tangents, "and then the tangents of tangents" (Stern 285). Ellison apparently felt the lectures had gone well. Unfortunately, Ellison did not receive the appointment. In 1962, his friend Saul Bellow was appointed to the Committee on Social Thought. Ellison was hurt and angry. Stern writes that during Ellison's lengthy stay as the White lecturer, he

> noticed another self-subversive element in him. I already knew that this confident, warm and charming man was pocked with insecurity, anger and bitterness, and that he countered these feelings with booze. He came to the house four or five times a week, and we drank martinis. He did not get drunk, only easy and weary. Then he stuttered, fumbled for words and occasionally turned sarcastic, angry. His vulnerability made me even fonder of him. (Stern 286)

Stern wrote further that although Ellison and Fanny never had children, Ellison did not despair: "He never made me feel sorry that he didn't have his own children. Not at all. He made the best of whatever came along, children or their absence" (286). About the long-awaited second novel, Stern remembered that Ellison had called him to report he was finished and was turning in the novel to his editors. With justifiable skepticism, having heard earlier announcements of the second novel, Stern believed that if there were no book, only groupings of scenes, there would be no detraction from Ellison, "the very visible man, complex, brilliant, ironic, generous, a bravely secret sufferer, a powerful charmer, the shaper of a richer answer to the American dilemma than anyone else has offered, the writer of one of the very good novels and some of the best essays of the century. That should be enough" (Stern 287).

John F. Callahan's contribution to the special *Callaloo* issue was an expanded version of the eulogy he delivered at Ellison's funeral, 19 April 1994, at Trinity Cemetery in New York City. During his eulogy, Callahan described Ellison as a master craftsman of words who always made him feel at home. Like many young intellectuals of the 1960s, Callahan had difficulty embracing American culture because of its vast contradictions. But Ellison encouraged him not to give up on his country, to love America, but on his own terms. On 1 March 1994, Callahan reflects, Random House sponsored a private dinner for Ellison's eighty-first birthday celebration. Among the celebrants was Albert Murray, Ellison's friend and Tuskegee classmate. At some point during the toasts, Ellison rose to his feet, slowly surveyed those gathered in honor of him, and brought his eyes to rest on Fanny. They looked at each other a long time, and Ellison simply spoke, "And Fanny. Fanny." For Callahan, this exchange was profound, for it typified Ellison's "way of acknowledging things which could not be said but had been experienced and were remembered" (Callahan 307). For Callahan, Ellison was both "friend and father" whose legacy was that of a "true American kinsman" who lives on through his "nourishing words" (309). Callahan could not grieve for Ellison because to do so meant grieving for himself. For a man of such "immense gifts and very American ambition," one has to remember his inviolable integrity as a writer, one who viewed life through the prism of literature and who saw himself working out of dual literary traditions: Euro- and African-American.

Ellison had not selected a literary executor before he died; eventually his wife, Fanny, requested that Callahan edit the novel on which Ellison had been working for more than forty years. Callahan had already edited two posthumous collections of Ellison's work: *The Collected Essays of Ralph Ellison* (1995) and *Flying*

Home and Other Stories (1996), and he would face many more challenges in the publication of Ellison's text. He undertook the daunting task of choosing selections from the vast arsenal of notes and drafts, and placing them in a sequential arrangement that might lend itself toward some accurate impression of the whole. Going through the papers, Callahan discovered two previously unpublished stories: "Boy on a Train" and "I Did Not Learn Their Names." These texts were published in the 29 April–6 May 1996 special edition of the *New Yorker* titled "Black in America." The end product of Callahan's work was Ellison's second novel, which draws from the richness of black cultural heritage. Callahan selected as the title *Juneteenth*—referring to the annual black celebration in parts of Texas, Louisiana, Arkansas, and Oklahoma of the Emancipation Day of American slaves on 19 June 1865, when the Union troops in Texas declared those states' slaves to be free. Callahan selected this title instead of Ellison's working title, *And Hickman Arrives*, which Ellison had used for one of the 1960 excerpts from the second novel.

Juneteenth was released posthumously in 1999. Rich in folklore and folk speech, like many of Ellison's previous works, *Juneteenth* is composed of various fragments of experience culminating in a focus on black religion and politics. Its major characters include the Reverend Daddy Hickman, a born-again jazz trombonist, and the Reverend Bliss, his light-skinned adopted son, who changes his name to Adam Sunraider. Sunraider eventually becomes a racist U.S. senator from the state of Massachusetts.

The novel is a long dialogue between the Negro preacher, Alonzo Hickman, and Senator Sunraider, the son of a white mother and a black father. At the beginning of the novel, Hickman is escorting members of his congregation to Washington, D.C., to celebrate the Juneteenth holiday at the Lincoln Memorial. While there, he hopes to visit the senator, with whom he has lost touch after Sunraider left Hickman's black community as a young man. Sunraider went to the North, first posing as a preacher, then working various jobs, including as a photographer for movie commercials, and finally winning the Senate election as a "race-hater." When Hickman goes to see the senator, he is refused entry by the secretary, who does not want to let "a black man" in to see her boss. Undaunted, Hickman escorts his church members to the Senate to hear Sunraider speak. After his speech, while the audience applause mounts, Sunraider notices a young black man leaning over a balcony, who opens fire on him. Sunraider sinks to the floor as the guards chase the fleeing gunman, and he hears a voice crying out, "For thou hast forsaken me," which he recognizes as Hickman's.

Hickman accompanies Sunraider to the hospital where they begin a long emotional exploration of their pasts in search of their identities. They recall how during revivals the young man would "be resurrected so that sinners can find life everlasting." Bliss would rise up out of a coffin that had been placed on the platform next to the preacher. They remember how, when there was a good cotton crop and the congregation had some money, revival meetings were a wonderful celebration where faith was well nourished: "We et 1500 loaves of bread, 500 pounds of catfish." Toward the end of their dialogue, the senator falls into a coma. In his dream state he sees a wild old woman shouting at him, "Shet up. I'll tell you who you really are." Throughout their dialogue, they are plagued by the problem of identity. Hickman views Bliss as a reconciler of American society. But Bliss has turned away from his former self in place of his newly constructed cultural identity.

From the dazzling range of idioms in its language, to the echoes of call-and-response in the black church, to the riffs and bass lines of jazz, *Juneteenth* offers jubilant proof that whatever else it means to be an American, it means to be "somehow black," as Ellison once wrote. For even as Senator Sunraider was bathed from birth in the deep and nourishing waters of African-American folkways, so too are all Americans. That idea is the cause for which Ralph Ellison gave the last full measure of his devotion.

The literary world turned out to be very skeptical of Ellison's posthumously released second novel. Some critics felt that Callahan was not the best individual to give shape to Ellison's legacy. Since he had no special connection to Ellison's past, they questioned Callahan's editorial decisions about what to include in Ellison's text. For example, if Ellison had wanted the novel to have a southwestern focus, that focus is not present in the published novel. In an effort to validate his role in Ellison's work, Callahan anticipated the concerns of the literary world in the introduction and afterword of the novel, where he assures the reader that every word in the novel is Ellison's. And he posits that he merely took Ellison's "multifarious, multifaceted, multifocused, multivoiced, multitoned" work and pared it down into a single, coherent, chronological story (J xxix).

Following the publication of *Juneteenth*, Albert Murray and Callahan edited and published *Trading Twelves: The Selected Letters of Ralph Ellison and Albert Murray* (2000), which details the lifelong dialogue between "two American men of letters whose importance only grows as the twentieth century passes away" (*TT* viii). This collection of letters offers the reader exposure to the lighter side of Ellison, the Ellison who "never stopped playing the dozens, never stopped practicing his craft, never stopped wrestling with America" (Guzzio 120). Plans for a scholarly edition of *Juneteenth* that will present a greatly expanded look at Ellison's conception of the work are well under way.

Because of the history of black life in America, Ellison found his love for the black community and his love for America difficult to reconcile. But he has been praised for his handling of this challenging issue. His work calls our attention to the complexities of life and encourages us to reach for a greater comprehension of the particular within the universal. From his frontiersmanlike experience in Oklahoma, which afforded him his first glimpse into his Americanness, to his use of fictional devices such as folklore, blues, myth, and symbol in his short stories, *Invisible Man*, and the posthumously published *Juneteenth*, Ellison has been primarily concerned with exploring how man determines his own reality and through that determination achieves personal freedom. Like the protagonist in *Invisible Man* who only sees more clearly after falling into a dark hole, Ellison believed that it was necessary to step outside of an externally constructed world to gain the clarity to see both the world and one's self inside. Ellison borrowed from the humor, irony, and bitterness of life to illustrate how inner freedom is possible by simply learning to transcend failures. Similarly, Ellison extended his life experience into his work for a broader, more universal application. He gave us young male protagonists in his fiction who are always engaged in some conflict through which they struggle to become more conscious of self, culture, and national history. These characters show force of will and echo the optimism and fortitude of the American spirit, values that Ellison himself held with deep conviction.

The measure of Ellison's triumph lies not so much in his work, but in the particular vision he imparted in it: that the sense of individual freedom must never be lost within or destroyed by the collective. Ellison's life, like his writing, was a constant negotiation, a struggle to sustain a degree of freedom in a hostile environment. The boundless inventiveness that Ellison learned to apply growing up on the profusely complex frontier, which he described as chaotic, encouraged his mind to soar and eventually found its way into his fiction. In the end, Ellison could find no better way to represent consciously and imaginatively the struggle of being American and Negro than in *Invisible Man*, the book that lays claim to an African-American experience that is also uniquely American.

REFERENCES

Busby, Mark. *Ralph Ellison*. Boston: Twayne, 1991.

Callahan, John. "Frequencies of Memory: A Eulogy for Ralph Ellison." *Callaloo: Ralph Ellison: A Special Issue* 18, no. 2 (Spring 1995): 298–309.

Ellison, Ralph. "Stormy Weather." *New Masses* 37 (1940): 20–21.

Forrest, Leon. "Ralph Ellison Remembered." *Callaloo: Ralph Ellison: A Special Issue* 18, no. 2 (Spring 1995): 280–83.

Graham, Maryemma, and Amritjit Singh, eds. *Conversations with Ralph Ellison*. Jackson: University Press of Mississippi, 1995.

Guzzio, Tracie Church. "Ralph Ellison." In *American Writers: A Collection of Literary Biographies*, edited by Jay Parini, 111–34. Detroit, Mich.: Scribner's, 2003.

Jackson, Lawrence. *Ralph Ellison: Emergence of Genius*. New York: Wiley, 2002.

Kirkland, Avon, dir. *Ralph Ellison: An American Journey.* Videocassette. California Newsreel, 2001.

O'Meally, Robert G. *Craft of Ralph Ellison.* Cambridge, Mass.: Harvard University Press, 1980.

Rowell, Charles, ed. *Callaloo: Ralph Ellison: A Special Issue* 18, no. 2 (Spring 1995).

Shor, Edith. *Visible Ellison: A Study of Ralph Ellison's Fiction.* Westport, Conn.: Greenwood, 1983.

Stern, Richard. "Ralph Ellison." *Callaloo: Ralph Ellison: A Special Issue* 18, no. 2 (Spring 1995): 284–87.

ELLISON IN
HIS TIME

"Creative and Cultural Lag"

The Radical Education of Ralph Ellison

William J. Maxwell

What does American democracy sound like? Thanks to Ralph Ellison, a student of the chromatic runs of guitarist Charlie Christian as well as the fractured syntax of poet T. S. Eliot, more than a few Americans now suspect that it sounds like jazz. While Ellison once pledged to high-flying confidant Albert Murray that he "wouldn't be a jazz critic for love or money" (*TT* 193), he spent crucial writing time in the dozen years after *Invisible Man* (1952) being just that. From 1955 through 1964, Ellison contributed a string of jazz-centered essays to fully visible periodicals such as *Esquire* and the *Saturday Review*. With painstaking elegance balancing spiked judgments, he surveyed everything from the frontier lyricism of singer Jimmy Rushing, to the cult of the brilliantly doomed alto saxophonist Charlie "Bird" Parker, to the speculative sociology of *Blues People* (1963), LeRoi Jones's pioneering study of black music in white America. Several of these pieces on jazz gained the status of small classics during the conquering twilight of Ellison's life, when his late 1960s reputation as an elitist sellout faded along with the militancy of the Black Arts movement. In the decade following his 1994 death, his race man's brand of cultural pluralism, committed to both "Negro American" invention and its bonds to American whiteness and American democracy, has grown into something approaching the orthodoxy of liberal academia. Ellison's recent elevation from overrefined relic to prophetic ancestor is thus often celebrated to the tune of his suggestion that African-American jazz is the rightful soundtrack to U.S. democratic principles. Listening to the antagonistic cooperation of the improvising soloist and the accompanying jazz ensemble, contemporary Ellisonians hear the Constitution's demanding synthesis of freedom and the common good, individual rights and governmental authority, the person and the People.

The present, then, is the best of times for Ellison's thoughts on jazz and the American way, reprinted in high style in Robert G. O'Meally's 2001 collection, *Living with Music: Ralph Ellison's Jazz Writings*, perhaps the only Modern Library volume with a soundtrack of its own (a CD compilation of Ellison's jazz favorites issued by Sony—no baloney). Still unheard amid the joyful noise of rediscovery, however, is the origin of Ellison's jazz thinking in his training as a black radical. Like the seeds of other lifetime habits, the first signs of Ellison's investment in a United States of "Jamocracy" can in fact be traced to his immersion in communism's Harlem stream from the late 1930s through the mid-1940s. Consider one indication of this ancestry, the rarely studied 1944 short story "In a Strange Country." Despite later sour grapes over the "loneliness, self-depreciation and self-pity" of the Bird's thin alto voice (*CE* 264), Ellison gives his sympathetic, semiautobiographical protagonist the most auspicious of the era's young names in jazz modernism: Parker. Ellison's second Bird is an African-American seaman first pictured seeking shelter from violent white Yanks in a Welsh pub during World War II, a conflict intent on teaching him that Nazis are not his most volatile foes. Warming to the healing sounds of an interracial jam session, he reveals a bohemian skepticism of nonartistic allegiances by paraphrasing his jazzman namesake, who once short-circuited a rap on religion by declaring himself a devout musician (O'Meally 70). "When we jam, sir," the literary Parker testifies, "we're Jamocrats!"—briefly united for a shared musical performance if not for the long, passive haul of common ethnicity or nationality (*FH* 143). At the close of the tale, however, Parker's pledge of allegiance has modulated into a more traditional key. Ellison's hero finds himself sobbing out the lyrics of "The Star-Spangled Banner," now able to hope for an American patriotism answerable to the interracial Jamocrats back home— but only after a stirring rendition of the communist "Internationale," the revolutionary workers' anthem, has kindled memories of "when he was a small boy" in the second line of jazz parades, "marching in the streets behind the bands that came to his southern town" (*FH* 145).

As critic Barbara Foley explains, these rapid-fire exchanges of song and identification reflect the fact that both nationalism and proletarian internationalism—the belief that workers have no country apart from their class—motivated Allied troops with leftist sentiments during World War II ("Reading" 336). This was a "global conflict," she notes:

> that, paradoxically, named itself the "Great Patriotic War" in the U.S.S.R. and was fought on a nationalist-cum-internationalist basis by all the communist forces involved. The 1944 readers of "In a Strange Country," accustomed to this paradox, would have been able to hold the tale's simultaneous claims to both nationalism and internationalism in contradictory suspension. (336)

For their part, 1944 readers close to Ellison on the Harlem Left— an audience accustomed to Duke Ellington concerts benefiting Soviet war relief—would also have appreciated the contradiction *within* the tale's claims of nationalism, and the paradoxical vehicle of its own suspension. Parker's love of country, as black as it is red, white, and blue, must align the southern jazz march, marked by pleasurable ethnic and regional particularity, with the American national anthem, generally welcoming in theory but painfully exclusive in racist practice. The "Internationale" does the connective trick, vocalizing a communism which had accented both black nationalist and "twentieth-century Americanist" themes during its coalition-building Popular Front of 1935–1940. In Ellison's "In a Strange Country," communism thus supplies needed passage to a pluralistic jazzlike Americanism, much as communism's bargain with nationalism ironically channeled the patriotism that made Ellison a left-wing target during the Vietnam War.

This is not to forget that Ellison's defense of American democracy in *Invisible Man* and after typically borrowed anticommunist terms. Like other disenchanted "fellow travelers" of his generation, former friends of communism who had never quite joined the party, he came to accuse American communists of scorning genuine national interests, institutions, and identities. "They fostered the myth that communism was twentieth-century Americanism," Ellison protested in 1967, "but to be a twentieth-century American meant, in their thinking, that you had to be more Russian than American and less Negro than either" (Graham and Singh, 126). *Invisible Man*, the Great American Anticommunist Novel, memorably dramatizes this common Cold War complaint by projecting communists as castrators of the American eagle. Yet the final patriotic creed of *Invisible Man*'s underground narrator could be lifted from Ellison's earlier hero Parker, a fellow jazz lover and wise literary grandfather who esteems communism's vow to prisoners of starvation. Both the Invisible Man and the too-conspicuous Birdman "affirm the principle on which the [United States] was built and not the men, or at least not the men who did the violence" (*IM* 574).

Why does *Invisible Man* tip its hat to Ellison's "Internationale"-loving sailor even while brilliantly restating standard-issue anticommunism, making lasting art from the same ideological cloth as *I Was a Communist for the F.B.I.*? This chapter will approach the question by reexamining Ellison's extended stay in communist territory during the Great Depression and the Second World War, a milieu he entered via the Harlem YMCA literally hours after his personal great migration to New York City. As the sympathetic relationship between *Invisible Man* and "In a Strange Country" suggests, the careers of the procommunist and postcommunist Ellison cannot be segregated as neatly as his liberal champions and radical critics assume. For one thing, these careers refuse easy translation into the conventional categories of youthful apprenticeship and mature independence. Ellison was pushing forty when *Invisible Man* finally emerged, and the notion of its author as a neophyte, overnight sensation neglected his editorships at flagship leftist journals, his dozens of earlier essays and book reviews, and his hundreds of completed pages of proletarian fiction. The renowned novelist who had won the National Book Award and the Albert Schweitzer Professorship was not eager to recall or republish such radical efforts, but their number and seriousness necessarily informed his postcommunist grasp of jazz, American democracy, and much else.

Meaningful continuities therefore mark the relationship between the fellow-traveling radical Ellison, a shadow still hibernating in the historical cellar, and the anticommunist liberal Ellison, an icon now routinely exposed in the first rank of American canons. Despite suggestions to the contrary sparked by the recent republication of some of Ellison's first stories, the most important such continuity does not involve the refinement of a unique, precocious black modernism amid the wasteland of depression-era naturalism. Ellison, whose New York comrades included Richard Wright, Langston Hughes, and bebop pioneer Charlie Christian, was not exactly outcast among Harlem radicals in admiring the experimental spunk of black vernacular culture and European-style avant-gardism, even the mingled absurdities and liberties of a race-crazy American century. Instead, the radical and liberal Ellisons are linked most significantly by an ongoing interest in the flux of historical leadership, African-American and otherwise, and in the contradictory possibility that being lapped by time's arrow can put one ahead of the curve. Ellison's residence in the far Left, this is to say, not only familiarized him with Marxist versions of linear history he would come to reject, but introduced him to the lasting terms of his disagreement. Harlem communism as much as anticommunism impelled his distinctive presumption that "the rear" may become "the avant-garde" (*IM* 572). When revisited as he met them, rather than as *Invisible Man* disowned them, Ellison's radical years take shape as an education in the intimate dialectic of belatedness and vanguardism—a dialectic that would structure Invisible Man's attitude to historical time in addition to Ellison's itinerary through the black communism of Harlem's "Negro metropolis."

In the Tracks of Scottsboro

Ellison managed to evade the blows of postwar McCarthyism through one major literary act—*Invisible Man*—and one consequential failure to write: he never signed a Communist party card. Yet many texts that Ellison produced before his famed novel, the great majority of them missing from *The Collected Essays* (1995) and other defining editions, display an eager, resilient support of communist ideas and programs. Just a year after his arrival in New York, he wrote his mother of his hatred of capitalism, "which offers a poor person practically nothing but work for a low wage from birth to death" (Jackson 189). Collectivization in the Soviet Union made him wish that they both could emigrate to the communist homeland and "live there" (189). Ellison's very first letter to Richard Wright ended with a slogan marrying his fledgling literary efforts to the famous final line of Marx and Engels's *Communist Manifesto*: "Workers of the world must write!!!!" (195). Later correspondence with Wright confessed that his experience at the communist-sponsored National Negro Congress was "almost mystical in its intensity" (Fabre 202).

When Ellison brought his worker-writing into print, his commitments to Marxism and to communist aesthetic policy remained frank. His 1940 review of Len Zinberg's *Walk Hard, Talk Loud*, a novel starring a young African-American boxer, celebrated "how far a writer, whose approach to Negro life is uncolored by condescension, stereotyped ideas, and other faults growing out of race prejudice, is able to go with a Marxist understanding of the economic basis of Negro personality" ("Negro" 27). In a 1941 roundup of Wright's *Native Son* and other examples of "recent Negro fiction," Ellison saluted the "new proletarian consciousness" among African Americans and the success of the John Reed Clubs and other communist literary groups that had directed black writers "toward an improvement and modernization of technique and enlargement of theme" ("Recent" 22). Elsewhere at the start of the 1940s, his critical prose dreamed out loud of the factory as labor's earthbound "cathedral," and denounced the "red-baiting" of black anticommunists, the Brotherhood chapters of *Invisible Man* not yet imaginable (*CE* 19, 21).

Once these chapters were invented and published, Ellison sometimes condemned American communism for its lap-dog responsiveness "to the necessities of Soviet foreign policy" during World War II (Graham and Singh 126). The conviction that an obedient party agreed to sidetrack African-American protest at the height of the war, together with lingering frustration over the negative response of black communists to *Native Son*, seems to have provoked Ellison's withdrawal from communist positions in the late 1940s. Yet life during wartime saw him publicly defend each twist in the communist line. Ellison attacked Father Charles E. Coughlin's "lynch mobs" as the war neared, setting the best in Franklin D. Roosevelt's New Deal democracy against the brutality inspired by Coughlin's homespun fascism ("Judge Lynch" 15). However, after the Soviet Union's shocking August 1939 nonaggression pact with Hitler, Roosevelt became a class enemy, and Ellison one "black Yank" who announced that he "was not coming" to save Europe from the fascist evil that capitalism had nourished (*CE* 15). When the Nazis shattered the nonaggression pact by invading the Soviet Union in 1941, Ellison to all appearances respected the demands of Soviet foreign policy, once more singing "the praises of national unity and [taking] an aggressive win-the-war stance" (Foley, "Rhetoric," 540). He was now a black Yank willing to come over, though preferably on egalitarian and relatively protected terms secured through left-wing contacts. In 1943, communist connections helped him avoid service in the Jim Crow army by prying open a spot in the merchant marines, then the most racially democratic branch of the U.S. military (Jackson 282–83). The sailor's yarn of "In a Strange Country," with its elaborate negotiations between American nationalisms and leftist cosmopolitanism, was one product of a tour of duty at sea that ended in April 1945.

Communism may or may not have saved Ellison's life by keeping him out of the infantry, but its intellectual world was his rock for a decade. When the published signs of Ellison's place in this world were concealed with the Cold War unveiling of *Invisible Man*, "quite an impressive c.v." was buried, notes Barbara Foley ("Rhetoric" 539). Ellison had joined forces with communism long enough to build this résumé for some specifically literary reasons. In the depression 1930s, a young writer's communism looked to be as natural as a banker's Republicanism; the professional and aesthetic future, after all, seemed firmly in the hands of the working class and proletarian letters. Ellison's affection for forward-looking art that "made it new," born with boyhood glimpses at Proust and Picasso in his mother's copies of *Vanity Fair*, thus alone made fellow-traveling desirable. The communism of the rising, post–Harlem Renaissance cohort of African-American writers seemed practically obligatory, moreover. William Attaway, Arna Bontemps, Sterling Brown, Frank Marshall Davis, Chester Himes, Melvin Tolson, and Margaret Walker joined Wright and Ellison in communist circles, crossing paths and trading theories at bars, automats, party-sponsored talks, and national conventions (Maxwell 1–12). Yet unlike some of these peers, Ellison also had an urgent nonliterary reason to stick with the party of the proletariat: he was consistently broke, or just one check from it, until he received the proceeds of a Rosenwald Fellowship in 1944 and married his second wife, the talented and steadily employed Fanny McConnell Buford, in 1946.

The root motive behind Ellison's procommunism—thirty formative years of impoverishment and low wages, punctuated by the worst depression in American history—is also the least discussed. High regard for his dissection of sociological caricatures of "the ghetto poor," among other things, has made social class a no-fly zone in Ellison criticism. Ellison himself, however, could argue even after his officially Marxist days that experiencing and understanding class difference was vital to American writers. Class alone did not determine the author's consciousness, he maintained, but a fluid consciousness of class indeed became more important "as the racial lines [gave] way" to the victories of the Civil Rights movement (Graham and Singh 204). During a 1971 interview, he described his own early "class identification" as "vague," though he associated this vagueness with the class-specific tradition of black "waiters, maids, nursemaids, and cooks," who knew from close observation "that all millionaires do not have good manners, nor are they all men of taste" (204). Whatever the novelistic value of such knowledge, proven in the

Mr. Norton episodes of *Invisible Man*, it came as the result of growing up a nonmillionaire. "I only know that we were poor as hell," Ellison admitted (203).

Lawrence Jackson, author of the first-ever biography of Ellison, reveals just how poor this was. By the time he was fifteen, young Ralph, born in Oklahoma City in 1913, had lived in more than a dozen separate apartments. Even before his adolescence, the "ragtag pilgrimage of the Ellison family," fatherless from 1916 to 1924, qualified as the source of the "boy's unspoken shame" (Jackson 44). The domestic work demanded of Ellison's mother, Ida, made the displacements unavoidable, "the result of a combination of miserable wages, unbearable conditions, and terminated contracts, probably more often by Ida's employers than her landlords" (44). At the start of the 1920s, her house cleaning earned her just $6 a week—worth about $57 in today's currency—with one-third reserved for the rent. Ida, a proud and highly literate woman who referred to herself as a "janitress" or "custodian" (44), encouraged Ralph's fascination with *Vanity Fair* and other far-sighted reading. She authorized his teenage trumpet lessons and dreams of symphonic composition: poverty was not to limit his horizons. An antidote to deprivation that she herself modeled was political. Ida was a serious socialist, willing to knock on doors to campaign for Eugene V. Debs, the left-wing folk hero who won 6 percent of the presidential vote in 1912 and 900,000 votes in 1920, the second time while behind bars for sedition. When off on his own in radical New York, Ellison wrote to his mother about Soviet wars on poverty not simply because they had suffered neediness together, but also because she had first taught him how anticapitalist politics might overcome it.

The young Ellison's program to escape his culturally rich but materially dismal Oklahoma boyhood culminated in his acceptance of a music scholarship to Alabama's Tuskegee Institute in 1933. Bookish romance and the Great Depression combined to send him to the world-famous black college as a hobo; by hitching a free ride on the rails, he calculated, he could travel in the liberated style of Huckleberry Finn and reserve especially scarce funds for a new Conn cornet (Jackson 88–89). Ellison's imaginative conversion of the Louisville and Nashville Railroad into

Mark Twain's Mississippi River did not end as planned, however. When his train pulled into the freight yards of Decatur, Alabama, "two white railroad detectives laying about them with the barrels of long nickel-plated .45 revolvers forced some forty or fifty of us, black and white alike, off the train and ordered us to line up along the tracks" (CE 769). "For me," recalled Ellison in 1976, "this was a frightening moment. Not only was I guilty of stealing passage on a freight train, but I realized that I had been caught in the very town where, at that moment, the *Scottsboro* case was being tried" (769).

In fact, the Scottsboro trial to which Ellison referred was just one of a series that tormented the "Scottsboro Boys"—nine young black hobos falsely accused of raping two white women on an Alabama train in 1931. By the time Ellison hitched his way to Tuskegee in the summer of 1933, the plight of the nine had become a national scandal, a symbol of the injustice of southern "legal lynching," and a cause célèbre for the Communist party. As the freshman-to-be was pulled from his boxcar, the party's International Labor Defense (ILD) was installed in Decatur, defying mob violence to represent the Scottsboro defendants in one of many retrials. With aid from the U.S. Supreme Court, the ILD would succeed in keeping all of the Scottsboro nine from the electric chair. Benjamin Davis and William Patterson, black communist lawyers who coordinated the Scottsboro support drive, would ensure that these legal victories helped to elevate the party to its greatest-ever popularity among African Americans. But the Ellison who anxiously lined up beside the tracks knew only part of this history. He suspected that he, too, might become a Scottsboro Boy doomed to execution, "a sacrificial scapegoat simply because I was of the same race as the accused young men then being prepared for death" (CE 769). When a set of white hobos decided to brave the .45s and make a break for it, Ellison therefore "plunged into their midst, . . . running far closer to the ground than I had ever managed to do as a high school football running back" (769). His Tuskegee Institute entrance photograph, showing a thin, sporty mustache and a freshly bandaged head wound, suggests that he was tackled and beaten before finding daylight. This frighteningly close call with

the fate of the Scottsboro nine favorably disposed Ellison to communist antiracism, proven as the National Association for the Advancement of Colored People (NAACP) wavered and the party
dove into the legal fray. It also accurately forecasted the dynamics
of his relationship to communist historicism, by which I mean
communism's self-conception as an actor-in-history. Not for the
last time, Ellison ran both behind and ahead of the black communist vanguard, arriving late to the scene of the Scottsboro defense, but escaping before the Scottsboro defendants, the last of
whom the ILD would not free until 1950. En route from strapped
teenager to upward-bound college man, he followed and jumped
the tracks of a party he learned to call "the locomotive of history" (Foley, "Rhetoric," 541).

In the Tracks of Hughes, Wright, and Herndon

By the end of his junior year at Tuskegee, Ellison's finances again
demanded hard traveling, this time a drawn-out bus ride to New
York City, where he intended to earn tuition money as a porter
on Hudson River cruise ships. A force looking like the locomotive of African-American literary history quickly presented itself,
however, and Ellison never returned to Alabama for his degree,
his first serious life blueprint discarded into Peter Wheatstraw's
cart. In July 1936, on just his second day in the city, Ellison walked
through the lobby of the Harlem YMCA and bumped into
Langston Hughes, then the poet laureate of African-American
communism as well as New Negro Harlem. Qualifying chat
about *The Waste Land* and Babette Deutsch's *This Modern Poetry*
concluded, Hughes set out to charm Ellison into the conviction
that adventurous modernist literature now tilted to the Left.
Copies of André Malraux, Cecil Day Lewis, and John Strachey's
"Literature and Dialectical Materialism" changed hands, with Ellison encouraged to read closely and report. Hughes also introduced his young acquaintance to the political face of Harlem
radicalism, bringing him along to meet Louise Thompson, the
best-placed African-American woman in the U.S. Communist
party and Ellison's entrée into Harlem party headquarters. But

Ellison's most crucial introduction from the older poet was to Richard Wright, whom Hughes convinced to send a curt post-card reading, "Langston Hughes tells me that you'd like to meet me" (Jackson 178).

Wright, whose proletarian verse Ellison knew through the *Partisan Review*, was just a few years older than the Tuskegee music major, but already rivaled Hughes in the breadth of his literary aspiration. When it came to Marxist theory, Wright's knowledge went far deeper than that of the Harlem Renaissance veteran. Ellison eagerly sat at Wright's feet as the latter wrote in his office at the Harlem bureau of the *Daily Worker*, the leading American communist newspaper. Impressed almost—but not quite—beyond criticism, the newcomer to the city pored over drafts of the hard-boiled stories soon collected in Wright's first book, *Uncle Tom's Children* (1938). As Lawrence Jackson describes it:

> Ellison gravitated to [Wright's workplace] as much as prudence allowed; there simply was no more interesting place to be than at the desk of a black writer engaged in the most pressing social and intellectual questions of the moment. The office of the *Daily Worker*, which was circulating the boldest articles on the race question in New York City ("Protests against Slugging Grow, Butcher Who Attacked Negro Boy Is Fired"), hummed like a place of consequence and radical struggle. (184)

Even more, the office hummed like the forward command post of African-American writing, the incubator of the literary future allied with communism, the pacesetter of a political future that would eliminate poverty in Oklahoma and beyond. At the Harlem bureau, Wright's onward-rushing prose took flight—prose Ellison placed in "the front rank of American fiction" and equated with the "take-off in a leap which promises to carry over a whole tradition" ("Recent" 22, 25).

To his credit, Wright was not content to see Ellison expend all his literary intelligence in appreciative reading. Taking the reins of *New Challenge*, a journal interested in Marxifying black letters, he solicited Ellison's first publication outside his college literary magazine, a review of Waters Turpin's 1937 novel *These Low Grounds*, which Ellison titled "Creative and Cultural Lag." Wright tapped one untried African-American voice to evaluate another. The novel in question was Turpin's first, encouraged into being by Edna Ferber, the author of *Show Boat*, who actually employed Turpin's mother. In Ellison's opinion, which reached print in the fall of 1937, Turpin's humble origin was more meaningful to his novel than his friendship with the well-to-do creator of Cap'n Andy and the Cotton Blossom. Unlike the swells of the Harlem Renaissance, Turpin had excavated "the rich deep materials" where black folklore met black labor (Ellison, "Creative," 90). In defining his novel's setting in relation to fields of black work— "the farming, oystering, and crabbing region of Maryland"— and in choosing a largely proletarian cast—"roustabouts, suds busters, bell boys, shoe-shine boys, coal men, ditch diggers and such"—he had crafted a "forceful and blunt" realism of black folk life (90). Praise was also due to Turpin's historical sweep, tracking four generations of an African-American family all the way from the Civil War to the Great Depression. "In *These Low Grounds*," Ellison explained, "we have the first attempt by an American Negro to essay a saga, and it is for this reason, if for no other, that Turpin's book merits reading" (90).

To Ellison's mind, however, Turpin's saga stumbled during its long historical journey. *These Low Grounds* failed to acknowledge the Marxist insight that psychological habits were historically variable. As a result, "the characters suffer, and . . . all seem to possess the same reaction to life, the same psychology; all of which bespeaks a certain lack of historical and political consciousness" (91). In language heavily indebted to Wright's decisive manifesto "Blueprint for Negro Writing," published in the very same issue of *New Challenge*, Ellison went on to insist:

> It is the Negro writer's responsibility, as one identified with a repressed minority, to utilize yet transcend his immediate environment and grasp the historic process as a whole, and his, and his group's relation to it. This cannot be accomplished with dull sensibilities, or by lagging in the cultural, technical, or political sense. (91)

By the grand phrase "the historic process as a whole," Ellison meant the process identified in the materialist conception of history hammered out by Marx, which held that the advance of productive forces in the economy set the course of class conflict and, in turn, the fundamental trajectory of human history. No foot-dragging behind these forces and the theoretical tools used to perceive and act on them could be forgiven in a literary realist who sought to capture the historical development of African Americans.

Hence the odd title of Ellison's initial foray into literary criticism, "Creative and Cultural Lag." "Negro writers have lagged sadly" behind "the Negro workers' struggle," declared Wright's "Blueprint" (54), and Ellison's review counted the ways. Turpin ignored communism and "lagged" in the "political sense," Ellison charged; he ignored most of the black-Left syntheses of Harlem's radical thinkers and lagged in the "cultural . . . sense"; he ignored the discoveries of literary modernism—"the techniques of his contemporaries," not yet imagined as averse to Marxism—and lagged in the technical sense (Ellison, "Creative," 91). (Years later, Ellison would charge that this last, technical lag in Turpin rendered him "an obstetrician attempting with obsolete instruments to aid a birth he sees only cloudily through blurred vision" ["Recent" 24].) In short, Turpin stranded the innovative historical saga of *These Low Grounds* behind the frontlines of contemporary (meaning Marxist) history—a history that Wright was busy injecting into the African-American canon, and Ellison was struggling to catch up with, in part through deeming a fellow apprentice to black writing behind the times. The "anxiety of influence" that critics have detected in Ellison's relationship to Wright thus initially centered not so much on a semi-Oedipal psychosexual contest as on Ellison's anxious belatedness before Marxist historical materialism, the then-cutting-edge philosophy of history to which Wright had migrated before him. As he debuted as a serious writer, Ellison knew enough to recognize that he lagged behind Wright as a Marxist literary intellectual, but that he just might pass other contenders for Wright's vanguard role by brandishing the related avant-gardist premises of modernism and communism. For now, he was content to stay in

front of Turpin and the rest of the pack, and behind the game defined by Wright, a young gun confident enough of the future to
call his thoughts on working methods a "Blueprint for Negro
Writing."

Yet Wright, too, feared being surpassed by the African-American communist with whom Ellison would do his most significant
work as a radical critic and editor. Prior to Wright's arrival in
New York to write for the *Daily Worker*, Angelo Herndon was the
most respected name in Harlem leftism. The cry of "Free Herndon and the Scottsboro Boys!"—eventually echoed in the pages
of "Blueprint" (54)—was first heard in the early 1930s at hundreds
of communist rallies, where Herndon rivaled the Alabama prisoners as the leading symbol of the party's blunt attack on southern apartheid. In Atlanta in 1932, he had led a march of the unemployed that led to his conviction by an all-white jury under an
1861 statute designed to prevent slave insurrection. The evidence
against him included communist pamphlets taken from his bed-
room and a stray copy of *Red Book* magazine, whose ruby-col-
ored cover alone the prosecutor thought was proof of guilt.
Herndon was ultimately saved from an eighteen- to twenty-year
sentence on the chain gang by Benjamin Davis and John H. Geer,
attorneys with the communist ILD and the first black lawyers "to
have sole control of a major civil rights case in the South" (Griffiths 622–23). Out on bond before his acquittal, he appeared at
dozens of party rallies, some of them featuring replicas of chain-
gang cages, perhaps the incitement for Brother Tarp's dented
chain-link memento in the Brotherhood section of *Invisible
Man* (Griffiths 623). In distinction to the less well-educated and
ideologically savvy Scottsboro Boys, Herndon was an articu-
late spokesman for communism. He was compared to Frederick
Douglass for his oratory, and recruited by Random House to
write a 400-page political autobiography, *Let Me Live*, issued in
1937 to applause from the *New York Times* and other mainstream
northern newspapers. Wright and Ellison, manning the cushy
cultural front in Harlem, had reason to feel "battle-scar envy" of
Herndon, as critic Frederick T. Griffiths suggests (631). Both also
had reason to admire and resent his literary priority: he published an unignorable account of black communist awakening

before either had placed a full-length work. To Ellison in particular, Herndon was another sign that the vanguard of Harlem radicalism was up and running—and risking its neck—well before he crossed paths with Langston Hughes.

Ellison finally caught up with Herndon in 1942, when he took a short-lived job as managing editor at a new journal named *Negro Quarterly*. Herndon himself, who served as editor in chief, was the main recruiter, considering Ellison "the most decently qualified black in New York" (Jackson 266). Editorial duties were to be split evenly. Herndon would raise funds and potential readers with his high profile; Ellison would run day-to-day operations and solicit authors; and both would set editorial policy. The resulting "Review of Negro Life and Culture" followed the "Double V" line on World War II visible in Ellison's story "In a Strange Country": its editorials advocated a dual victory over Axis fascism and American Jim Crow. Its articles addressed a constituency wider than the Communist party, but remained within the orbit of Harlem anticapitalism, for which the party still provided the majority of debating points. The journal's offices on West 125th Street bisected an ideological range that stretched mainly from the party faithful to the party skeptical—from Herbert Aptheker, the diehard communist historian of Negro slave revolts, to Richard Wright, preparing his first anguished critique of party dogmatism in the form of "I Tried to Be a Communist" (1944).

Critics have tended to read Ellison's contributions to *Negro Quarterly* as abstract variations on Wright's budding anticommunism, and as direct preparation for the antimaterialist theory of politics endorsed in the culmination of *Invisible Man*. Closer to the truth, however, is that Ellison's work for the journal extended his fascination with the communist-fed dialectic of belatedness and vanguardism, and predicted the imaginative resolution of its tensions that energizes his history of invisibility. Ellison's signed piece "Transition," a spring 1942 review of William Attaway's novel *Blood on the Forge* (1941), is a case in point. Like many later readers, Ellison recognized Attaway's work as a major fictional reflection on the Great Migration, the mass exodus that directed Ellison and millions of other African Americans from the South to the North after 1910. The book's special contribution to understanding this epochal event, believed Ellison, was its Marxist comprehension of "two areas and eras of Negro experience, those of the semi-feudal plantation and the industrial urban environments" ("Transition" 89). Attaway, a frequent presence on the Harlem Left, correctly discerned that his historical "source material receives its dynamic movement from the clash of two modes of economic production" (89). He knew that the South differed from the North as a semifeudal mode of production differed from a wholly industrial-capitalist one. He realized, apropos of Ellison's title, that the greatest metamorphosis of the Great Migration consisted in the transition from feudalism to capitalism, a passionate concern of Marxist historians since the broad strokes of Marx and Engels's *German Ideology* (1845–1846).

Yet Ellison's review goes on to find the historical cognition of *Blood on the Forge* limited, and for reasons similar to those discussed in his evaluation of Turpin's *These Low Grounds*. Attaway, Ellison maintains, squandered his progressive focus on migration between modes of production by failing to grasp history and Marxist historiography in all their contemporaneity. Nostalgic for the ways of southern black folk, he lagged behind the knowledge that not all migrants had been deadened by the Great Migration. In the process, he fell behind the creative-technical vanguard of African Americans, who were able to conceive of the transition in flexible, scientific terms. Ellison complains that *Blood on the Forge* contains no such vanguard "center of consciousness, lodged in a character or characters, capable of comprehending the sequence of events" (90)—thus anticipating his famous attack on Wright's inability to produce a protagonist as insightful as Wright himself. He hints that the needed center of consciousness might look a lot like his editor in chief, Angelo Herndon, "the most conscious Negro type, the black trade unionist," who seized the intellectual breakthroughs that compensated for the losses of industrialization (91).

New to Ellison's vanguardist vocabulary, however, is the suggestion that historical vision and initiative might also stem from some of the masses who campaigned for Herndon, masses who linked the bygone with the trailblazing. "Attaway grasped the destruction of the folk, but missed its rebirth on a higher level," Ellison protested. "Nor did Attaway see that the individual which emerged, blended of old and new, was better fitted for the problems of the industrial environment" (90). This criticism divulged a conclusion at odds with the most linear Marxist accounts of historical development, yet one true to Ellison's belated path through Harlem communism. Beneath the Hegelian terminology of rebirths and levels, he proposed that arriving late to the black metropolis, combining down-home ways and the latest intellectual devices, supplied resources for superior leadership. Ellison's thesis was not completely without Marxist precedent. Between the lines, he argued that the most conscious black migrants in northern factories—and, by extension, at Harlem's *Negro Quarterly*—shared the status of the trend-setting colonized workers invoked in Leon Trotsky's controversial theory of "uneven and combined development." Ellison's folk, like Trotsky's "colonial proletariat," were empowered to vault directly from feudalism to the anticapitalist forefront by uniting "backward" features with those drawn from the most advanced stages of capitalist development. Whatever the implications of taking theoretical cues from Trotsky while supporting a Stalinist political party, Ellison's thesis had the advantage of narrowing his own historical lag behind Wright, Hughes, and other black communists. His literary criticism was no longer just a footnote to Wright's "Blueprint"; he was ready to issue his own diagram for treating the "aching past" as "a guide and discipline for the future" (Ellison, "Transition," 92).

Portions of this diagram can be found in Ellison's best-remembered contribution to *Negro Quarterly*, an editorial comment in the final, spring 1943, issue that he may have hashed out with Herndon. Ellison here translates his advice to African-American authors such as Turpin and Attaway into advice to "Negro leaders" more generally ("Editorial" 300). Black captains of business and politics were obliged to narrow their distance from the black majority by tightening their grip on the innovative, wherever it could be found. "They must integrate themselves with the Negro masses," Ellison advised. "They must be constantly alert to new concepts, new techniques and new trends among other peoples and nations with an eye toward appropriating those which are valid when tested against the reality of Negro life" (300). "When needed concepts, techniques or theories do not exist" elsewhere, black leaders "must create them" themselves, accepting the model of the black war workers, who were mastering "hitherto unavailable techniques" and winning the "equivalent . . . of a major military objective," behaving like the avant-garde in its original, military incarnation (301). Yet effective African-American leaders were also required to explore the novel path to power in the seemingly random and backward "myths and symbols which abound among the Negro masses" (301). "Much in Negro life remains a mystery," Ellison remarks in a slyly anthropological voice. "Perhaps the zoot suit contains profound political meaning; perhaps the symmetrical frenzy of the Lindy-hop conceals clues to great potential power" (301). For cultural leader Ellison, at least, these questions could not be more rhetorical. In the antiefficient extravagance of the hipster's padded suit; in the mock-primitive dance honoring Charles Lindbergh's mechanical leap into the stratosphere, he saw evidence of the unpunctual futurism of black urbanity. While Turpin, Attaway, and official black leadership balked at authentic contemporaneity and unwittingly assisted "the Jim Crow retardation of the flow of the Negro folk consciousness" (Ellison, "Recent," 24), Harlem's street-level avant-garde nabbed such contemporaneity from behind, creating a wartime subculture of uneven, combined, and imminent development. Ellison never fully enjoyed or valued bebop, this subculture's incipient art music. But he shared its love for lindy-hopping at the Savoy, savoring the bands' hard-driving swing and the dancers' fast-moving stylization of his thoughts on impeding and exceeding historical time-as-usual.

In the Tracks of the Hep-Cat Subway

In the aftermath of the merchant marines, the shifting urgencies of World War II communism, and the folding of *Negro Quarterly,* Ellison retreated from radical Harlem and entered the neighborhood of *Invisible Man.* "It all began during the summer of 1945," he recalled, "in a barn in Waitsfield, Vermont," where the insistent voice of the shapeless narrator descended on him as he recuperated from city exhaustion (*IM* vii). Yet this beginning did not abruptly end Ellison's reflection on the topics that had kept him coming back to the Harlem bureau of the *Daily Worker*. Among the "things once obscure falling into place" during the composition of *Invisible Man* were what Ellison called "political activities observed during my prewar days in Harlem" (xvi). He "had agitated . . . for the release of Angelo Herndon and the Scottsboro Boys," he recollected, "and had been part of a throng which blocked off Fifth Avenue in protest of the role being played by Germany and Italy in the Spanish Civil War" (xvii).

The style in which *Invisible Man* replaced and reimagined Ellison's agitation for communist causes remains a primary contribution to the anticommunist imagination—among the last such contributions, in fact, still regularly assigned in high school and college surveys of American literature. Given the declining fortunes of Whittaker Chambers's *Witness* (1952) and other anticommunist classics following the collapse of the Cold War, students required to read Ellison's novel have little reason to doubt that U.S. anticommunism was piloted by African Americans weary of party racism. Wright's *Native Son*, sometimes the title just preceding *Invisible Man* on the syllabus, helps to seal this impression. The truth is more complicated, however, as Ellison's best-informed and least-forgiving recent radical critic emphasizes. For Barbara Foley, the turbulent ingenuity of Ellison's novel, stretching naturalism to meet the surreal, does not prevent him from lazily reproducing anticommunist clichés. "Ellison's own experience of the left during the years represented in the Harlem section of *Invisible Man* was not one of unremitting bitterness and betrayal," she asserts, and thus could not be "the source of the novel's overwhelmingly negative portrayal of the Brotherhood," Ellison's ironic euphemism for the party ("Rhetoric" 541). Foley submits that the widespread American "discourse of anticommunism," already "maturing rapidly in the late 1940s," was the true inspiration for the book's grievance against Brother Jack and other tokens of communist blindness, foreignness, and callous will-to-power (542). Significantly, more than a handful of

Invisible Man's initial reviewers agreed in advance with the heart of Foley's argument. Lloyd L. Brown and other black communists placed the novel within an evolved "Richard Wright–Chester Himes school" of anticommunist maneuvers (32), underscoring that Ellison's lag behind Wright's communism was followed by a lag behind Wright's anticommunism. More surprisingly, novelist Saul Bellow, an ally of Ellison's genius with no love lost for communism, admitted that he did not "think the hero's experiences in the Communist party are as original in conception as the other parts of the book" (28). Richard Chase, a liberal academic critic soon to write the influential history *The American Novel and Its Tradition* (1957), complimented Ellison's "sheer richness of invention," but similarly complained that "not all of Mr. Ellison's communists escape cliché" (36, 37). No reviewer of any persuasion, meanwhile, escaped the conclusion that Ellison's Brotherhood and the American Communist party were meant to be one and the same.

Foley's objection to the secondhand outrages indicted in the anticommunism of *Invisible Man* thus would not have shocked too many of the novel's original readers. Among other strengths, her work directs us to a forgotten element in the novel's early reception history, an element that illuminates underexplored ties between *Invisible Man* and an array of anticommunist texts, from Chester Himes's novel *Lonely Crusade* (1947) to Arthur Schlesinger, Jr.'s historical study *The Vital Center* (1949). At the same time, however, Foley's argument encourages a presumptive isolation of Ellison's radical and liberal careers—careers joined, to her mind, only as immediately experienced procommunist facts are related to borrowed anticommunist distortions. *Invisible Man*'s many meditations on existential and historical time, for their part, tell a different story of relationship, continuing a dialogue on vanguardism and belatedness whose outlines were revealed as Ellison bolted from the scene of Scottsboro, and whose dramatic unfolding began as he emigrated to Harlem communism.

Quick visits to two of *Invisible Man*'s most pointed deliberations on time and history will have to make this final case. In Ellison's well-known prologue, the transparent narrator introduces several of the historiographical tropes that the novel proceeds to probe, combine, and integrate into its own narrative procedures. History is said to move by "contradiction," a claim not too far removed from the Marxist account of history as class conflict (*IM* 6). It is said to fly "not like an arrow, but a boomerang," a specification that ranks circular theories of a history that hurts above overconfident linear ones, the Brotherhood's arrogant, Marxist "science of history" not excluded (6). Most interestingly, however, the novel's prologue compares such abstractions of historical time to the peculiar sense of time proper to invisibility—a sense best captured in the poetry made when jazz trumpeter Louis Armstrong "bends that military instrument into a beam of lyrical sound" (8). With invisibility, the narrator explains, "you're never quite on the beat. Sometimes you're ahead and sometimes behind. Instead of the swift and imperceptible flowing of time, you are aware of its nodes, those points where time stands still or from which it points ahead" (8). These much-discussed sentences disclose Ellison's remarkable range of intellectual interests and sympathies, his equally intense study of philosopher Henri Bergson, novelist William Faulkner, and master-of-syncopation Louis Armstrong, all modernists leagued against the invariable forward motion of the factory clock. For good measure, these sentences also contain a profane in-group joke on "CP" or "colored people's" time, said to run an hour or two behind the imperial world standard coordinated in Greenwich, England (Graham and Singh 204). No less, however, do these famous lines reflect a set of concerns over historical authority that had consumed Ellison since his introduction to the "CP time" of the Communist party. The theory of seemingly backward historical leadership developed in the pages of *Negro Quarterly* here becomes a mini-philosophy of the existential experience of blackness in and through time. The precise referents have changed, as has the particular field of application, but the distinctive stress on rapid shuttling between the vanguard and the rearguard—"sometimes you're ahead and sometimes behind"—remains.

Jump to chapter 20, the second deliberation on history in *Invisible Man* that fuses the radical and liberal Ellisons. Near the climax of the narrator's showdown with the Brotherhood, he enters the subway—since Ezra Pound's "In a Station of the Metro" (1916), a favorite modernist double for the classical epic underground where the future meets the past. His head is turned by a trio of boys who appear to have abandoned themselves to the tempo of invisibility. With "their legs swinging from their hips in trousers that ballooned upward from cuffs fitting snug about their ankles; their coats long and hip-tight with shoulders far too broad to be those of natural western men" (*IM* 440), they walked directly off the pages of *Negro Quarterly*, promising to solve the riddle of the zoot suit Ellison posed in 1943. At first, the narrator answers the enigma of their profound political meaning in the negative. "They were men outside of historical time, they were untouched, they didn't believe in Brotherhood" (440)—in short, they signified the profound political impotence of evading history's upwardly spiraling or arrowlike path. Something snaps, however, and the narrator begins to approach the hipsters' riddle through the dissenting historical terms that inform the prologue's discussion of Armstrong, set earlier in the novel's page order but later in its boomeranging timeline. "Who knew but they were the saviors, the true leaders, the bearers of something precious?" the narrator asks. "What if Brother Jack were wrong? What if history was a gambler, instead of a force in a laboratory experiment, and the boys his ace in the hole?" (441).

By the chapter's end, the question marks have all but disappeared. The dawning leadership of the boys is seen to rest on their understanding of history's gambling arbitrariness, its lack of scientific predictability. Just as in the prologue, however, the ability to outperceive those selling the "swift and imperceptible flowing of time" (8) is enmeshed with the capacity to look both ahead and behind. The boys impress the narrator as "men of transition," migrants "speak[ing] a jived-up transitional language full of country glamour," hard-core modernists who nonetheless "should have disappeared around the first part of the nineteenth century, rationalized out of existence" (440, 441, 442). They are the heirs of the migrants Ellison unveiled in his Attaway review, "Transition"—a newly arrived metropolitan vanguard synthesizing the old and the new and reinventing the folk in the subterranean heights of the subway. In an introduction to *Invisible*

Man written thirty years after its first publication, Ellison cites Faulkner to instruct readers that "what is commonly assumed to be past history is actually as much a part of the living present" (*IM* xvi). For all its anticommunism, this novel's still-animated past included the Ellison who thought and agitated his way through Harlem communism—an Ellison who, finally, in 1952, supplied a version of the African-American leadership class he had sought in *New Challenge* and *Negro Quarterly*, an invisible band radical enough to refuse distinctions between "the rear" and "the avant-garde" (*IM* 572).

WORKS CITED

Bellow, Saul. "Man Underground: Review of *Invisible Man* by Ralph Ellison." 1952. In *The Critical Response to Ralph Ellison*, edited by Robert J. Butler, 27–29. Westport, Conn.: Greenwood, 2000.

Brown, Lloyd L. "The Deep Pit: Review of *Invisible Man* by Ralph Ellison." 1952. In *The Critical Response to Ralph Ellison*, edited by Robert J. Butler, 31–33. Westport, Conn.: Greenwood, 2000.

Butler, Robert J., ed. *The Critical Response to Ralph Ellison*. Westport, Conn.: Greenwood, 2000.

Chase, Richard. "A Novel Is a Novel: Review of *Invisible Man* by Ralph Ellison." 1952. In *The Critical Response to Ralph Ellison*, edited by Robert J. Butler, 35–37. Westport, Conn.: Greenwood, 2000.

Ellison, Ralph. "Creative and Cultural Lag: Review of *These Low Grounds* by Waters Turpin." *New Challenge: A Literary Quarterly* 2, no. 2 (Fall 1937): 90–91.

———. "Editorial Comment." *Negro Quarterly* 1, no. 4 (Winter–Spring 1943): 295–302.

———. "Judge Lynch in New York." *New Masses* 33 (15 August 1939): 15–16.

———. "Negro Prize Fighter." Review of *Walk Hard, Talk Loud* by Len Zinberg. *New Masses* 37 (17 December 1940): 26–27.

———. "Recent Negro Fiction." *New Masses* 40 (5 August 1941): 22–26.

———. "Transition." Review of *Blood on the Forge* by William Attaway. *Negro Quarterly* 1, no. 1 (Spring 1942): 87–92.

Fabre, Michel. "From Native Son to Invisible Man: Some Notes on Ralph Ellison's Evolution in the 1950s." In *Speaking for You: The Vision of Ralph Ellison*, edited by Kimberly W. Benston, 198–216. Washington, D.C.: Howard University Press, 1987.

Foley, Barbara. "Reading Redness: Politics and Audience in Ralph Ellison's Early Short Fiction." *JNT: Journal of Narrative Theory* 29, no. 3 (Fall 1999): 323–39.

———. "The Rhetoric of Anticommunism in *Invisible Man*." *College English* 59, no. 5 (September 1997): 530–47.

Graham, Maryemma, and Amritjit Singh, eds. *Conversations with Ralph Ellison*. Jackson: University Press of Mississippi, 1995.

Griffiths, Frederick T. "Ralph Ellison, Richard Wright, and the Case of Angelo Herndon." *African-American Review* 35, no. 4 (2001): 615–36.

Jackson, Lawrence. *Ralph Ellison: Emergence of Genius*. New York: Wiley, 2002.

Maxwell, William J. *New Negro, Old Left: African-American Writing and Communism between the Wars*. New York: Columbia University Press, 1999.

O'Meally, Robert G. *The Craft of Ralph Ellison*. Cambridge, Mass.: Harvard University Press, 1980.

O'Meally, Robert G., ed. *Living with Music: Ralph Ellison's Jazz Writings*. New York: Modern Library, 2001.

Wright, Richard. "Blueprint for Negro Writing." *New Challenge: A Literary Quarterly* 2, no. 2 (Fall 1937): 53–65.

A Delicate Ear, a Retentive Memory, and the Power to Weld the Fragments

Steven C. Tracy

> I am now satisfied that the future of music of this country must be founded upon what are called negro melodies. This must be the real foundation of any serious and original school of composition to be developed in the United States.
> —Antonín Dvořák, "The Real Value of Negro Melodies"

> My basic sense of artistic form is musical. . . . I think that basically my instinctive approach to writing is through sound.
> —Ralph Ellison, "A Completion of Personality"

I

When European composer Antonín Dvořák came to America as director of the National Conservatory of Music in 1892, he brought with him a profound interest in the potentialities for music on American soil. In fact, just six weeks before he and his family left Bohemia for America, he began his cantata *The American Flag*, opus 102. This interest, of course, reflected Dvořák's artistic aesthetic. His emphasis on how Romantic, particularly nationalistic, issues influenced the artistry of the classical composer, and by extension the literary artist as well, is borne out in his late nineteenth-century pronouncements concerning the nature and future of the American school of music as it would emerge in the twentieth century.

American artists had been struggling with the question of American identity since the country's inception, trying to determine what was unique about and characteristic of the American landscape and people, and searching for distinctive forms and techniques to express those ideas. In "Music in America," published in *Harper's New Monthly Magazine* in 1895—the year Dvořák resigned from the conservatory—Dvořák opined that "the germs for the best of music lie hidden among all the races that are commingled in this great country" (Tibbetts 377), and indicated a particular interest in "negro melodies" (Tibbetts 355) as a primary source for a national American art. Anticipating the arrival of the quintessentially American artist, Dvořák continued, "The music of the people is like a rare and lovely flower growing amidst encroaching weeds. Thousands pass it, while others trample it underfoot, and thus the chances are that it will perish before it is seen by the one discriminating spirit who will prize it above all else" (Tibbetts 377–78). This idea regarding the natural productions of the folk seems to stem from Johann Herder, who was influential in the development of Romanticism through his notions about folklore—which he called "a spontaneous, indigenous expression of the collective soul of a people" (Bell 156)—and its importance to and influence on "high art." It was an idea that helped prompt many budding Romantics and nationalist writers to seek in their own folklore, national mythologies, and peasant life the national expression which would become the basis for their artistic productions.

Naturally, this one discriminating spirit, as Dvořák termed it, would need to have special qualities to be able to recognize the potentialities of the material: "a delicate ear, a retentive memory, and the power to weld the fragments of former ages together in one harmonious whole" (Tibbetts 378). And the artist must be capable of a broad, discerning appreciation of materials: "Nothing must be too low or too insignificant for the musician. When he walks he should listen to every whistling boy, every street singer or blind organ-grinder" (Tibbetts 378). That is, the power of the national must be rooted in the expressive temperament and diversity of the local. The truly great artist will see in the whistler and the organ grinder the strength and beauty of the nation, and unite them in a profoundly great vision that produces a comprehensive and transcendent art.

Is there a better description of the artistry of Ralph Ellison?

Ellison himself felt that the quest for identity was the central great theme of American literature (Plimpton 329). Indeed, he sought in his works to describe and explain the American character through the delineation of African-American experiences in this country as they affected the nature of the country as a whole. He saw the varied experiences of a range of peoples in this country as commingled, crucially intertwined in a way that made defining America without the paradoxes and dilemmas occasioned by the gap between American ideals and realities hopelessly delusory. Ellison's reference to Dvořák's Ninth Symphony, *From the New World*, in chapter 5 of *Invisible Man* makes clear Ellison's recognition of American syncretism in art. The narrator hears in the selections played proudly at the chapel ceremony following Homer A. Barbee's speech strains of "Swing Low, Sweet Chariot," the favorite spiritual of his mother and grandfather and a proud connector to the heritage of African-American art. Nonetheless, however harmoniously Dvořák blends European classical music and spirituals in his work—and it is primarily in the *Largo* section, after all—the narrator cannot bear the Horatio Alger–type, American-dream mythology and illusory optimism of Barbee's speech in juxtaposition with the music, and so rushes from the chapel and the (non)sight of the blind bard Barbee. Indeed, one of the central questions of Ellison's text is how the artist (narrator), having gained insight into the nature of his country and world, can express it adequately and comprehensively and, further, how he can respond socially and politically once he emerges from his artistic cocoon. In their works, both

Dvořák and Ellison attempt to place American art in a larger context, and both, like composer-conductor-musicians, marshal the various elements into compositions that make profound cultural and, in Ellison's case especially, political statements about what the artist is to do with America. Ellison's narrator seems poised to emerge from underground as the novel ends, and in fact has already emerged in creating his narrative, but the question of what to do in the flawed and exploitative world of America above ground still daunts him. And us.

2

In that sublime 1940 orchestra constructed around the particular strengths of saxophonist Ben Webster and bassist Jimmie Blanton, Duke Ellington possessed perhaps his finest concentrated artistic opportunities and achievements. As composer, orchestrator, bandleader, and soloist, Ellington was responsible for bringing his hard work and discipline to a variety of tasks that affected the group's artistic, popular, and financial success. Envisioning the scope of the group's palette based on his own aesthetic and the musical personalities of its members; integrating its common and varied experiences and modes of expression; encouraging a free, artistic exchange of ideas both in formally composed and improvisational performance; composing and selecting the repertoire based on that vision and experience; selecting and ordering the set list based on venue; providing thematic flow, establishing appropriate tempo within songs, and pacing the entire set itself; connecting to the ancestors, the audience, and the descendants in artistically and socially meaningful ways—these are only some of those duties so marvelously managed by Ellington. His compositions and the solos set within them were sound stories, rooted in a particular place and time but having in their purview a universal appeal. They were, to paraphrase Ezra Pound discussing his concept of an image, emotional and intellectual complexes liberated in two-and-a-half minutes of time. Ellington achieved such a high level of identification with his band that, indeed, sounding like Ellington meant sounding like the conversations among the voices of members of his band. From his earliest work with the Washingtonians, Ellington's work possessed this "communal spirit" which "would mark much of the work of the Ellington orchestra" (Hasse 81). The presence of saxophonist Ben Webster, an individual voice capable of both roaring magnificence and tender caressing in his instantly recognizable, blues-based style, gave Ellington the dynamic soloist he needed.

Blanton's arrival on the Ellington scene in 1939 was an auspicious occasion not only for Blanton and Ellington, but for jazz itself. Plucked from the St. Louis bar scene by Ellington after band members reported Blanton's remarkable talent to their leader, the bassist brought to the ever-restless imagination and invention of Ellington a new role for the bass in the orchestra. No longer was the bassist's role of timekeeper, relegated to the background—an estimable role not to be undervalued—sufficient. Now the instrument strutted proudly beyond its former boundaries into the alleys and boulevards of greater melodic freedom and invention. Now it was more of an equal partner in the technical and intellectual and emotional world of the jazz band. In accompaniment, solo, and tone, the bass had arrived at its new jazz orchestral role with this young turk so conversant with its tradition and so ebullient in his expansion of it. And it arrived in the band context in the Ellington composition recorded by the group in March 1940 entitled "Jack the Bear." The composition's title has been identified as stemming from the African-American folklore tradition or from the nickname of either a Harlem bass player or a rent-party pianist/dope addict/gambler named John Wilson. "The Bear" was also Ben Webster's nickname for Blanton. Jack the Bear was part oral legend and part urban reality transmuted by verbal ingenuity into an irrepressible trickster image exuding confidence and power. Now the master bandleader, the tough and tender soloist, the vibrant pulse, and the disciplined aggregation entered the personality of Jack the Bear and made beautiful music at the frontier of big band jazz.

When Ralph Ellison's anonymous narrator claimed Jack the Bear for his identity in the prologue to *Invisible Man*, surely these four pieces of Ellison's own artistic puzzle were in place. After all, by the late 1930s and early 1940s, the music of Ellington had assisted in helping Ellison to understand that "jazz possessed possibilities of a range of expressiveness comparable to that of classical European music" (GT 220), especially music of the Romantic tradition, with which Ellington associated himself through such compositions as "The Harlem Suite" or "Tone Parallel to Harlem," recorded just four months before the release of *Invisible Man*, and "Such Sweet Thunder." Ellington himself, pushing on the artificial boundaries of American musical categorizations and exclusivity with wit and ingenuity, was "an urbane version of the trickster" (Hasse 343), one who used not only the bear character employed later by Ellison, but also the rabbit character of folklore in the title of his classic 1940 recording "Cotton Tail." Now this Ellisonian aggregate trickster voice on the frontier of American fiction would make his own music with the various rural and urban, oral and written, legendary and historical voices of his life.

At its best, Ellington's group achieved transcendent personal and artistic connections and success. He helped bring jazz into its big band (and international) artistic maturity without losing the essential connection to individual expression and improvisation so important since the music's inception. And Ellington managed to develop and maintain for his group a high level of visibility from the 1920s until the year of his death in 1974, and even beyond. And what Ellington did! It's a lot like being a novelist. It's a lot like being Ralph Ellison.

3

We should understand Ralph Ellison as a literary artist in the context of musical traditions, traditions that were emerging out of the nationalistic nineteenth-century Romantic and the burgeoning twentieth-century modernist aesthetics, understood and worked out with a strict discipline of form. Ellison's first significant formal teacher-mentor was Zelia Breaux, who was in charge of the music curriculum in African-American schools in Oklahoma City. Like many upwardly mobile, middle-class African Americans in the 1920s, Breaux believed in the elevating power of classical music, and inculcated the lessons of discipline in her students in their artistic endeavors. But she also appreciated folk arts and even opened the Aldridge Theater, where locals could experience great vernacular artists like Bessie Smith, Ma Rainey, and King Oliver (Jackson 56–57). Ellison praised her great gifts to him as "the freedom to broaden our personal culture by absorbing the cultures of others" and her introduction of the idea of the artist's need for discipline (*GT* 136).

This "basic compatibility of the mixture of classical and vernacular styles" (*GT* 136) is reflected in Ellison's references to (primarily African-American) classical music figures in his essays (Hazel Harrison most frequently, but also Marian Anderson, Roland Hayes, Leontyne Price, Simon Estes, and Jessye Norman, among others), short stories (Roland Hayes in "I Did Not Learn Their Names"), and novels (Dvořák in *Invisible Man* and Sissieretta Jones in *Juneteenth*). But it is also reflected in his concern with composing and orchestrating larger forms that weave various musical motifs into an extension of oral elements into a written medium. Ellison's lessons with tutor Ludwig Hebestreit in the early 1930s included discussions of "structure, chord patterns, modulations, and other composition and conducting techniques" (Jackson 68–69), which provided the budding musician with solid formal training, enough to make Ellison think of being a conductor himself. The Ellison who had hoboed to Tuskegee in depression-plagued 1933 with dreams of composing Wagnerian symphonies by his twenty-sixth year found a professor, William L. Dawson, whose own work transforming African-American folk music into classical pieces such as the *Negro Symphony No. 1* (1934) seemed to anticipate Ellison's own aspirations. Unfortunately, Dawson's distaste for jazz and blues and inability to appreciate the modernist uses of the imagination drove an inevitable wedge between the two (Jackson 122), though Ellison's 1971 "Homage to William L. Dawson" indicates a fondness and profound respect for Dawson's achievements. Ellison's disagreements with music faculty at Tuskegee were softened by the kindnesses of classical pianist and teacher Hazel Harrison, who unfortunately never recorded commercially, but whose artistry and friendship buoyed the young music major.

In all, his formal, classical teachers offered Ellison technical, intellectual, and emotional support in varying degrees. Breaux also provided a general sense that the uses avant-garde composers were making of African-American vernacular and popular music were entirely appropriate and natural developments. What Dvořák had done with a spiritual in his *From the New World*, or Scott Joplin with ragtime in *Treemonisha* (1911), Stravinsky in *Ragtime* (1918) and later his jazzy *Ebony Concerto* (1945), or the ragtime, blues, and jazz experiments of Darius Milhaud, Paul Hindemith, George Antheil, George Gershwin, Ernst Krenek, William Grant Still, and William L. Dawson in the 1920s and 1930s, and even later Morton Gould and Leonard Bernstein, were necessarily neither incongruous nor ludicrous. And it was this type of modernist openness to experimentation and cross-genre pollination that helped lead to Ellison's mature writings.

4

Of course, we should not underestimate the influence of Ellison's informal teacher-mentors, those musicians to whom he was exposed in the clubs of his youth and with whom he performed, as well as those whose music he encountered on recordings. Ellison's work—novels, short stories, essays, and interviews—celebrates his encounters with blues, jazz, spirituals, and gospel music, emphasizing, importantly, how he was not only entertained but enlightened and instructed by these musicians. This is important because in the 1920s, 1930s, and 1940s—and even beyond then—many people were not ready to claim artistic status for performers of nonclassical African-American music. Beyond that, those who might have appreciated the artistic value of vernacular music may well not have been able to envision how it might be "elevated" to the artistic status it deserved, nor how it might instruct artists from other disciplines in its aesthetic. Ellison himself, after all, felt it necessary to establish a kind of "blues school" of literature (Jackson 296–97) in the early 1940s, dissatisfied, perhaps, by the way the music had been appreciated and employed even by such earlier authors as Langston Hughes.

Blues and jazz were frequently associated in the popular mind with illiteracy, drug abuse, and dissipation rather than creativity, inspiration, and discipline; they might have suggested primitivistic abandon-turned-entertainment rather than heritage and individuality transmuted into art. In a 1921 article in the *Ladies' Home Journal* entitled "Does Jazz Put the Sin in Syncopation?" Anne Shaw Faulkner quoted Dr. Henry van Dyke as saying, "As I understand it, [jazz] is not music at all. It is merely an irritation of the nerves of hearing, a sensual teasing of the strings of physical passion" (Walser 35–36). Interestingly, a War Department education manual from 1944 views jazz as the product of "an inbred, feeble-stocked race, incapable of development," and characterizes it as "sterile," despite its associations with physical passion (Lemke 59), positing both a physical and intellectual impotence thrashed out in the realm of bestiality that parallels the racist assumptions that made *Invisible Man*'s Trueblood a symbol to the white community and an embarrassment to the black when he impregnates his daughter. In fact, even among some more educated and presumably more sympathetic minds the music might not have found its proper appreciation. This may have been for reasons of racism—in 1925 folklorist Dorothy Scarborough found the mind of the Negro "not essentially logical," with "considerable lack of coherence in thought" (272)—or class distinction: in 1940 W. E. B. Du Bois called jazz "caricature" and the performers "entertainers of the white world" (202–3). Of course, there were those who appreciated jazz as an art, magazines devoted to jazz such as *Jazz Hot* and *Down Beat* in the 1930s, and even classes dealing with jazz in America as early as the 1930s. But Ellison was clearly among those who felt that jazz needed to be elevated to its proper level of artistic appreciation.

Generally speaking, spirituals had been the most highly regarded African-American music since the nineteenth century, with James Weldon Johnson editing two important collections of spirituals in the 1920s. Appreciation of jazz as an art form just began to emerge in the late 1930s and early 1940s in book form in the work of Charles Edward Smith, Frederic Ramsay, Iain Smith, and later Rudi Blesh. As far as the blues, it wasn't until 1959, with the appearance of Sam Charters's *The Country Blues*, that real appreciation of the art of the blues performer emerged in book form. Ellison, of course, realized that African-American vernacular and vernacular-based music could both instruct and please, and could also serve as the basis for the "high art" that Alain Locke, James Weldon Johnson, and Langston Hughes felt was still to come.

Ellison made clear the centrality of vernacular music to an African-American aesthetic, and his own, in his review of former Beat, future Black Arts movement writer LeRoi Jones's *Blues People* in 1964. Disagreeing with Jones's pronouncement that a slave could not be a man, Ellison described the slave musician as someone who "realized himself in the world of sound." The music was, in other words, a central means of establishing identity for the individual and provided a sense of liberation in a world that enslaved: "the art . . . was what we had in place of freedom" (*SA* 254–55). Ten years later, Ellison related his own artistic approach to that of the slave musician he described: "I think that basically my instinctive approach to writing is through sound" (*CE* 797). In other words, Ellison's art is realized in that world of sound, and Ellison as an artist finds his form, function, and technique in that same milieu. For example, in a 1992 address, Ellison responded to published research on his grandfather Big Alfred Ellison by demonstrating how the history and legacy of slavery led to his own musical-artistic response: "My reaction at finding my personal connection with slavery and emancipation stated in words was such a mixture of tragedy and comedy that it filled me with a blueslike laughter which caused my wife to ask what had come over me" (*CE* 853). What had come over him was the profound intensity and emotion of the moment of recognition of the sublimity of his forebears' technique and skill in grasping and expressing the nature of African-American life in the American system. His response was to join them in vernacular expression, to acknowledge and employ their expression and that of African-American vernacular music, secular and sacred, in order to negotiate his own situation.

In an essay on Mahalia Jackson, Ellison called attention to the influence of Bessie Smith on Jackson, and noted that Jackson had endured the type of grievous experiences that helped produce the bedrock blues singer as well (*SA* 214–15). Thus when Ellison references spirituals, gospel, jazz, and blues, while he may be speaking of an individual genre, the spirit he is invoking cuts across genres to "a spirit beyond the tragic" (*SA* 140) that found expression in them all, as well as in the work of writers he admired, such as Ernest Hemingway. Thus are the various genres banded together, but also united with a larger context of expression that is both universal and multidisciplinary. Ellison told interviewers in 1955 that he felt it was possible for readers to understand his work without a background knowledge of the folklore involved because, like jazz, "there's no inherent problem which prohibits understanding but the assumptions brought to it" (Plimpton 327). Unfortunately, because assumptions about the nature, artistry, and value of African-American vernacular music had been formed, it was necessary for Ellison, in both his fiction and nonfiction, to unpack the superfluous and misinformed baggage of American culture regarding African Americans in general—as reflected in such films from Ellison's lifetime as *Birth of a Nation* (1915), *Green Pastures* (1936), *Gone with the Wind* (1939), and *Cabin in the Sky* (1942)—and jazz specifically, and bring his own estimate to bear on those attitudes.

Ellison's discussions of jazz in his writings are the work of an artist intent upon illuminating, like the protagonist of *Invisible Man*, the limitations that ignorance, neglect, and presupposition imposed upon African Americans and their culture. Louis Armstrong's legendary response to the query "what is jazz?"—that if you have to ask, you'll never know—rings true, and yet a wordsmith like Ellison, who makes connections between jazz and his own written tradition, believed that trying to do so, both in essays and fiction, could help people hear what their minds wouldn't let them. As such, he made a number of pronouncements about the music that connected to his modernist literary aesthetic in order to garner jazz the serious attention it deserved. It is difficult, for example, not to hear Eliot's "Tradition and the Individual Talent" behind Ellison's 1958 pronouncements that "true jazz is an art of individual assertion within and against the group" and that "each solo flight, or improvisation, represents (like the successive canvases of the painter) a definition of his identity as individual, as member of the collectivity and as a link in the chain of tradition" (*SA* 234). In these statements, Elli-son unites literary, musical, and visual arts; high art and vernacular art; and the individual and the group. Moreover, he references the title of a high-profile 1941 Charlie Christian recording with one of Benny Goodman's inte-grated bands ("Solo Flight")—the primary soloist being an African-American innovator—associated, possibly, with the ideals of Romantic aspiration in the mythic story of Daedalus and Icarus, which illuminates the rewards and dangers of jumping at the sun. And the 1927 flight of Charles Lindbergh in his *Spirit of St. Louis* monoplane, which made Lindbergh an international hero, seems squarely in the background as well. Clearly, the solo flight of the jazz musician could be of great musical, mythical, and his-torical importance.

Furthermore, Ellison emphasized that jazz was not merely the result of uninhibited, instinctual passion, but conscious craft and discipline: Ellison reported that the jazz bands typically re-hearsed far more than the school band, but appeared to possess more enjoyment and freedom than school bands allowed. The "wild, transcendent moments" of jazz band performances that produced the most inspired solos "depended upon dedication to a discipline" that prevailed even under the crowded rehearsal conditions of places like Halley Richardson's shoeshine parlor (*SA* 154–55). Ellison returned time and again to the influence of the discipline, devotion, and technical mastery exercised by jazz artists on his own work ethic and aesthetic, marshaling "the fun-damentals of his instrument and the traditional techniques of jazz—the intonations, mute work, manipulation of timbre, the body of traditional styles" in the service of "being reborn" and finding "his soul" (*SA* 208–9). From Charlie Christian, Jimmy Rushing, Hot Lips Page, Walter Page, Count Basie, and countless other jazz musicians from his youth, Ellison learned to take his craft seriously, to ply it consciously and assiduously in the service of self and group definition and actualization. One did not shut down part of one's identity, the intellect, to achieve jazz expres-sion through pure passion; rather, emotion and intellect served and supported each other in the service of transcendent expres-sion. At a time when many conceived of jazz as a kind of "spontaneous overflow of powerful emotions"—and not recollected in tranquillity—Ellison's insistence upon the contributions of deliberateness and depth of technique was a serious corrective.

This kind of serious commitment to craft and imagination made the jazz performer a role model not only as an artist but as a human being. Given that since even before the 1920s, the importance of African Americans presenting a proper and dignified (read: middle-class) image for the progress of the race exerted a strong pull on upwardly mobile blacks, Ellison's 1964 statements on the matter were pointedly remarkable: "Looking back, one might say that the jazzmen, some of whom we idolized, were in their own way better examples for youth to follow than were most judges and ministers, legislators and governors" (*SA* xiv). Placing the jazz performer ahead of the representatives of the systems of law, religion, and government as exemplars of proper modes of discipline and behavior was quite an emphatic criticism of the supposedly respectable representatives of American society, a radical re-envisioning of the proper (or improper) status of the misunderstood jazz musician.

5

Given his reconsideration of the importance of the jazz musician, it is understandable that throughout his written work Ellison discusses jazz and its performers with a greater frequency than any other musical genre. In his essays, Ellison mentions an array of performers from the roots of jazz in ragtime (Scott Joplin, Jelly Roll Morton, Fats Waller) to early purveyors of embryonic jazz (James Reese Europe, King Oliver) to jazz's first generation of stars (Louis Armstrong, Duke Ellington, Coleman Hawkins) to the stars of the swing and big band era (Count Basie, Charlie Christian, Lester Young, Jimmy Rushing, Benny Goodman) to the beboppers of the 1950s (Dizzy Gillespie, Charlie Parker, Miles Davis, Thelonius Monk). His short story "A Hard Time Keeping Up" mentions the Gershwin jazz staple "Summertime," and the title of his World War II–era short story "Flying Home" (1944) comes from the song that was initially an interracial collaboration of jazz performers Benny Goodman and Lionel Hampton, later made popular as a big band vehicle by Hampton. On Hampton's 1942 Decca recording, the remarkable Illinois Jacquet, struggling to establish an individual identity on his instrument, found his voice and pointed the way for rhythm-and-blues saxophonists to come with a seminal solo that was a triumph of integration of the individual and group. At one point, we hear Jacquet and a riffing horn section trading repeatedly on the same note, but liberated by a beautifully intertwined rhythmic complexity, creating a relentless swing that, when the octane was upped by Jacquet two years later at the *Jazz at the Philharmonic* concerts on the tune "Blues," created a frantic prototype for the honking and screaming R&B saxophone style. Style, technique, discipline, imagination, individual voice, group identity, and a breakthrough to the new and innovative—it was an Ellisonian dream. Clearly Jacquet's soaring solo informs the symbolism of Ellison's story of an African-American flyer trying to emerge from the wreckage of his life in order to "transcend his limitations" again, while at the same time clarifying his relationship to his "racial group" through his dealings with the black "peasant" who finds him. By bringing together these themes with contemporary African-American experiences in the military during World War II and the popular and groundbreaking recording, Ellison created an extremely rich emotional, intellectual, political, and cultural complex of meaning.

The musician Ellison mentions most frequently in his essays is also the jazz figure that plays the most prominent role in his fiction, Louis Armstrong. Armstrong's name first turns up in Ellison's 1943 short story "That I Had the Wings," where the powerful crowing of a rooster earns him the nickname "the Louie Armstrong of the chickens" (*FH* 53). Significantly, the young boys see Louie the rooster as defying tigers, signifying monkey-style, and inventing new notes for the trumpet that nobody has heard yet. It is a harbinger of Ellison's role for Armstrong in his first novel. Interestingly, initially Ellison had planned to employ Buddy Bolden in the role Armstrong ultimately took in *Invisible Man*. It was a masterful switch, and one that plays out very well historically, thematically, and aesthetically in the novel. Armstrong, the presiding genius of jazz in the twentieth century, a major jazz innovator who refocused jazz on the soloist rather than on ensemble playing, was nonetheless by this point seen by many as the caricature and entertainer of the white race as Du Bois commented in *Dusk of Dawn*. The clowning, mugging image of Armstrong, handkerchief in hand and bright smile shining like a lighthouse on the sea, playing pop tunes in front of a big band, became fixed in the popular mind, while musicians of the bebop generation that emerged in the mid-1940s sought the status of artistic respectability in place of the label of entertainer and the function of providing dance music. Dizzy Gillespie, for example, who recognized Armstrong's great contributions to jazz and his own style, nevertheless bemoaned Armstrong's "plantation image" because he felt that white audiences would expect the same type of demeanor from him (Walser 168). Criticism from the Left berated Armstrong for gleefully reaping the benefits of the capitalist system by abandoning his New Orleans roots for commercial appeal and not retaining his artistic integrity, though his return to the small-band New Orleans jazz format with his All Stars in 1947 was welcomed by some. Unfortunately, Armstrong even developed the image of an "Uncle Tom," despite the fact that he spoke out about Eisenhower's inaction following the Orville Faubus–Little Rock incident in 1957 and occasionally commented on racial matters to the press thereafter. The question becomes, who was Armstrong: the revolutionary jazz performer or the smiling image before the mainstream American public?

One answer is that Armstrong was both, the trickster using a mask to make his forays across social and musical boundaries without exposing himself to too much danger in the process. America in the 1940s was still Jim Crow territory, after all, and Armstrong the entertainer needed his southern and northern dates to sustain himself financially. Surely, economics influenced his decisions. But certainly Armstrong continued to demonstrate his remarkable genius, though no longer avant-garde, throughout his career. Even at the end, he took naïve or innocuous lightweight songs and transformed them through his highly individual style, vocal timbre, and personality. It is a point that

Ellison himself makes in "Change the Joke and Slip the Yoke," where he terms Armstrong's boundary-challenging clowning abilities "Elizabethan" (*SA* 67). Ellison confronts the problem in *Invisible Man*: how far must and can an African American go to gain opportunity, to succeed? What does it mean to succeed, and how far is too far? Readers continue to argue over the final choice of Tod Clifton to be a street vendor selling Sambo dolls. Just what was he thinking?

The song that Ellison presents Armstrong performing in that acoustic deadness underground in the prologue to *Invisible Man* is full of particular significance as well. The words to "(What Did I Do to Be So) Black and Blue?" were written by Andy Razaf for the *Hot Chocolates* revue in 1929, and set to music by Fats Waller. Generated in response to a threatening directive by mobster Dutch Schultz to provide a funny song featuring a woman singing about how tough it is to be black (!), Razaf responded with a revolutionary protest song that broke the boundaries of the current subject matter on the Broadway stage, courting danger, he knew, in writing it and yet, under threat from Schultz (and perhaps from the implications of his own refusal to confront the situation head on), courting danger if he didn't. This condition, of course, recalls that of Trueblood in the novel, whose need to move without moving in his situation with his daughter proves so vexing. The Razaf-Waller song negotiates the situation through honest, superbly crafted lyrics and a melody perfectly adapted to their blues inflections stretched into a pop-song format, beautifully sung by Edith Wilson. Armstrong recorded the song in June of that same year, and his version, which was interestingly not issued in the race series set aside for African Americans but in OKeh's white series, could be considered a courageous choice of material (Singer 217–20).

What Armstrong does with the lyrics, however, is interesting. Whereas the original song actually has three stanzas, Armstrong sings only roughly one-third of them, a composite of stanzas two and three. What he eliminates are the most overt intraracial elements of the song, those dealing with the social stratification by skin color within the African-American community, that spawned an entire industry of skin-lightening and hair-straightening products. Lyrically, then, he places greater emphasis on the interracial tragedy of such lyrics as "My only sin is in my skin" and "I'm white inside, it don't help my case." More important is the fact that the first half of his recording is wordless, a musical introduction to the theme that presents a triumphantly inventive and technically advancing Armstrong delineating the emotional parameters of what it means to be black and blue. The pun of the title becomes clearer and more ironic. The interracial violence symbolized by the reference to bruising (black and blue), modulated to refer to skin color and the mental state produced by such mistreatment (black and blue), is transformed into a transcendent statement by a black man in the idiom of the black blues. It is truly the triumph of art over social limitations, at least in an immortal three-minute spinning slab of black shellac, which turns out to be no small thing in itself. When the narrator says that he wants to hear five recordings of the performance simultaneously, he is clearly referring to his desire to replicate Armstrong's revolutionary artistry, to increase the ranks, as it were, and to put that "military instrument" (*IM* 8) to its musical and lyrical battle with the racial status quo. The recording exemplifies the notion of making poetry out of being invisible and reminds, perhaps, Armstrong's social critics just what he had done, overtly and covertly, with his artistry.

In this sense, Armstrong the trickster has the last laugh. Significantly, the performer Armstrong frequently had a huge grin on his face, like the bank the invisible protagonist tried so assiduously to dispose of, but Armstrong was aware of the value of the smile. While Armstrong could expose the exultant that arose from the tragic, he could also expose the underside of the upbeat as well. For example, his 1927 recording of "Twelfth Street Rag" brilliantly signifies on the conventional versions of the tune, which are generally rollicking, uptempo fingerbusters. Armstrong turns it into a blues, with gutbucket tempo and inflections that almost mock expectations through the tension he creates between the plodding tempo and his magnificent rhythmic liberties. His rhythmic complexities within this slowed-down setting are so daring, so challenging, that they defy any easy melodic journey in favor of an exploration of how the twists and turns of the blues life transform the style and tenor of the story.

A number of African-American artists, Langston Hughes among them, had been critical of middle-class audiences that had been unwilling or unable to see past the carefree surface of cabaret performance to the "tingle of a tear" underneath (Rampersad 412). In *Invisible Man*, the veteran's admonition for the narrator to learn to look beneath the surface can be seen in the context of Ellison's desire to have listeners hear beneath the surface of jazz to its creative and emotional core, or be tricked into illusions of understanding that continue to render jazz invisible in mainstream American culture. Louis Armstrong as trickster, playing with subject matter, sense of time and rhythm, and the polarities and uncertainties of African-American life from a vernacular-based but individually creative vantage point, frames and stands at the center of *Invisible Man*.

Juneteenth, too, refers to jazz performers like Sam Nanton and Jimmy Rushing, as well as songs such as Louis Armstrong's "Struttin' with Some Barbecue," a Hot Five recording that plays off the stereotypes in the title with virtuoso breaks highlighted by stop-time choruses. The novel is also peppered with references to musical elements like having a new rhythm (*J* 130), keeping to the rhythm (131), trusting the inner beat (131), and using a solo-rhythm-break pattern as Hickman plans a strategy for dealing with Bliss's mother (306). Clearly the notion of listening to one's musical heartbeat to help establish identity and strategies for living informs the text. Of course, the style of the novel combines Faulknerian techniques with the call-and-response patterns prominent in African-American music, blended so skillfully that it recalls Ellison's claims that he found Eliot's rhythms in *The Waste Land* to be closer to jazz than those of many African-American poets (*CE* 203). Ellison, in fact, found Eliot's "artful juxtaposition of earlier styles" to be similar to the techniques of Louis Armstrong (*SA* 225). Ellison's main character, Hickman, is identified with an instrument himself: he is, borrowing from the James Weldon Johnson volume of oral sermons that championed the poetic artistry of that tradition, "God's Trombone," an instrument of deliverance as a preacher generally and as Bliss's mentor specifically. The tune he plays is brimming with African-American vernacular materials, both literally and symbolically.

6

It was a track Ellison had always followed. In addition to Ellison's numerous references to jazz in his work, he dealt very specifically with the blues as well. Indeed, some would argue that is difficult to speak of jazz without reference to the blues—and we haven't done that here—and that to do so would be somewhat artificial. While true, it should be pointed out that there are many kinds of blues that are relatively untouched by jazz, and even some jazz that seems little informed by the blues. Still, though it seems clear that Ellison saw the connections between the various genres of African-American vernacular music, it also seems best to discuss Ellison's treatment and uses of the blues unto themselves, while making the requisite connections that Ellison acknowledged in his works.

A good bit of Ellison's familiarity with the blues, if we assume it is reflected in the references in his work, came through jazz. Jazz players, of course, used the musical and lyric patterns of the blues in their works, as well as the sounds found in earlier rural blues performances—blue notes, straining, bending, and growling—in blues and nonblues structural settings. For many, the blues feeling is felt to be central to jazz, and the performers Ellison most appreciated—the Blue Devils, Jimmy Rushing, Count Basie, Ellington, Armstrong—were all fully conversant with and masterful at working with the blues tradition. However, as we look at the performers classified as blues musicians whom Ellison mentions in his essays, for example, we find primarily the so-called classic blues singers of the vaudeville tradition, which employed many jazz musicians as accompanists—Bessie Smith, Ma Rainey, Ida Cox, Clara Smith, Chippie Hill—and stars like Leroy Carr, whose immense hits with "How Long Blues" and "In the Evening" passed over significantly into the jazz repertoire. Articles on all of these performers were appearing in the important jazz journals (blues journals didn't emerge until the 1960s) of the 1940s and 1950s—*Record Changer, Jazz Forum, Jazz Journal,* and *Down Beat,* among others—and a number of them were either part of reissue programs (Bessie Smith) or still recording with jazz backing (Chippie Hill for Circle Records in 1946) at the time.

Versatile Sammy Price, a talent scout and session pianist as well as a performer of blues, jazz, and pop songs, also merits brief mention.

By and large, however, the rural folk blues tradition receives scant attention in Ellison. Although we know that Oklahoma was not one of the major blues centers with regard to providing artists for the recording industry, it did boast a blues scene that included John T. "Funny Papa" Smith, Thomas Shaw, and perhaps the mysterious artist known as "Freezone," who sang of going back to Oklahoma to marry an "Indian squaw" ("Let the big chief Indian be my daddy-in-law"). However, Ellison makes little mention of this milieu. Even among the letters to and from Albert Murray, the folk blues performers mentioned are in relation to the release of *Big Bill Blues* by Big Bill Broonzy, who arguably developed into an urban blues musician but whose emergence on the crossover music scene with the *From Spirituals to Swing* concert in 1938 and as a blues ambassador to Europe in the 1950s returned him to his rural roots. The performers are mentioned in a letter written to Ellison by Murray (*TT* 156), who makes one other reference to Leadbelly (*TT* 34).

The major exception with regard to Ellison's references to blues performers is his extensive use of yet another trickster character, Peter Wheatstraw, in *Invisible Man* and, later, in *Juneteenth* (178, 294). His syncopated speech patterns, including adding quick, jivey tag endings to words and phrases ("daddy-o" and "Stingeroy") and bragging about himself with an onrush of words run together—"I'maseventhsonofaseventhson"—(*IM* 176) mark him as a primary purveyor of vernacular music effects in speech. Used to symbolize the narrator's separation from his folk roots, the character seems to be a composite of elements of vernacular culture rather than any real person. However, in an interview with blues researcher Leroy Pierson, Ellison acknowledged that he had actually known and played in St. Louis bars with a famous blues singer whose recording name was Peetie Wheatstraw, from whom Ellison took the character's "general personality and patterns of speech" (Garon 64) and whose own career contains the prominent employment of trickster elements. Ellison's knowledge of this blues singer and his use in the texts indicate once again Ellison's employment of elements of the vernacular music tradition to very specific purposes that are illuminated by closer knowledge of the sources.

Wheatstraw, whose real name was William Bunch, began recording in 1930 under the assumed name, and all of his recordings featured this identification, usually with the subcredit "The Devil's Son-in-Law," though on two occasions he is dubbed "The High Sheriff from Hell." A popular performer in St. Louis, he recorded 164 sides that frequently sold well, indicating that as a performer he captured the race record–buying public's interest. In fact, when he died in a car-train collision on 21 December 1941, his obituary ran at the top of the front page of *Down Beat* magazine, and *Variety* and *Billboard* included short notices as well. Musically, Wheatstraw likely served Ellison's fictional purposes because he had generated an instantly recognizable, individual style both as a musician and a singer. His singing style, in fact, spawned a number of imitators drawn to his distinctive verbal touchstone, the phrase "ooh, well, well," which he used to help pace and pattern a fair number of his lyrics. Thus, Bunch exemplified the strength of the performer who established for himself a strong musical identity.

That identity also involved his generating a specific image of himself for his audience, which must be understood in the context of the folklore tradition he knew from his birthplace of Ripley, Tennessee, from where he was raised in Cotton Plant, Arkansas, and from his hoboing through the southern states as documented in a number of folklore sources at the time. The names "Peetie" and "Wheatstraw" seem to draw on elements of African-American folklore related to magic charms and spells. "Peetie" recalls the Ki-Kongo *Petro* gods, who made things burn in a positive, healing sense (also referring to the singer's devil-related nicknames), and "Wheatstraw" suggests the southern folk belief that straws of wheat could help discover the identity of a future spouse, in addition to being able to make warts disappear. The names, then, associate the singer strongly not only with the folk tradition but with superstitions that would lend him a certain mystical status. That status was enhanced by his use of the folklore motif of marrying the devil's daughter—thus becoming the devil's son-in-law—that established his credentials as a powerful figure who could consort with and seduce the devil's daughter but also, as the folktale goes, work with that daughter to resist, outwit, and defeat the devil. It established this Wheatstraw as a powerful outlaw figure, a trickster, one who both embraces and transcends his association with the devil because the devil is an authority figure who ought to be resisted. The appeal of outlaw figures in African-American folklore seems to stem from this knowledge, that when one exists in a system where established authority is evil and repressive, the bad man becomes the good man because of this relativity of values, a knowledge particularly obvious given the Jim Crow treatment suffered by African Americans in the twentieth-century South. It was an important block in the building of an identity that would appeal to his audience through both folkloric and social familiarity, while setting him apart as an individual with a distinct identity. This Wheatstraw, then, was "walking magic, challenger of systems, and asserter of self and freedom" (Tracy 56) in a hostile world that sought to limit individuality and freedom in the African-American community.

Additionally, in the lyrics in his recordings, Wheatstraw strives to create a tough, jivey, urban image of a beleaguered urban laborer negotiating a difficult world, which appealed to a record-buying audience and a general African-American population that was becoming increasingly urban following the Great Migration, and thus was anxious to see and hear expressions of African-American urban life in their music. This trend was noticeable in the emergence of a variety of popular blues performers such as Memphis Minnie, Big Bill Broonzy, Tampa Red, and Sonny Boy Williamson, all of whom performed by the mid- to late 1930s more sophisticated, combo-oriented blues without losing their crucial connections to their rural traditions. As such, Wheatstraw represents the transplantation and adaptation of the southern African American to the type of seemingly promising but ultimately hostile northern environment that the protagonist of Ellison's novel faces, as well as a potential solution to the restrictions placed upon life and identity in that environment through his tricksterism.

Ellison's Wheatstraw is a character in possession of but not enslaved to the blueprints (read: blues identity) he carts around— that is, he understands that the plans can be changed, and that the ability to improvise when the plans are changed to someone else's advantage makes a difference to one's sanity and survival. "You have to stick to the plan," the protagonist naïvely offers, to which the worldly wise Wheatstraw replies, "You kinda young, daddy-o" (*IM* 175). He also realizes something else that the narrator must learn in order to protect himself in a deceitful world: appearance is not reality. Just as the vet has told the protagonist to look beneath the surface of things, and as the yam man would do later, so Wheatstraw sings a traditional blues lyric (recorded in 1936 by Jimmy Rushing in a song entitled "Boogie Woogie") that is also a repository of this wisdom. Unfortunately, the protagonist doesn't understand the lyric. To him, it describes the ugliness of a woman with "feet like a monkey / legs like a frog" (*IM* 173), which prevents him from appreciating her real importance, what she can do with what she has: love in a special and powerful way that causes the singer to love her more than himself. Interestingly, Ellison does not provide the final words to the blues stanza he quotes, so the reader does not quite know exactly how the sentiment wraps up or is resolved intellectually or emotionally within the framework of the blues stanza. If it ends with the words Rushing sings, it is quite illuminating. Although there is, of course, a value in finding a partner that one can love more than oneself, there is also a danger in subsuming one's identity in another for, as Rushing sings, "Come to find out baby was loving somebody else." Thus the lyric turns back on itself twice, by describing the woman in physically repugnant terms, then talking about how she transcends appearances, and then describing the deceit that still exists in their relationship. In the lyric progression, then, it replicates the unexpected reversals, twists, and turns the protagonist faces in his circuitous route to enlightenment, as well as those we all face in our lives. Remarkably, it is all there in this brief blues lyric. The blues singer and the blues, then, are revealed as repositories of folk wisdom that have a continued and complex relevance to the necessary education of the protagonist in the novel. The fact that the protagonist can't quite figure out the blues singer, but that he feels a simultaneous estrangement from and attraction to his personality, reveals the protagonist's divided consciousness and loyalties.

Of course, the novel demonstrates other uses of the blues, with references to blues songs "Back Water Blues" (Bessie Smith), "The First Shall Be Last and the Last Shall Be First" (Wheatstraw), and "Jelly Jelly" (Billy Eckstine). There are, in fact, profound stylistic, emotional, intellectual, and structural elements of the blues in *Invisible Man*. There is the call-and-response pattern in theme, structure, episode, and language, as in the echoes of his grandfather's advice and the regular recurrence of the idea of looking beneath the surface. The importance of folk roots, the down-home "shit, grit, and mother wit" so common in the blues, is emphasized, as is the importance of the relation of the individual to the community negotiated in the artistry of the blues singer. The protagonist connects with the homeless couple, Mary (who sings the disaster song "Back Water Blues" as a way of transcending the disaster), Wheatstraw, the yam man, and the community in general through his work with the Brotherhood. The language is laced with material from blues songs or the philosophy reflected in them. The protagonist is a speaker who has created his own blues voice, a joking trickster in the language of the blues, laughing to keep from crying, demonstrating in the novel that he has had trouble all of his days, but also offering the flickering belief that the sun is gonna shine in his back door some day. It exemplifies Ellison's justly famous definition of the blues as "an impulse to keep the painful details and episodes of a brutal experience alive in one's aching consciousness, to finger its jagged grain, and to transcend it, not by consolation of philosophy but by squeezing from it a near-tragic, near-comic lyricism" (*SA 78*). Ellison strove for that in the content and style of his writings all his life.

Ellison also casually refers to a woman playing boogie woogie in church (*IM 497*), highlighting the common origins of sacred and secular African-American folklore that were nonetheless sometimes sharply divided in the Christian community because of the "sinful" nature of the blues, to the obvious detriment, in Ellison's mind, of understanding and appreciating African-American vernacular music. Ellison mentions in *Juneteenth* a Laura Minnie

Smith (possibly fictional, though a Laura Smith who recorded blues sides and one sacred coupling between 1924 and 1927 is on record), who "could battle Bessie Smith note for note, tone for tone, and on top of that was singing the Word of God" (*J* 135). The development of gospel music through the combination of church music and the blues by such performers as Tom Dorsey, who is mentioned as "flirting with God" in *Juneteenth* (135), Arizona Dranes, and Rosetta Tharpe in the late 1920s to early 1930s, and Mahalia Jackson's well-known appreciation for the artistry of blues singer Bessie Smith, which Ellison acknowledged (*CE* 251), expose the myth of separation and celebrate the free interplay of various genres of vernacular music.

Some commentators from the 1960s on have tended to write about songsters, for example, as if they were only blues artists, thus blocking out the parts of their repertoires that held less interest to a nation in the midst of a blues revival. For example, the notion of Robert Johnson as tortured blues genius does not quite jibe, for some, with reports that in person he was known to play pop songs such as "My Blue Heaven" for tips. Somehow it "corrupts the purity of his art" to be seen as a mere entertainer, though not to see him as that serves to make the real person disappear—exactly the point Ellison was making in *Invisible Man*. As the issue of "purity" in the Liberty Paints section reveals, purity is frequently built on an illusion best exposed and dispelled. Celebrating all of the ingredients of a complicated, juice-swapping mix is not only most honest, but most healthy as well. That interplay is also celebrated by the inclusion in Ellison's texts of various folk rhymes and tunes that were common in the African-American community. Ellison employs "Buckeye the Rabbit" (241–42) and the sardonic "Pick Poor Robin Clean" (193) in *Invisible Man*. "Make Me a Pallet on the Floor" is sung as a soothing lullaby in *Juneteenth* (314). The frequently obscene rhyming game "the dozens" turns up in both "A Coupla Scalped Indians" (*FH* 70–71) and *Invisible Man* (241–42). Various folk rhymes are used for their emotional and intellectual value (as well as to portray adolescent behavior in the style of Richard Wright's "Big Boy Leaves Home" in the short stories "Mister Toussan" and "Afternoon") in "King of the Bingo Game" and in Ellison's interview for the *Paris*

Review (*CE* 214–15). In "Mister Toussan," Ellison goes so far as to quote a folk story formula rhyme at the beginning of his story to place his work firmly within the folk tradition. Religious tunes such as "No Hiding Place" (*CE* 479), "Heab'n" (*FH* 24), "Wings of a Dove" (*FH* 48–50), and "Amazing Grace" (*FH* 70) echo in various works, as do call-and-response oral sermons (9–10) and "Go Down Moses" (313) in *Invisible Man* and in "Mister Toussan," and "Let Us Break Bread Together" (136, 139, 169) and "Listen to the Lambs" (169) in *Juneteenth* (in addition to mention of the actual group Whitby's Heavenly Harmonizers). We encounter a range of songs of this type in the repertoires of songsters who recorded in the 1920s and 1930s, such as Jim Jackson, Frank Stokes, Luke Jordan, Mississippi John Hurt, and Geeshie Wiley and Elvie Thomas, who are labeled more widely as blues per-formers though their repertoires were somewhat broader than what that genre has encompassed in its traditional definitions, which tend to focus on musical and lyric structure rather than emotional content. Ellison seems to be acknowledging the limi-tations of those labels in his casting a broad, inclusive net around African-American vernacular music in his work. In this he erases boundaries and creates a democratic communal space in his fic-tion that requires acceptance and understanding of these per-spectives, even as it interrogates their shifting subjective mean-ings. As the protagonist of *Invisible Man* says, "Old Bad Air is still around with his music and his dancing and his diversity" (*IM* 581), embraced by Louis Armstrong, who knew the value of his con-tribution, the protagonist, and Ellison himself.

In the work of certain forebears like Langston Hughes and Richard Wright, whose *Black Boy* Ellison felt represented the "flowering—cross-fertilized by pollen blown by the winds of strange cultures—of the humble blues lyric" (*SA* 80), Ellison sensed an attempt to own the blues tradition, but he wished to utilize a more comprehensive network of stylistic and thematic blues devices in tandem with other African-American vernacular music and Euro-American literary theory and technique to ex-pose the depth and breadth of importance that the African-American tradition could and did have for the art of expression worldwide. Ellison's critics may contend that Ellison was reaching for a reflected glory for African-American music by associating it with European technique and philosophy, or was attempting to show off his erudition with grandstanding riffs on high art. However, at the time of his publication of *Invisible Man*, many whites were frequently not ready to acknowledge the contributions of African Americans, with *Brown v. Board of Education*, lunch counter sit-ins, bus strikes, and civil rights marches not yet materialized. It seems more likely, then, that Ellison was merely awakening to and illuminating for his audience the artistic and intellectual contributions that had been there in front of their faces all along. As in Dvořák's *New World*, the world exposed and created by Ellison and his protagonist in *Invisible Man* and the world of Hickman, whose nickname "God's Trombone" recalls the words of James Weldon Johnson's "The Creation," "I'm lonely— / I'll make me a world" (17), Ellison wished to illuminate the unfathomed world of African-American music in his writing.

Just the kind of thing that a man with a delicate ear, a retentive memory, and the power to weld the fragments might do.

WORKS CITED

Bell, Bernard. "Folk Art and the Harlem Renaissance." *Phylon* 36 (1975): 155–63.

Broonzy, Big Bill. *Big Bill Blues*. London: Cassell, 1955.

Du Bois, W. E. B. *Dusk of Dawn*. New York: Harcourt Brace, 1940.

"Freezone." "Indian Squaw Blues." *Rare Country Blues*. Document 5170, n.d.

Garon, Paul. *The Devil's Son-in-Law*. London: Studio Vista, 1971.

Hasse, John Edward. *Beyond Category: The Life and Genius of Duke Ellington*. New York: Simon and Schuster, 1993.

Jackson, Lawrence. *Ralph Ellison: Emergence of Genius*. New York: Wiley, 2002.

Johnson, James Weldon. *God's Trombones*. 1927. Reprint. New York: Penguin, 1972.

Lemke, Sieglinde. *Primitivist Modernism: Black Culture and the Origins of Transatlantic Modernism*. New York: Oxford University Press, 1998.

Plimpton, George, ed. *Writers at Work: The* Paris Review *Interviews.* 2d ser. New York: Viking Compass, 1965.

Rampersad, Arnold, ed. *The Collected Poems of Langston Hughes.* New York: Random House, 1994.

Scarborough, Dorothy. *On the Trail of Negro Folk-Songs.* 1925. Reprint. Hatboro, Pa.: Folklore Association, 1963.

Singer, Barry. *Black and Blue: The Life and Lyrics of Andy Razaf.* New York: Schirmer, 1992.

Tibbetts, John C., ed. *Dvořák in America, 1892–1895.* Portland, Oreg.: Amadeus, 1993.

Tracy, Steven C. "The Devil's Son-in-Law and *Invisible Man.*" *MELUS* 15, no. 3 (Fall 1988): 47–64.

Walser, Robert A., ed. *Keeping Time: Readings in Jazz History.* New York: Oxford University Press, 1999.

RECORDINGS RELEVANT TO *INVISIBLE MAN*

Armstrong, Louis. "Black and Blue." *Portrait of the Artist as a Young Man.* Columbia 57176.

———."Twelfth Street Rag." *The Hot Fives and Sevens,* vol. 2. Columbia, CK44253.

Broadie, Elder. "You Got to Move." *Gospel Singers and Preachers.* Document DOCD5585.

Carr, Sister Wynona. *Dragnet for Jesus.* Specialty SPCD-7016-2.

Dranes, Arizona. *Complete Recorded Works.* Document 5186.

Dvořák, Antonín. *Symphony No. 9: From the New World.* Teldec T2-73244.

Eckstine, Billy. "Jelly Jelly." *Earl Hines: Piano Man.* RCA 6750-2-RB.

Eliot, T. S. "The Waste Land." *The Caedmon Treasury of Modern Poets.* Caedmon 2006.

Ellington, Duke. "Jack the Bear." *The Blanton-Webster Band.* RCA 5969-2-RB.

Four Girls. "Old John the Rabbit." *Field Recordings,* vol. 8. Document 5598.

"Freezone." "Indian Squaw Blues." *Rare Country Blues.* Document 5170.

Griffin, Sin Killer. "The Man of Calvary." *Field Recordings,* vol. 5. Document 5579.

Heavenly Gospel Singers. "Lead Me to the Rock." *Complete Recordings in Chronological Order,* vol. 1. Document 5452.

Lightnin' Hopkins. "The Dirty Dozens." Raglan LP 51. Reissue. *Recorded in Houston, Texas, 1954 and 1959.* Document Private Issue.

Jarrett, Pigmeat. "Pigmeat's Name." *Snow on the Roof, Fire in the Furnace.* June Appal no number.

Johnson, James Weldon. "The Prodigal Son." *God's Trombones.* Lexington LP7716.

Jones, Eddie. "The Dozens." *One String Blues.* Takoma CDTAK 1023.

Jordan, Luke. "Pick Poor Robin Clean." *The Songster Tradition.* Document 5045.

Morton, Jelly Roll. "Buddy Bolden Blues." *Last Sessions.* Commodore CMD403.

Platt, Moses. "Clear Rock," "Run, Nigger, Run." *Field Recordings,* vol. 6, *Texas.* Document 5580.

Reagon, Toshi. "John Brown's Body." *Africans in America.* Rykodisc 90444.

Richardson, Benny, and Group. "Grizzly Bear." *Wake Up Dead Man.* Rounder 2013.

Robeson, Paul. "No More Auction Block." *Every Tone a Testimony.* Smithsonian Folkways 47003.

Rushing, Jimmy, and Count Basie. "Boogie Woogie." *The Complete Decca Recordings.* GRP611.

Smith, Bessie. "Back Water Blues." *The Complete Recordings,* vol. 3. Columbia C2K47474.

Southern Sons. "Go Down Moses." *I Hear Music in the Air.* RCA 2099-2-R.

Speckled Red. "The Dirty Dozen." *Complete Recorded Works.* Document 5205.

Tuskegee Institute Singers. "Live a-Humble." *Complete Recorded Works.* Document. 5549.

Various Artists. "Signifyin' Monkey." *Get Your Ass in the Water and Swim Like Me.* Rounder 2014.

Waters, Muddy. "My John the Conqueror Root." *The Complete Muddy Waters.* CD Red Box 3.

Wheatstraw, Peetie. "Devil's Son-in-Law," "Pete Wheatstraw." *Peetie Wheatstraw,* vol. 1. Document 5241.

———. "The First Shall Be Last and the Last Shall Be First." *Peetie Wheatstraw,* vol. 3. Document 5243.

———. "Peetie Wheatstraw Stomp Pt. 2." *Complete Recorded Works,* vol. 4. Document 5244 .

Wiley, Geeshie, and Elvie Thomas. "Pick Poor Robin Clean." *Mississippi Blues*, vol. 1. Document 5157.

SELECTED ADDITIONAL RECORDINGS
RELEVANT TO ELLISON'S WRITINGS
AND AESTHETIC

Christian, Charlie. *The Genius of the Electric Guitar*. Columbia CK40846.
Cox, Ida. *Complete Recordings in Chronological Order*, vols. 1–4. Document 5322–25.
Dawson, William L., and Duke Ellington. *Orchestral Works*. Chandos 9909.
Ellington, Duke. *Early Ellington (1927–1934)*. RCA 6852-2-B.
Gillespie, Dizzy. *The Complete RCA Victor Recordings*. Bluebird 66528-2.
Hampton, Lionel. *Hamp: The Legendary Decca Recordings of Lionel Hampton*. Decca GRD-2-652.
Jackson, Mahalia. *The Apollo Sessions, 1946–1951*. Pair PCD 2-1332.
Jacquet, Illinois. *The Illinois Jacquet Story*. Proper Box 49.
McShann, Jay. *Jumpin' the Blues*. Proper PVCD 131.
Moten, Bennie. *Bennie Moten's Kansas City Orchestra (1929–1932)*. RCA 9768-2-RB.
Page, Hot Lips. *Pagin' Mr. Page*. ASV 5347.
Parker, Charlie. *Boss Bird*. Proper Box 46.
———. *The Complete Savoy Studio Sessions*. Savoy ZDS 5500.
Rainey, Ma. *Complete*, vols. 1-5. Document 5156, 5581–84.
Rushing, Jimmy. *Every Day*. Vanguard 79607-2.
Smith, Bessie. *The Complete Recordings*, vol. 1. Columbia C2K47091.
Still, William Grant, William Dawson, and Duke Ellington. *Symphony No. 2: Negro Folk Symphony/Harlem*. Chandos 9226.
Various Artists. *Jazz Kansas City Style*. Pearl 1036.
———. *Kansas City Piano*. Decca 79226.
———. *Ralph Ellison: Living with Music*. Columbia/Legacy 85935.
———. *The Real Kansas City*. Columbia CK64859.
———. *Selection of Original Sounds of Kansas City*. Golden Sounds 773.
Webster, Ben. *Big Ben*. Proper Box 37.
Young, Lester. *The Kansas City Sessions*. Commodore CHD402.
———. *The Lester Young Story*. Proper Box 8.

"Something Warmly, Infuriatingly Feminine"

Gender, Sexuality, and the Work of Ralph Ellison

James Smethurst

Critical assessments of the representation of women in the work of Ralph Ellison, particularly the novel on which his reputation ultimately rests, *Invisible Man*, often seem at odds. Claudia Tate argues that "like underground station masters of the American slave era, these female characters assist the Invisible Man along his course to freedom" (164). Ann Folwell Stanford asserts that Mary Rambo "stands out as the only positively memorable woman character in the novel (out of a cast of almost twenty black women characters)" (118). And even Mary Rambo is a limited character whom the narrator sees as hardly human. Yet these two statements are not as irreconcilable as they first appear. Gender and sexuality are absolutely crucial to Ellison's cultural vision—and crucial to his success as an artist and as a public intellectual, to employ a vague and overused term.

Ellison's success can, of course, be attributed in part to the amazing tour de force that is *Invisible Man*. However, as many critics have noted, both critically and approvingly, much of the power of *Invisible Man* lies in its status as a prominent product of the cultural Cold War, powerfully engaging that ideological moment. What is somewhat less observed is the degree to which this power does not reside in the critiques of specific individuals and organizations, particularly the Communist party—critiques which even anticommunist contemporary reviewers of the novel found to be the least convincing aspect of the novel. Rather, the engagement with the larger ideological conversations and conflicts of the cultural Cold War, especially concerning questions of the individual and the masses and of the relationship of the individual to high culture and to mass culture, give the novel much of its charge. Constructions, to employ another overused term, of femininity (and masculinity) and homosexuality (and effeminacy) and how they inflect and mirror notions of race are major ingredients of an aesthetic and social vision that placed a novel by an African American at the center of American literature for the first time in the history of the United States.

My focus will be on *Invisible Man* since, again, it is the foundation of Ellison's literary reputation and exists in a sort of symbiotic relationship with his essays. *Invisible Man* forces us to pay attention to the essays, and to a large extent illustrates them; the essays in turn interpret or frame interpretations of the novel—though they are often a sort of conscious interpretative feint or distraction on the part of Ellison. The posthumously published novel *Juneteenth* is an interesting document. The fact that it exists is in itself a testament to Ellison's enduring stature since it had to be laboriously assembled from a mass of uncompleted manuscripts by John Callahan. However, rather than securing Ellison's place as a novelist, it is Ellison's position, established by the reception of *Invisible Man*, that secured its publication.

The gender politics of Ellison's essays are worth at least a brief comment. One of the arresting things about them is how little women figure other than in his short but well-known essay on Mahalia Jackson, "As the Spirit Moves Mahalia," and the early sketch about Harlem life, "The Way It Is." In Ellison's discussions of his literary and artistic ancestry, women, black or white, appear virtually nowhere. Of course, Ellison was famously ungenerous toward earlier black writers generally and extremely competitive with his contemporaries and even the younger artists who followed him. Not that Ellison was remarkable in that regard, since he came of age in an extraordinarily competitive time when many writers seemed obsessed not simply with their careers, but with how they ranked among their peers. Richard

Wright, after all, was notably vicious toward his black predecessors in "Blueprint for Negro Writing," and Ernest Hemingway's mean-spirited recollections of F. Scott Fitzgerald's anxiety about the size of his penis in *A Moveable Feast* are more extreme than anything Ellison ever put into nonfiction prose.

However, the relative invisibility of women in Ellison's essays should not blind us to the overall importance of women in his larger body of work, particularly *Invisible Man*. As Stanford notes, one striking aspect of *Invisible Man* is that there are really no fully positive representations of women, black or white, in it. As Carol Sylvander pointed out in one of the earliest essays examining the representation of women in the novel, Ellison relies on familiar female types or stereotypes in a relatively straightforward manner that seems strange for a work so taken with "the peculiar disposition of the eyes" of Americans, black and white, when it comes to truly seeing the unnamed narrator-protagonist as an individual human (77). These types are largely (and broadly) sorted by race in ways that, again, are odd given what appears to be the individualistic, antiessentialist trajectory of the novel. They are odd in the sense that the black women appear to be stereotypically "Negro" in many respects—though the stereotypes could be said to come as much from within the African-American community as from outside it. Similarly, white women embody a long-held modernist gendering of a mass culture that is simultaneously dehumanizing, emasculating, insipid, and seductive. This sorting is linked to those who sexually desire and are desired by the narrator and those who feel no such attraction to him and (at first glance) inspire no carnal longing in him.

A curious, if little remarked, feature of the novel is the lack of sexual attraction that the narrator exerts on black women as opposed to a desire to mother him. It is not that no one finds the narrator attractive. A number of white women are drawn sexually to him. There is a wealthy and nameless member of the Brotherhood who couches her wish to be seduced in "teach me the beautiful ideology of the Brotherhood." There is also Sybil, the wife of a Brotherhood leader, who demands that the protagonist rape her. And Emma, the wife of Brother Jack, the head of the Brotherhood, clearly has a predatory sexual interest in him—

though she seems so "hardened" and treacherous that even the usually clueless narrator knows to stay away.

He also draws at least one white man. After his expulsion from college by its director, Dr. Bledsoe, the narrator attempts to visit various northern white trustees of the college, seeking a job. When the narrator goes to see the trustee Mr. Emerson, he gets no further than Emerson's son, an ironic conflation of the old-line New England Emersonian intellectual establishment, where art and philosophy intersect with old money, and the gay Harlem Renaissance figure Carl Van Vechten, embodying a gay interracial scene where bohemianism meets old and new money. Emerson's son insists on casting himself as Huckleberry Finn with the narrator as Jim—a not very subtle reference, as many commentators have noted, to the critic Leslie Fiedler's notorious 1948 essay, "Come Back to the Raft Agin, Huck Honey," which argued that an unconsummated homoerotic relationship between Huck and Jim marked Twain's novel and exemplified how the homosocial in American literature and culture was symbolically displaced onto interracial relationships.

In the sort of parodic doubling typical of Ellison's approach to literary subtexts, Emerson's son's imposition of Twain (and Fiedler) on his relationship with the narrator is both ridiculous and apt, another version of American blindness that insists on its juvenile innocence while indulging adult desires, crimes, and follies of every sort. A crucial aspect of this incongruous mélange of innocence and adult desire is the assumption that the white faux child, Emerson's son, would direct the younger black man much as Huck imagines himself to dominate Jim—and much as a white male might ideally dominate his "natural" spouse, a white woman. There is then implicitly another displacement— gender onto interracial relationships—so that this Emerson is both a boy and a white man and the narrator is both a black man and a sort of white woman. As we will see, this homology between the narrator and white women, strangely homoerotic and hyperheterosexual at the same time, is crucial in describing the narrator's existential predicament as well as marking the movement of his ultimate liberation.

The black women in the novel most concerned with the narrator (and most attractive to him in a nonsexual way) are such motherly characters as Mary Rambo and the old woman of the Harlem eviction scene. They are basically asexual. The nonmotherly black women are quite different, both actively sexual and sexually active. However, black women (and black men) show little carnal interest in the narrator. The notable exception is during his masquerade as the rounder/numbers runner/jackleg preacher, Rinehart. Of course, this is an ironic masquerade since Rinehart is pure mask himself. Tellingly, as soon as these black women realize that the narrator is not Rinehart, which is to say that he is more than mask, more than dark glasses and a hat, they recoil from him in fear, anger, and even disgust. These moments (along with the brief scene where a fellow college student asks the narrator to carry a cryptic, yet sexually charged message to her lover) reveal, among other things, the sexual agency of black women. In other words, these women demonstrate an open sexual interest in black men—and sometimes a willingness to trade sex for money or other material gains; only they are not interested in *him*.

This pattern of interest and disinterest is apparently reciprocated by the protagonist. Rarely does the narrator describe black women as attractive. There are the older, motherly black women, who are generally large and, again, relatively sexless. The most prominent of these figures is, of course, Mary Rambo, the southern migrant who takes in the narrator after a horrifically surrealistic industrial accident at the Liberty Paints factory and his subsequent "treatment" by a squad of mad scientist-doctors, who seem to have escaped from a grade-B monster movie. They also include the "old singer of spirituals" in the prologue (a slave who both loved and hated her master and the father of her children, the children who murdered their father), the old woman whose eviction leads to the protagonist's first encounter with the Brotherhood, and the church women who form much of the congregation of the con man Rinehart. These women scarcely exist as people with individual personalities. Rather, as is generally the case with women and dark-skinned black characters in the work of one of Ellison's most prominently acknowledged literary ancestors, William Faulkner (as opposed to light-skinned, male, possibly Negro characters, such as Joe Christmas), these women are types, unself-conscious embodiments of natural or social forces rather than characters with specific humanity:[1] "Nor did I think of Mary as a 'friend'; she was something more—a force, a stable, familiar force like something out of my past which kept me from whirling off into some unknown which I dared not face" (*IM* 258).

From the novel's publication, critics have seen Mary Rambo and the other, less-prominent "motherly" black women in the text as revisions of the mammy figure of plantation literature and works in other genres inspired in part or in whole by the plantation literature tradition, such as the films *Birth of a Nation* and *Gone with the Wind*. While there may be some truth to this association, they are more closely related to the figure of the Negro mother, a sort of embodiment of the African-American folk spirit and culture. This figure and the related trope of Mother Africa were old hallmarks of African-American literature, dating back to the nineteenth century. Like the mammy figure, the Negro mother is typically older, large, dark-skinned, and nonsexual. Like the mammy, the Negro mother is, as the name suggests, nurturing, but she is also a catalyst of race pride, urging on her actual or figurative children, as in Frances Harper's "Aunt Chloe's Politics," Langston Hughes's "From Mother to Son," or Lorraine Hansberry's *Raisin in the Sun*. Strangely, though the motherly black women in *Invisible Man* recall to the narrator his southern roots and the old folks back home, his actual mother and grandmother, unlike his grandfather, figure nowhere in the novel. In this, *Invisible Man* resembles *The Souls of Black Folk* where W. E. B. Du Bois uses his "grandfather's grandmother" to embody an original (and partially lost) African culture and sensibility, which is then passed on to his "fathers" without any further mentions of "mothers."

Generally, younger black women in the novel are described neutrally, often as "plain," whether thin or plump. Even in the bar-whorehouse, the Golden Day, the "girls" are "small skinny," "small plump," and "a brown-skinned woman with red hair." The one exception is the second of Rinehart's girlfriends to mistake the protagonist for her lover before recoiling from the narra-

tor in anger after his confession that he is not Rinehart. He later
has a sexual fantasy about her:

> And just as I caught sight of the glasses I remembered grasp-
> ing Rinehart's girl's hand. I lay there unmoving and she
> seemed to perch on the bed, a bright-eyed girl with her glossy
> head and ripe breasts, and I was in a wood afraid to frighten
> the bird away. Then I was fully awake and the bird gone and
> the girl's image in my mind. What would have happened if I
> had led her on, how far could I have gone? (511–12)

But even in this case, this fantasy is based on a sort of double im-
personation: he must fool her and fool himself. She is not interested in him as himself (whoever that might be), and his interest
in her is through Rinehart. Apparently she, and sexually attractive black women in general, were invisible to him until he "became" Rinehart. In short, the black women of the novel are either mothers or sexual agents, sometimes whores veering close
to the familiar Madonna and whore stereotypes, while, as we will
see, white women in the novel are both domestic, often house-
wives (though not mothers as far as we can tell), and sexual. Even
the least domestic of the Brotherhood women, Emma, plays a
sort of hostess role for Brother Jack.

The narrator's physical attraction to some white women is far
more pronounced, in the sense both of explicit statement and of
the concrete details devoted to bodily descriptions. It is worth
noting that as there are different types of black women in the
novel, so are there different sorts of white women. One type can
be thought of as a gatekeeper or assistant, perhaps drawn from
the work of Franz Kafka. As will be noted later, Kafka's novels
and short stories are full of aged, somewhat ridiculous, and apparently infirm or damaged father figures who nonetheless rise
from their apparent weakness or mildness to terrifying displays
of power. These threatening figures often have assistants whose
purpose seems to be to ward off, impede, or direct the protagonist. In *Invisible Man*, this assistant is most commonly female and
generally, though not always, white. The secretaries of Mr. Bates
and the other trustees of the college who block the narrator in

"friendly and encouraging" ways fall into this category. So does the nameless "girl" who directs the narrator toward his meeting with Brother Jack and the Brotherhood after the eviction scene.

Then there are the unavailable beautiful white women who inspire blurrily defined and overlapping lust and murder in the heart of the protagonist. These women draw on the African-American trope of America as beautiful and seductive, yet treacherous and murderous, as seen, for example, in Gwendolyn Brooks's poem from the 1945 *A Street in Bronzeville*, "Negro Hero," which describes American democracy as a "fair lady" "with her knife lying cold, straight, in the softness of her sweet-flowing sleeve" (49). The first of these figures in *Invisible Man* is the "magnificent blonde" in the battle royal chapter, a sort of Hollywood bombshell or pinup composite of Jean Harlow and Jane Russell (and anticipating Marilyn Monroe) with "breasts firm and round as the domes of East Indian temples" and an American flag tattooed on her belly (*IM* 19). The narrator declares that he wanted "to caress her and destroy her, to love and to murder her"(19). However, even the apparently clueless narrator realizes that to act on such urges, or even reveal that he has such urges, would result in his death. Other beautiful and desirable but unavailable white women include the college trustee Mr. Norton's dead daughter, whom the narrator only sees in an engraved miniature, and Emma, Brother Jack's mistress with a "hard, handsome face." Both Emma and the engraving of Norton's daughter awaken strange feelings of déjà vu in the narrator, as if they remind him of someone or something. They are, in fact, variations on the magnificent blonde of chapter 1.

However, other white women, including the nameless woman who asks him to teach her "the beautiful ideology of the Brotherhood" and Sybil, are not beautiful or handsome in the same manner as the blonde, Norton's daughter, and Emma. The unnamed woman is attractive, "a small delicately plump woman with raven hair in which a thin streak of white had begun almost imperceptibly to show" (411). But she is hardly the sort of "bombshell" described in the first chapter. Sybil is described in less appealing terms: "She would soon be a biddy, stout, with a little double chin and a three-ply girdle. A thin gold chain showed around a thickening ankle. And yet I was becoming aware of something warmly, infuriatingly feminine about her. I reached out, stroking her hand" (519). Yet in both cases, the narrator is sexually drawn to these women, who do not seem to possess the overwhelming and somewhat remote allure that the magnificent blonde, Emerson's daughter, and Emma do. Interestingly, as the joining of "warmly" and "infuriatingly" here suggests, these women do inspire some of the same emotional ambivalence that the more distant white women do.

Of course, the fact that all of these women provoke such ambivalent but intense desire is precisely the point. This desire is not because they are all beautiful, or that he thinks that they are all beautiful. Only in the case of the Rinehartian sexual dream does a black woman produce anything like this response—and she is described as a mixture of bird and woman, a sort of desirable harpy. Again, even the whores of the Golden Day apparently do not move the narrator in this way. It cannot be simply that the author is not drawn to whores, since the blonde of the battle royal and Emma are strippers, whores, or represented as so mercenary that the distinction is meaningless. Even in the case of Rinehart's "lovely girl," the narrator is far less sensually concrete in his picture of her than even that of Sybil. And when his fantasy of her has passed, he immediately resolves to act like Rinehart, but decides to pursue "a [white] wife, a girl friend, or secretary of one of the leaders" of the Brotherhood (512). This pursuit is allegedly for information, but one in which the pull of the "infuriatingly feminine" cannot be avoided.

In fact, the one truly sensual portrait of a black person in the novel is that of the Brotherhood youth leader, Tod Clifton: "And now close up, leaning tall and relaxed, his arms outstretched stiffly upon the table, I saw the broad, taut span of his knuckles upon the dark grain of the wood, the muscular, sweatered arms, the curving line of the chest rising to the easy pulsing of his throat, to the square smooth chin" (363). Even Clifton's knuckles are sexy. Interestingly, even though the narrator describes Clifton as "very black and very handsome," he suggests that this attractiveness is the result of racial mixture rather than racial purity. The narrator goes on to say that he watched Clifton warily, thinking of him as a potential rival. Clifton here recalls the young men of the marijuana- and jazz-induced dream of the prologue, who are the children of the old slave woman and her master and who beat the narrator for questioning their mother too sharply. In short, one sees much of the same ambivalent combination of desire and hostility that characterizes the response of the narrator to a range of white women, but not to black women.

Of course, the narrator is presented as a sort of naïf, a picaresque hero who appears to learn some important lesson only to fall into the same trap in somewhat different form. In this, despite Mr. Emerson's homosexual fantasy, which sees the narrator as Jim, he much resembles Huck Finn, who often seems to have reached some sort of epiphany about race on a raft on the Mississippi with Jim and then repeatedly abandons Jim only to find himself in one impossible situation after the other before he "lights out for the territories." The protagonist of *Invisible Man* also (and literally) drops out of society, falling into an open manhole while being chased by a racist mob.

One might assume such a naïf to be sexually inexperienced and uncertain. And perhaps he is. But he lets drop hints that he might be more experienced than one might expect. In the second chapter, he recalls from his clean, well-lighted hole the campus from which he was expelled: "Many times here at night, I've closed my eyes and walked along the forbidden road that winds along the girl's dormitory" (34). One gets the feeling that he may have walked that road with his eyes open, and yet the longing, especially the sexual longing for black women, is a note sounded briefly and not repeated. Similarly, in the next chapter, the narrator mentions in passing that he seldom went to the Golden Day "except with some of the fellows when word got out that a bunch of new girls had arrived from New Orleans" (73). Now, secret visits to the women's dorm at a historically black college and trips to a brothel with "the fellows" hardly indicate either sexual sophistication or a sexual ease with black women. But moments like these suggest a dimension to the narrator's emotional landscape that neither he nor Ellison seem to have much interest in developing. Perhaps they exist to reassure the reader of the narrator's normalcy.

This naïve normalcy is extraordinarily important in the cultural vision promoted by the novel. One of the claims that Ellison makes is that the official or dominant consciousness of the United States is marked by a willfully arrested male emotional development that enshrines a sort of erotically charged preadolescence. This sort of consciousness can be seen in the narrator's picture of a romantic wooden bridge on campus that will never see any lovers' meetings, in Mr. Norton's incestuous longing for his dead daughter, and, again, Emerson's role playing, which casts the younger narrator as an older black man and himself as a white boy. In other words, the peculiar and willful blindness of the United States with respect to race that the narrator first posits at the beginning of the prologue is bound up with an equally willful sexual infantilization that in part relies on contradictory notions of a wild and unrestrained black sexuality and of a black passivity and subservience in which black men mirror white women with their warm but infuriating femininity.

It is worth noting that it is difficult to find any examples of a real or imagined sexual relationship that is not, in the novel's terms, perverse and/or mercenary. When the magnificent blonde of the first chapter is last seen, she flees from the room after being tossed among the white men watching the battle royal between the young black men, her terror mirroring that of the narrator. Norton is reduced to a semiconscious hysteria by the sharecropper Jim Trueblood's story of incest, which brings to the surface Norton's own incestuous desire for his dead daughter. The whores of the Golden Day reflect on the randiness of rich and respectable white men who reenact their dreams about black sexuality behind closed doors. Sybil fantasizes being raped by the narrator whom she transmutes from his Raskolnikov-like ineffectual ambivalence and uncertainty into "a strong big brute," a popular culture, Popular Front composite of Joe Louis and Paul Robeson in his most "middlebrow" mode as the singer of "Old Man River" from the musical *Showboat*. As Claudia Tate points out, this fantasy is complicated since it involves rape as a consensual act—though it has to be said that the fantasy of rape as a subliminally consensual act ("she asked for it") is the familiar stuff of heterosexual male pornography and rape defenses (170). Emma clearly desires the narrator even if the exact nature of her desire is less clear than that of Sybil. However, the narrator senses that an affair with Emma would be too dangerous because of her essentially mercenary relationship with Jack. Even the "lovely girl" of the narrator's one overt attraction to a black woman is being conned by Rinehart.

In mapping how gender and sexuality work in the novel, the relationships between men and between women and men seem compounded of Freud's *Totem and Taboo*, the ancient Greek myth of Kronos eating his children, the story of Cain and Abel, and the work of Franz Kafka. (Relationships between women are tellingly absent.) The mythic dream of the prologue in which the old slave woman's sons have banded together and killed their white father and master particularly draws on Freud in a manner that lacks the parodic intertextual relationship that characterizes most of the novel's engagement with other texts. Yet, after that beginning, the father figures of the novel—Norton, Bledsoe, Ras, Lucius Brockway, and Jack—are more Kafkaesque, older, often apparently declining, faintly ridiculous, or ineffectual figures who suddenly rear up in some threatening or terrifying manner. Of course, one difference is that where in Kafka these figures, and their ubiquitous assistants, frequently block the protagonist from any sort of movement, the father figures of *Invisible Man* keep the narrator in perpetual motion. Unlike the omnipotent father figure of *Totem and Taboo*, who possesses all the women that the sons desire, and like the fathers of Kafka, Ellison's fathers are strangely asexual or impotent. One reason that the white women of the Brotherhood pursue the narrator is that their white Brotherhood partners are so unsatisfactory in bed. There are also the non-Freudian, non-Kafkaesque folk trickster father/teacher figures, such as the grandfather, Peter Wheatstraw, Brother Tarp, and perhaps Jim Trueblood, who try to direct the narrator through indirection, through an awareness of the properties of invisibility.

The relation of the protagonist to black brother figures (as opposed to the white Brothers) mixes love and hate in nearly equal measure, recalling the narrator's feelings about the magnificent blonde. Beginning with the sons who attack him in the prologue's dream through the "brawler" Tatlock, whom he fights in the battle royal of chapter 1, Tod Clifton, Brother Hambro (the black member of the Brotherhood who brings disciplinary charges against him), and Rinehart (whose presence is weirdly marked by his absence)—all these brothers are potential and often actual rivals. Yet, as seen above in the description of Tod Clifton, his attraction to these brothers often seems greater and more erotically charged than any he feels for black women.

There are really no sister figures of any race in the novel and, as we have seen, no black girlfriends, wives, or partners of the narrator—in short, no black female peers. There are mother figures, but as the narrator says with respect to Mary Rambo, these women are really only principles, natural forces with little or no consciousness or self-consciousness. Mary herself is generous and nurturing but, for the narrator, also unbearably narrow, trapped in clichés of racial uplift and self-improvement. The white women in the novel are hardly motherly or sisterly. Even as lovers they are condescending and oddly controlling and submissive at the same time, demanding that the narrator dominate them intellectually and sexually (which seem to come to the same thing for the unnamed woman and for Sybil).

In this regard, Ellison's revision process is quite revealing. As Barbara Foley notes in "From Communism to Brotherhood," in earlier drafts, the white woman who serves as an intermediary between the narrator and the Brotherhood after the Harlem eviction scene has a far larger role. In these drafts, the woman, Louise, modeled perhaps on the leftist novelist Sonora Babb, with whom Ellison had an important romance, is much more sympathetic as a character than any white member of the Brotherhood in the final version She appeals to the narrator for not only her physical attractiveness, but also her honesty and thoughtfulness.

Similarly, earlier versions of the novel reveal Mary Rambo to have a much more developed and vivid personality than she does in the published text of the novel. As Stanford argues, this depth is hinted at in Rambo's statement, "I'm in New York, but New York ain't in me, understand what I mean. Don't git corrupted" (*IM* 249), displaying a brief liveliness of character and thought (Stanford 21–24). Apparently, excised passages in which Rambo actually rescues the narrator from the hospital, partially releasing the protagonist and reviving him with herbs from her 104-year-old root-working mother, were cut late. These passages, based in part on interviews in Harlem that Ellison conducted for the Federal Writers Project in the 1930s, appeared as a separate story, "Out of the Hospital and under the Bar," in 1963. Ellison, in an author's note to the story, said that he regretted the excision and thought that Mary Rambo "deserved more space in the novel and would, I think, have made it a better book" (Ellison 245). However, Ellison is often an extremely unreliable commentator on his own work. In fact, the removal of the passages fleshing out Mary's personality a bit and giving her more agency (even if she remains a comic embodiment of the Negro mother in many respects) and the virtual elimination of Louise as a major character make perfect sense in terms of the overall shape of the novel.

Invisible Man is a neomodernist novel that in some ways wears its connection to early twentieth-century modernism on its sleeve and yet is in many respects ambivalent about European and North American modernism. While it is dangerous to generalize about the large body of work associated with modernism, it is worth noting that many of its key texts are anti-individualist and anti-Romantic. The story of Joyce's *Ulysses*, a crucial subtext for *Invisible Man*, is in part the reconstitution of family and the transcending of various sorts of individual alienation. Both Eliot and Pound described and decried in their various ways the breakdown of organic community in "the West" and its replacement by mass culture. Fitzgerald's Gatsby is a literally self-fashioned man whose dreams of greatness center on a woman with a voice that sounds like money and whose vocabulary for expressing those dreams seems to be a closet full of expensive shirts. In Nathanael West's 1933 *Miss Lonelyhearts* (in which the triangle of the protagonist, his boss, Shrike, and Shrike's wife, Mary, resembles and may have been the model for the relationships between Jack, Emma, and the narrator in *Invisible Man*), there is both a critique of mass culture and a sense of resignation to the facts that resistance is futile and assimilation inescapable.[2] West's protagonist is not only a man with a Christ complex, but by implication suggests that Christ was a man with a Christ complex. Even in Hemingway, the heroism of the individual is in keeping on while facing the void of modern existence. That is to say that the individual acts because that is the best one can do. While one might read this macho individualism as heroic, there is rarely a sense of triumph about it and often it ends in death.

As has been noted since the earliest critical response to *Invisible Man*, the novel ends on a note of triumphant heroic individualism. Or rather, the note is one of limitless individual potential, a note that, as Berndt Ostendorf points out, does not harmonize with high modernist pessimism or even the anti-individualist optimism of Joyce (107–10). Perhaps that is why André Malraux with his transposition in *Man's Fate* of the Dostoevskian protagonist into a revolutionary hero whose individual act is truly heroic—and oddly individualistic in the service of a collectivist ideology—made such a deep impact on Ellison.

However, the novel is postmodern in a sense as well as neomodern in that it engages not only the European and American modernist writers of the early twentieth century, but also scholarly reassessment of nineteenth-century American literature under the rubric of the "American Renaissance" taken from F. O. Matthiessen's 1941 study, *American Renaissance*. In many respects, as Alan Nadel argues, Ellison's novel engages in a similar project of assessing and reconceiving the legacy of nineteenth-century American literature. *Invisible Man* extends the usual suspects of American Renaissance studies (Emerson, Thoreau, Hawthorne, Melville, Whitman, and sometimes Poe) to include the slave narrative, particularly those of Frederick Douglass—anticipating similar extensions of course syllabi a few decades later. Of course, as we have seen, Ellison's novel frequently had a parodic relationship to those texts. Yet the final note of heroic potential (and potential heroism) in which the protagonist is going to do something great, tomorrow, is unabashedly Emersonian. While this Emersonianism may, as Nadel suggests, combine with what Ellison took to be a Melvillian awareness of evil, there is a sense of triumph (or impending triumph) at the end of *Invisible Man* that is missing in the work of the mature Melville (Nadel 104–23). In Bledsoe's poisoned recommendation letter is a restatement of the ironic invocation of *The Great Gatsby*'s retreating green light, which one thinks one will be able to catch tomorrow.

Only the restatement seems to be made in complete seriousness—unless Ellison is having a joke on us in getting us to believe
in the narrator at the end of the novel much like Fitzgerald in
Gatsby lures us into believing Nick Caraway despite what should
have been his suspicious protestations of brutal honesty.

Ostendorf contends that Ellison's optimistic American individualist revision of modernism derives from his reading of jazz
and the jazz aesthetic. Certainly, such a reading is used by Ellison
to authorize his vision of the vocation of the artist. Ellison also
draws on a view of the jazz tradition to justify his version of his
literary genealogy in which the rhythms and allusions of late
1920s and 1930s jazz, particularly in the work of Louis Armstrong
and such leading southwestern "territory" musicians as Benny
Moten and Jimmy Rushing, are seen as having a closer relationship to the modernism of T. S. Eliot, F. Scott Fitzgerald, and
Ernest Hemingway than to writing produced by his immediate
black literary predecessors and by African-American contemporary writers.[3]

However, this neomodernist American Renaissance revision
of modernism in a distinctly male, macho modality is not restricted to Ellison's text. As Serge Guilbaut provocatively posited
in *How New York Stole the Idea of Modern Art*, the United States,
particularly New York, became the center of the art world
with the rise of abstract expressionism. Abstract expressionism's
(and New York's) new international ascendancy was shaped by
the emerging Cold War in the post–World War II United States,
rejecting older leftist modes of aesthetics and politics while
maintaining a radical formal stance. Like Ellison, many of the abstract expressionists had participated in the cultural and political
movements of the communist Left during the 1930s and early
1940s, but had moved away from the Communist party—sometimes with a sojourn in the circle of the then-Trotskyist and anti-
Stalinist journal *Partisan Review*. The work of these artists, such
as Willem DeKooning, Robert Motherwell, and, most famously,
Jackson Pollock, enshrined various sorts of abstraction—though
some link to their radical political past was occasionally retained,
as in the title of Motherwell's *Homage to the Spanish Republic*. This
art was framed by such critics as Harold Rosenberg and Clement

Greenberg (and somewhat ambivalently by *Life* magazine) as a heroic rejection of both totalitarian ideology and aesthetics, notably communism and Marxism, and American mass culture, which was sometimes explicitly linked to communist Popular Front ideology and cultural work. As Guilbaut points out, this criticism found at least a partial echo in the anticommunism and extolling of individualism of Arthur Schlesinger, Jr., in his influential manifesto for a "new liberalism" in such essays as the 1948 "Not Left, Not Right, but a Vital Center," which he would elaborate in *The Vital Center: The Politics of Freedom* (1949)—though Schlesinger was perhaps less invested in the avant-garde than Greenberg (Schlesinger 187–94).[4] Even the personas that many of the abstract expressionists (and their critics) adopted often drew on a heroic macho individualism. Jackson Pollock, who embraced a sort of Wyoming cowboy image, was perhaps the most extreme. But other members of the circle that hung out at the Cedar Tavern and the Artists Club on East Eighth Street were constantly challenging each other to fist fights—a predilection lampooned by younger and often openly gay artists of the next generation, many of whom maintained a famously close engagement with popular culture.[5]

However, it is not so much Ellison's rejection of ideology as such that struck such a powerful chord at the onset of the Cold War. Interestingly, quite a few anticommunist critics of the novel found Ellison's portrait of the Brotherhood unpersuasively two-dimensional in its negativity. For example, Irving Howe, a vociferous critic of the communist Left, claimed, "Ellison makes his Stalinists so stupid and vicious that one cannot understand how they could have attracted him" (21). In any event, as Lloyd Brown pointed out in the communist journal *Masses and Mainstream*, such caricatures were unremarkable as part of "the central design of American Century literature" (31). The novel's rejection of nationalism, notably as figured by the Garveyesque Ras, aggravated some prominent Black Arts activists in the 1960s and 1970s.[6] But such a rejection in the early 1950s when, as Lorenzo Thomas argues, such nationalism was virtually underground would not strike much of a chord outside the black community—and perhaps not so much in it (137–40). This is not to say, of course, that the rejections of the Left and of nationalism are not important components of the narrator's heroic individualism (or heroic potential).

In the end, the heroism of the novel is a rejection of the masses and mass culture for an individual subjectivity. As Andreas Huyssen points out, for much of modernism, the masses, particularly mass culture and its consumers, are coded as female—as seen in T. S. Eliot's *The Waste Land*, Ezra Pound's "Hugh Selwyn Mauberly," and even Langston Hughes's "The Negro Artist and the Racial Mountain" (where the "Philadelphia clubwoman" is used as an icon of middlebrow, middle-class Negro mediocrity)— though Hughes had a far more complicated relationship to popular culture than did Eliot or Pound (Huyssen 44–53). Again, Sybil's "big black buck," her lens for seeing the narrator, may depend on an old stereotype reaching back to early attacks on Reconstruction, but its vocabulary is the much more contemporary popular culture figures of Louis Armstrong and Paul Robeson. It is this feminized mass culture at war with the male individual, the Thurber cartoon (as the narrator characterizes his interaction with Sybil), which is rejected. Of course, this vision is ironically complicated since it relies in no small part on the myth of a hypersexed, hypermasculine black man, though as we shall see, this myth finds a parallel in mass-culture notions of female sexuality so that black male hypersexuality can be strangely feminine.

This rejection also has a complicated relationship to feminism and the Communist party variant of Marxism in the 1930s and 1940s. Organized feminism in the United States was at a relatively low ebb between the 1920s and the beginnings of second wave feminism in the 1960s. However, to a large extent the Communist party and its institutions provided a crucial link between first wave and second wave feminism. Quite a few scholars have claimed, and *Invisible Man* itself argues, that the Communist party was marked by male chauvinism and hostility to "bourgeois" feminism. Certainly, its top leaders were all male until Elizabeth Gurley Flynn's tenure as national chair in the early 1960s.[7] However, as other critics have pointed out, the communist Left and its ideological positions on "the woman question" provided both a vocabulary and institutional space in which feminist issues and concerns could be articulated, debated, and sometimes successfully addressed within a leftist context.[8] Not surprisingly, a number of the most important early originators of second wave feminism and women's studies in the United States, such as Betty Friedan and Gerda Lerner, had backgrounds in the communist Left.

The protagonist and the Brotherhood see the narrator's reassignment to the woman question by Brother Jack as a demotion, a punishment. Again, this vision of the place of gender issues in the Brotherhood pecking order would seem to accord with feminist and postfeminist visions of communist hypocrisy on these issues. However, the novel differs in that the reader, too, is made to feel that such an assignment is inherently a step down. The (white) women of the Brotherhood are so caught up in mass-culture fantasies of race and sex that even if feminist ideals did have any value (within the frame of the novel), these women are too deluded, too intellectually weak to see them. While the narrator is able, ultimately, to leave behind the Brotherhood and its ideology, there is no sense that any of the women have the spiritual or intellectual resources to do so. And, as noted above with respect to Ellison's remaking (removal, really) of the character Louise, this denial of agency to the Brotherhood women is, as the Communist party liked to say, no accident. In fact, the women of the Brotherhood, and the Brotherhood's (and Communist party's) use of the woman question, represent what is seen as a fundamentally dishonest and intellectually bankrupt engagement with mass culture. In this, Ellison echoed various attacks on the Popular Front in *Partisan Review* and other journals associated with the New York intellectuals, which blamed, in part, the communist Left for the circulation of middlebrow culture among American intellectuals.[9]

In *Invisible Man*, those who might be termed the controllers (for example, the audience at the battle royal, Bledsoe, and Brother Jack) are male. These men seem to run the system. Perhaps they do run the system, but they are caught in it as well. Bledsoe, for example, clearly understands invisibility and blindness, two foundational principles of the system, better than the narrator, in whom Bledsoe sees an earlier, more naïve self. But

Bledsoe also is strangely blind. It is true that Bledsoe is able to benefit personally from his manipulation of the role that white people expect him to play. He speaks of his ability to get himself "power, influence, contacts with powerful and influential people—and then stay in the dark and use it" (*IM* 145). But he only has power so long as he does what the true power, "rich white folks power," wants him to do. Similarly, Brother Jack seems to be in control, seems to understand the underlying principles of society better than the narrator but is revealed as literally visually impaired when his glass eye pops out.

Beyond these controllers are those who evade control in various ways. These figures are male too. They are also black. The narrator's grandfather, the yam seller, Peter Wheatstraw, Jim Trueblood, and Brother Tarp are all sort of folk tricksters, who are able to partly evade complete control and mass culture by living according to older cultural codes of resistance through indirection. As he looks through Rinehart's dark glasses, the narrator discovers the possibilities of invisibility in the relatively new urban ghetto of the North:

> In the South everyone knew you, but the North was the jump into the unknown. How many days could you walk the streets of the big city without encountering anyone who knew you? You could make yourself anew. The notion was frightening, for now the world seemed to flow before my eyes. All boundaries down, freedom was not only the recognition of necessity, it was the recognition of possibility. And sitting there trembling I caught a brief glimpse of the possibilities posed by Rinehart's multiple personalities and turned away. It was too vast and confusing to contemplate. (499)

Rinehart seems to be the ultimate self-centered individualist. He is in fact a creature of mass culture—all rind and no heart. In many respects, he is Bledsoe without illusion. But where Bledsoe understands the possibilities of what might be thought of as Booker T. Washington–era invisibility, Rinehart understands the possibilities of urban mass culture and embraces it. He is a true postmodernist.

Once again, the black women in the book are different. They are neither controllers nor evaders. As in Faulkner's work, they have no true self-consciousness. The white women in the novel are controlled and instruments of control. These women are often victims whose conditions and even emotional responses echo those of black men, especially the narrator—as seen in the first chapter where the white men of the battle royal audience physically abuse the magnificent blonde. And they sometimes rebel ineffectually as when Brotherhood women sexually pursue the narrator—though often with the approval of their husbands and lovers. Indeed, though these women pursue the narrator at least in part through a sense of the inadequacy of their Brotherhood husbands or lovers, they are in fact a means through which the Brotherhood exerts control over the narrator, raising the old anticommunist claim that the Communist party used white women as a sort of bait to draw in and control black men.[10] At the same time, the nameless woman, Sybil, and even Emma are on the margins of the Brotherhood (as the name suggests). There are really no female Brotherhood activists—much less leaders. Again, Ellison basically excised the only female Brotherhood character with any degree of agency, self-consciousness, and integrity by the time he produced the final draft of the novel.

These white women remain bound by mass culture as seen, for example, in the gold chain willingly worn around Sybil's ankle—which contrasts with the broken link of chain from his prison-gang shackles that Brother Tarp carries. Sybil's rebellion against her husband is shaped by the popular culture vision of "the big black buck." In a sense, Ellison's rendering of Sybil anticipates Foucault in that an attempt to police racial boundaries (and power relationships) through the use of the image of the black savage rapist has ironically created or focused the very desire it was supposed to repress. Of course, this rendering of the "forbidden fruit" syndrome and its dangers is part of a long line of discussion in African-American literature and culture. In any event, the narrator oddly rejects his actual participation in this vision while reinforcing it in Sybil by leading her to believe that he did play the role in which she cast him. This has the result of heightening his individualism since *he* knows what he did while reinforcing the collective social vision articulated by Sybil (and him to her). These women are also tools used by the controllers, which even the often clueless narrator is able to sense. Again, he avoids Brother Jack's girlfriend, Emma, because he knows that Jack would use her against him somehow.

It is worth noting that not only does the narrator need to literally fall out of history in order to gain the sort of distance that allows him a space from which he can potentially reemerge as the individual triumphant (in some unspecified manner), but somehow the horrific hallucinatory castration scene near the end of the novel's final chapter (before the epilogue) is an integral part of the process. It is as if such castration is necessary so that the "warmly, infuriatingly feminine" (as he describes Sybil) mass culture embodied in white women, and the desires it inculcates, no longer has any purchase (so to speak) on him.

Yet ironically it is this castration that confirms or reconstitutes his manhood. As noted above, in many respects the fitful passivity and rebellion of white women shaped by a naïve or unconscious consumption of mass culture mirrors that of the equally naïve, though variously rebellious narrator. This link between white women and the narrator is first drawn in the terror that the narrator believes he sees in the eyes of the magnificent blonde, which he thinks matches his own. The image of the "big black buck," which is the flip side of black subservience, matches female "nymphomania," which is the reverse of feminine domesticity, the familiar types of the Madonna and the whore, seen most clearly in the narrator's encounter with Sybil. His assignment to speak on the woman question can be seen as a demeaning statement on the part of Brother Jack and the Brotherhood, implying that he *is* a sort of woman—an insult that he feels acutely. Even the rebellions of both the women and the narrator are often used by the male controllers.

However, the resemblance ends as the protagonist assumes his final identity as the self-conscious heroic individual while the white women are left behind in dreamland. In an odd way then, given the novel's assault on black nationalism, there is an echo of the traditional nationalist tropes of racial emasculation and the reclamation of manhood that are embodied in the novel by Ras. However, unlike the nationalists, it is an individual manhood that is reconstituted—a reconstitution that depends largely on a vision of white women and mass culture (really, white women as mass culture).

Similarly, Mary and the motherly black women of the novel embody a relatively passive vision of the folk, but without the conscious agency of, say, Jim Trueblood or the narrator's grandfather. There are moments where the novel hints that she might have such agency, where there are, to use a slightly dated term, aporia in which we see that she might be something different— and, as noted above, Ellison's earlier versions of *Invisible Man* in fact gave Mary Rambo much more agency and self-consciousness so that she would more nearly resemble one of the novel's male folk instructors of the narrator. The narrator feels something for these women, but, as we have seen, it is neither desire nor, finally, respect. In the end, however, the reader is most strongly left with the notion of Mary as a sort of passive force or principle, a feeling that is reinforced by the description of her racist coin bank, which she possesses without any apparent (to the narrator, anyway) irony or self-awareness. Again, this could be compared to Brother Tarp's use of the chain link as a tool of memory and self-knowledge.

The protagonist of *Invisible Man* rejects various ideologies of the masses, whether nationalism or Marxism (including 1940s Marxist variations of feminism), and mass culture through this heroic individualism that engages modernism while significantly revising and transposing it into an Emersonian frequency. As Irving Howe remarked long ago, literary expressions of heroic individualism were not remarkable in the moment of the high Cold War (22). One thinks of such divergently heroic individuals as Augie March in Saul Bellow's *The Adventures of Augie March* (1953), Moses Herzog in Bellow's 1964 *Herzog*, and Neil Klugman in Phillip Roth's *Goodbye Columbus* (1957). Like Ellison's narrator, and no doubt influenced by Ellison's novel, their heroism relies on strangely dependent relationships with consumer culture–identified women that are both mothering and murderous and that enable the protagonists to liberate themselves even as they finally reject those relationships.

But none of these expressions could match the tour de force of Ellison's novel with its incredibly wide-ranging reconsideration and revision of nineteenth-century European and American literature (including African-American literature and culture) as well as of modernism in the Cold War moment. Again, it was not simply the novel's open anticommunism that made it a premiere work of that moment. Rather, as with the "action painting" of Pollock and its framing by Clement Greenberg, Thomas Hess, and Harold Rosenberg, it is the powerful engagement with the ideological underpinning of the Cold War and the American Century, which was also aimed at demolishing Marxism and other sorts of ideological competitors in a way that did not solely rely on stories of actual acts of perfidy and betrayal by particular individuals and organizations, but attempted to foreclose whole ideological (and aesthetic) positions. As a result, *Invisible Man*, unlike, say, *Native Son*, became not merely a popular and important novel, but also a key *American* text that became virtually inescapable on any syllabus in a modern American novel survey class long before the widespread existence of courses, seminars, programs, and departments in African-American studies.

While, as we have seen, the relationship between *Invisible Man* and modernism is more vexed than is sometimes allowed, the ideological (and aesthetic) thrust of the novel does absolutely rely on various neomodernist framings of gender and sexuality and their intersection with American conceptions of race. The peculiar thing about these framings in a book that is so concerned with sight and blindness, with vision and revision, is that they draw upon such familiar types of American and African-American high and popular culture without much apparent self-reflection—to the degree that anything can be taken straight in such a parodic work. So, in the end, both Stanford and Tate are correct. There are virtually no positive portrayals of women in the novel (and even the most positive are troubling), and women are absolutely central to the ideological and artistic project of the book.

NOTES

1. Ellison also cites Twain's use of women to embody "established values" as a model for his use of gender in his early fiction (Graham and Singh 196–97). One could also invoke Flaubert's Emma Bovary as an important predecessor of the white women in *Invisible Man*—though in the course of *Madame Bovary*, Emma is humanized in a way that Sybil or the nameless Brotherhood woman never are.

2. Ellison denied that West exerted any influence on him, claiming that he only read West's work after he finished *Invisible Man* (Graham and Singh 71). This may be true, but, again, it is worth noting that Ellison was often reluctant to admit any debt to the work of American contemporaries or near-contemporaries, black and white.

3. For a well-known example of Ellison's use of jazz to authorize his vision of the artist generally, and his own claims of literary ancestry specifically, see "Hidden Name and Complex Fate" (*SA* 144–66). Interestingly, Ellison famously held the self-consciously modernist musicians of bebop and the various schools of avant-garde jazz that followed them in low regard.

4. Both Greenberg and Schlesinger were heavily involved with the CIA-funded Congress for Cultural Freedom and the American Committee for Cultural Freedom. The former group fought the cultural Cold War abroad while the latter aimed at eradicating the remnants of the Popular Front and its legacies in the arts and academy of the United States. As Paul Buhle points out, Schlesinger played a key role in facilitating and shaping the CIA's efforts with artists and intellectuals (263–64). For a more detailed examination of the role of Greenberg, the American Committee for Cultural Freedom, and the CIA in promoting abstract expressionism (and combating what Greenberg saw as residual Stalinism), see Saunders 252–78.

5. Andy Warhol makes a telling critique of the macho zeitgeist of the Cedar Tavern scene, social epicenter of the high abstract expressionist era, in his memoir *POPism*. He asks incredulously if one could imagine him asking Roy Lichtenstein to "step outside" because he had insulted one of his soup cans. "How corny," Warhol concludes (15).

6. Ellison asserted vehemently in an interview that Ras was not based on Garvey. Rather he claimed that Ras was a sort of embodi-

ment of his own anger at white liberal paternalism. However, it is hard to believe that Ras's description and Caribbean accent were not supposed to evoke Garvey and various neo-Garveyite nationalist leaders in Harlem during the 1920s, 1930s, and 1940s (*SA* 181).

7. For important studies of the Left and women's literature during the 1930s that emphasize the shortcomings of the Communist party regarding "the woman question" while asserting how women artists combated or circumvented those failings, see Rabinowitz and Coiner.

8. For an examination of radical literature of the Great Depression that is much more positive about the communist Left and the role of women artists within it, see Foley, *Radical Representations*, 213–48.

9. For example, Robert Warshow claimed that the "Stalinists" seduced much of the intelligentsia into embracing a debased middle-brow culture, which he defined as "mass culture of the educated classes" (3–5).

10. For brief discussions of this claim and the vexed reception of relationships between black men and white women in the Communist party by black female communists and the Harlem community generally, see Naison (136–37) and McKay (232–37). Though Ellison was notably disinclined to acknowledge black literary influences, the final chapter of McKay's *Harlem: Negro Metropolis*, "Sufi Abdul Hamid and Organized Labor," draws a picture of Harlem political life, including a vitriolic critique of the Communist party, that much resembles Ellison's.

WORKS CITED

Brooks, Gwendolyn. *Blacks.* 1987. Reprint. Chicago: Third World, 1992.

Brown, Lloyd. "The Deep Pit." 1952. In The Critical Response to *Ralph Ellison*, edited by Robert J. Butler, 31–33. Westport, Conn.: Greenwood, 2000.

Buhle, Paul. "How Sweet It Wasn't: The Scholars and the CIA." In *The New Left Revisited*, edited by John McMillan and Paul Buhle, 257–72. Philadelphia, Pa.: Temple University Press, 2003.

Coiner, Constance. *Better Red: The Writing and Resistance of Tillie*

Olsen and Meridel Le Sueur. New York: Oxford University Press, 1995.

Ellison, Ralph. "Out of the Hospital and under the Bar." In *Soon, One Morning*, edited by Herbert Hill, 242–90. New York: Knopf, 1963.

Fiedler, Leslie. *Collected Essays*. New York: Stein and Day, 1971.

Foley, Barbara. "From Communism to Brotherhood: The Drafts of Invisible Man." In *Left of the Color Line: Race, Radicalism, and Twentieth-Century Literature of the United States*, edited by Bill V. Mullen and James Smethurst, 163–82. Chapel Hill: University of North Carolina Press, 2003.

———. *Radical Representations: Politics and Form in U.S. Proletarian Literature, 1929–1941*. Durham, N.C.: Duke University Press, 1993.

Graham, Maryemma, and Amritjit Singh, eds. *Conversations with Ralph Ellison*. Jackson: University Press of Mississippi, 1995.

Guilbaut, Serge. *How New York Stole the Idea of Modern Art: Abstract Expressionism, Freedom, and the Cold War*. Chicago, Ill.: University of Chicago Press, 1983.

Howe, Irving. "A Negro in America." 1952. In *The Critical Response to Ralph Ellison*, edited by Robert J. Butler, 21–22. Westport, Conn.: Greenwood, 2000.

Huyssen, Andreas. *After the Great Divide: Modernism, Mass Culture, Postmodernism*. Bloomington: Indiana University Press, 1986.

Jackson, Lawrence Patrick. *Ralph Ellison: The Emergence of Genius*. New York: Wiley, 2002.

McKay, Claude. *Harlem: Negro Metropolis*. 1940. Reprint. New York: Harcourt Brace Jovanovich, 1968.

Nadel, Alan. *Invisible Criticism: Ralph Ellison and the American Canon*. Iowa City: University of Iowa Press, 1988.

Naison, Mark. *Communists in Harlem during the Great Depression*. New York: Grove, 1984.

Ostendorf, Berndt. "Ralph Waldo Ellison: Anthropology, Modernism, and Jazz." In *New Essays on Invisible Man*, edited by Robert O'Meally, 95–121. New York: Cambridge University Press, 1988.

Rabinowitz, Paula. *Labor and Desire: Women's Revolutionary Fiction in Depression America*. Chapel Hill: University of North Carolina Press, 1991.

Saunders, Frances Stonor. *The Cultural Cold War: The CIA in the World of Arts and Letters*. New York: New Press, 2000.

Schlesinger, Arthur, Jr. *The Vital Center: The Politics of Freedom*. Boston: Houghton Mifflin, 1949.

Stanford, Ann Folwell. "He Speaks for Whom? Inscription and Reinscription of Women in *Invisible Man* and *The Salt Eaters*." *MELUS* 18, no. 2 (Summer 1992): 17–31.

Sylvander, Carolyn. "*Invisible Man* and Female Stereotypes." *Negro American Literature Forum* 9, no. 3 (Autumn 1975): 77–79.

Tate, Claudia. "Notes on the Invisible Woman in Ralph Ellison's *Invisible Man*." In *Speaking for You: The Vision of Ralph Ellison*, edited by Kimberly Benston, 163–72. Washington, D.C.: Howard University Press, 1987.

Thomas, Lorenzo. *Extraordinary Measures: Afrocentric Modernism and Twentieth-Century American Poetry*. Tuscaloosa: University of Alabama Press, 2000.

Warhol, Andy, and Pat Hackett. *POPism: The Warhol '60s*. New York: Harcourt Brace, 1980.

Warshow, Robert. *The Immediate Experience: Movies, Comics, Theatre and Other Aspects of Popular Culture*. 1962. New York: Anchor, 1964.

The Integrated Literary Tradition

Alan Nadel

Ralph Ellison's connections to nineteenth-century American authors have been extensively discussed by numerous critics as well as by Ellison himself. From his earliest days as a writer, as his collected essays make clear, Ellison was profoundly concerned with the literary canon and with his relation to it. The *Collected Essays* discusses at length, over a fifty-year period, the range of influences that forged Ellison's personal canon out of canonical American literature.

In "Twentieth-Century Fiction and the Mask of Black Humanity," an essay written in 1946 just prior to his beginning work on *Invisible Man*, Ellison discusses the importance of Twain, Emerson, Thoreau, Whitman, and Melville from a perspective particularly unique in the 1940s: that these writers were significant because they understood, in the context of the social and political tensions of their times, that the Negro represented the call to their—and to their readers'—humanity. "This conception of the Negro as a symbol of Man," Ellison explained, "—the reversal of what he represents in most contemporary thought—was organic to nineteenth-century literature" (*CE* 88). Thus "Huck Finn's acceptance of the evil implicit in his 'emancipation' of Jim represents Twain's acceptance of his personal responsibility for the condition of society" (*CE* 89). At a time when the dicta of New Criticism dominated American literary scholarship, Ellison's insistence on reading American literature not only as historical but also as consciously political represented a significant divergence from conventional practice, a divergence that was to inform Ellison's critical perspective throughout his career. That career embraced his work as an essayist, lecturer, scholar, and fiction writer. Thus, his extensive criticism—always occasional—blends seamlessly with his fiction to comprise a rich, lifelong investigation of the American canon and the factors that shaped it.

Ellison's investigation included lectures, essays, and richly allusive fiction that places details from and aspects of American literature in contexts that impel the reader to experience them afresh and thus to confront—however subtly—the history and the prejudice that rendered certain meanings and readings invisible. In this regard, therefore, integration represents Ellison's understanding of America's cultural history—even when obstructed by laws or social values—and equally his aesthetic and critical practice. Because his fiction integrates its own literary tradition, moreover, it is integrated with his criticism. Both the criticism and the fiction pursue a common goal, although by very different means: to reveal the way in which Negro[1] America has always been integral to white American culture and knowledge, even when it comprised the visible contradiction to the nation's articulated principles.

Thus, like his essays and lectures, Ellison's novels pursue a very Ellisonian understanding of America's integrated heritage. Specifically, Ellison as a critic returned repeatedly over the course of his adult life to a small number of profoundly influential figures: Melville, Crane, Emerson, Twain, James, Hemingway, Eliot, and, in the long run perhaps most significantly, Faulkner. The only black writer whom Ellison engaged with comparably explicit attention was Richard Wright. As a result, perhaps, Ellison's connections to his Negro American heritage have been most widely noted in regard to blues musicians and characters out of Negro folklore. Ellison, nevertheless, could only create his visibly integrated literature because of a Negro literary tradition as well as a white tradition, and the purpose of this essay is to detail some of the ways Ellison, in his essays and in his fiction, has pursued both as an artistic goal and as a moral imperative— aspects of writing Ellison never wished to separate from one another—the cause of integration.

Interpreting the Canon

One particularly important and sustained objective for Ellison was demonstrating that the white canon already contained the Negro as a source of its moral imperative. This is the thesis of the essay I quoted at the outset, "Twentieth-Century Fiction and the Mask of Black Humanity." In "Society, Morality, and the Novel," written in 1957, Ellison argued that the strength of *Moby-Dick*, *Huckleberry Finn*, and *The Bostonians* was that "each is concerned with the moral predicament of the nation" (*CE* 704), that their authors realized that the novel was "bound up with our problem of nationhood" (704). Hemingway too, Ellison explained, "was as obsessed with the Civil War and its aftermath as any Southern writer" (*CE* 709). In 1964, Ellison pointed out:

> The contradiction between [America's] noble ideals and the actualities of our conduct generated a guilt, an unease of spirit, from the very beginning, and . . . the American novel at its best has always been concerned with this basic moral predicament. During Melville's time and Twain's, it was an implicit aspect of their major themes; by the twentieth century and after the discouraging and traumatic effect of the Civil War and the Reconstruction it had gone underground, had become *understated*. Nevertheless . . . it is to be found operating in the work of Henry James as well as that of Hemingway. (*CE* 206–7)

Of equal importance in developing the modernist style of *Invisible Man* were Joyce and Eliot, writers he encountered early and to whom he returned often. Although he had gone to Tuskegee to study music, in his second year Ellison read *The Waste Land*, "and that," he explained, "although I was unaware of it, was the real transition to writing" (*CE* 202): "*The Waste Land* seized my mind. I was intrigued by its power to move me while eluding my understanding. Somehow its rhythms were often closer to those of jazz than were those of the Negro poets, and even though I could not understand then, its range of allusion was as mixed and as varied as that of Louis Armstrong" (203). From Eliot, in other words, Ellison learned the art of bricolage, the construction of a cultural moment through the reassembly of the however fragmentary bits of that moment's artifacts and traditions (an art for which the blues had already laid the groundwork). By 1937, he had come to realize that "in my uninstructed reading of Eliot and Pound, I had recognized a relationship between poetry and jazz music, and this led me to wonder why I was not encountering similar devices in the work of Afro-American writers" (*CE* 659–60). Joyce was particularly helpful in demonstrating how this high modernist technique could be employed in the service of an extended prose narrative.

Invisible Man is thus replete with nods to Eliot and Joyce. One of the two epigraphs prefacing the novel, for example, comes from Eliot's play *Family Reunion*. The quote is a statement about identity, misperception, blindness, and ultimately tragedy: "I tell you it is not me you are looking at, / Not me you are grinning at, not me your confidential looks / Incriminate, but that other person, if person / You thought I was: let your necrophily / Feed upon that carcase." In addition to underscoring the relationship between vision and identity that provides a central motif in *Invisible Man*, the inscription also acknowledges Eliot's technique of updating Greek tragedy by employing modernist poetics.

Near the beginning of chapter 2, Ellison makes another direct allusion to Eliot, using key images from *The Waste Land* to describe the school as a "flower-studded wasteland, the rocks sunken, the dry winds hidden, the lost crickets chirping to yellow butterflies" (*IM* 37). The novel begins as well with two pointed allusions to Joyce's *A Portrait of the Artist as a Young Man*. The first is the initial head-butting incident described in the prologue, in which the invisible man assaults a man for making a racial slur and yells, "Apologize! Apologize!" (*IM* 4), echoing Stephen Dedalus's refrain: "Apologize / Tear out his eyes / Tear out his eyes / Apologize,"[2] an allusion that links the violence to blindness, in the same way that the Eliot epigraph does.

That blindness, however, in the context of Ellison's adaptation, employed modernist technique in relation to issues specific and central to Ellison's historical moment and conscious goal. To put it most simply, half of the tradition he wished to evoke using these modernist techniques was invisible. That invisibility, moreover, assumed myriad forms. Negro contributions to American culture had been largely ignored or marginalized, or surreptitiously appropriated, and/or misrepresented. In addition, the role that the presence of Negro Americans had in creating the social and historical conditions for the nation's greatest literature and art had been repressed and at times even consciously suppressed. Ellison believed this was the case because the presence of Negro Americans and everything they represented about American history comprised a threat to the nation's conscious claims to sovereignty. Since slavery and its aftermath, in other words, contradicted the very principles that justified the nation, Ellison argued in 1967 that James, like Emerson before him, as well as his contemporaries Twain and Crane, understood that in the second half of the nineteenth century:

> The United States had reached a moment of crisis, and in fact
> . . . he was writing during a new period in the life of the nation, when the lyrical belief in the possibilities of the Constitution and the broadness of the land was no longer meaningful. Mindful that hundreds of thousands of men had died in the Civil War, James knew for his own time what Emerson knew for his. . . . What James realized was that the old enduring evil of the human predicament had raised its face, revealing itself within this land. (CE 759–60)

Ellison returned to this theme again in 1976: "The great writers of the nineteenth century and the best of the twentieth have always reminded us that the business of being an American is an arduous task, as Henry James said, and it requires constant attention to our consciousness and our conscientiousness" (CE 781). From Ellison's perspective, however, the literary criticism that canonized writers such as Emerson, Melville, Twain, and James did so through a lens that filtered out the racial dynamics instrumental in their works. The works, in a word, were *whitewashed*. An important factor in the difficult "task" of being an American, therefore, was created by the fact that "the contradiction between [America's] noble ideals and the actualities of our conduct generated a guilt, an unease of spirit, from the very beginning, and . . . the American novel at its best has always been concerned with this basic moral predicament. During Melville's time and Twain's, it was an implicit aspect of their major themes" (*CE* 206–7).

Thus Ellison's "arduous task" was multifarious. In addition to demonstrating how the presence of Negro culture and the issues surrounding slavery and race empowered the American writers Ellison considered most significant, Ellison also wanted to show how those authors provided the literary tradition for Negro American authors. Repeatedly, Ellison emphasized the fact that despite being raised in segregated Oklahoma, and traveling through the segregated South to attend Tuskegee, an all-Negro college, he was as much the heir to the great works of literature, art, and music as any American, regardless of race. In Macon County, Alabama, he points out, "I read Marx, Freud, T. S. Eliot, Pound, Gertrude Stein and Hemingway. Books which seldom, if ever, mentioned Negroes were to release me from whatever 'segregated' idea I might have had of my own human possibilities" (*CE* 164). "Anything and everything," he explains in the 1964 introduction to his first collection of essays, *Shadow and Act*, "was to be found in the chaos of Oklahoma; thus the concept of the Renaissance man has lurked long within the shadow of my past, and I shared it with at least a dozen of my Negro friends" (*CE* 50). Although not intending when he first came to New York to become a writer, Ellison came nevertheless steeped in literary tradition and literary knowledge.

At that point Richard Wright played an important role in the formation of Ellison's literary values by sharing with Ellison the writers that influenced Wright's craft: "[Wright] was very conscious of technique. He talked about it not in terms of mystification but as writing know-how. 'You must read so-and-so,' he'd say. . . . 'You must learn how Conrad, Joyce, Dostoevsky get their effects.' He guided me to Henry James and to Conrad's prefaces, that type of thing" (*CE* 73–74). Ellison's knowledge of the Euro-American literary tradition, in other words, was not sui generis; it was available to anyone who read, and it was shared by the best writers of all races.

This point is crucial to understanding Ellison's sense of integration, which is lodged in practices that recognize strains of the American experience that have always been present in ways that are not only integrated but, in fact, inseparable. Just as white American music, dance, and humor are the composite of multiracial, multiethnic influences, so Negro American literature reflects the legacy of a literary tradition that is anything but monoracial. In emphasizing the fact that he and Wright drew from a common well, Ellison was arguing that black writers had the right (and the obligation) to be judged *as* writers. He was also making clear that the "white" writer could not claim to be the exclusive heir to the estate of Western art and thought. If Ellison insisted that he and Wright and any other Negro author be judged by canonical standards, to the extent that they met those standards they had to be included in the body of the nation's "influential" writers. It was exactly because they had engaged the tradition that they could become part of it.

In other words, if Ellison sought to craft a novel that met the high modernist standards of twentieth-century literature, he saw the task as endemic to his social responsibility as a Negro author. In order to speak effectively as a fiction writer (as opposed to, for example, a sociologist) about Negro American experiences, Ellison indicated emphatically that he had to perfect the craft of writing equal to his ambitious themes.

The result, *Invisible Man*, is a novel employing richly allusive modernist techniques that refer to major works of the American canon in contexts that impel reinterpretation. By identifying the self-deluding trustee, Mr. Norton, with Emerson's trustees of the consciousness, Ellison demonstrated how easily Emersonian self-reliance, denuded of its historical specificity and moral imperative, could be misread to ends completely inconsistent with Emerson's ideals. Because the rebellion of vets in the Golden

Day echoes the slave ship rebellion in Melville's "Benito Cereno," Ellison's rendition shows that foregrounding the issue of race and slavery makes it impossible to identify Melville with his naïve protagonist, Captain Delano, an interpretation that was conventional wisdom at the time Ellison was writing *Invisible Man*.

Equally popular, in that period, was a view of *The Adventures of Huckleberry Finn* that focused upon the escape from society at the expense of the ways in which the novel forced the reader to engage the social problems—especially those surrounding race and slavery—that relentlessly defied the characters' attempted escapes. At its most extreme, the escape was figured, in criticism contemporaneous to the writing of *Invisible Man*, as representing the homoerotic allure of the racial Other as an alternative to the constraints of domesticity. In *Invisible Man*, Emerson's son, as a parody of this version of Huck, shows how inadequate such a figure is to the social demands of the nineteenth century, unresolved and thus resonant with the invisible man's twentieth-century predicament.

For Ellison, one strength of the American experience was a kind of cultural democracy that made it possible for him to discover American and world literature on his own, in such a way as to recognize that they engaged the social responsibility of the novel and thus how important the Negro was to that engagement. A far darker aspect of the American experience was the asymmetry with which American culture acknowledged the cultural democracy that, even in its most repressive mode, it was incapable of preventing. That is the dark place of the invisible man, the underground world of American culture on which, in *Invisible Man*'s prologue, the narrator desires to shed light. The overilluminated room whence the novel's narrative emanates is saturated by the musical strains of Louis Armstrong, the inventor of the jazz solo, the international representative of Negro American music, who drew upon and integrated myriad strains of American musical performance traditions. Literary traditions equally, albeit more obliquely, saturate the room, a point made clear by the Faulknerian dream interlude that begins with the narrator's hearing "a spiritual as full of Weltschmerz as flamenco" (*IM* 9). The integrated musical strains—spiritual, weltschmerz, flamenco, blues—move to the site of racial integration, the slave auction, the funeral for the master killed by the slaves who were also his sons. "The object of my fictional imagination," Ellison said in 1969, "is American society and the American experience as experienced fundamentally by Negroes, and I find it impossible to deal with either in isolation, for they are intricately united in their diversity" (*CE* 430).

Invisible Man, Negro Folklore, and Autobiography

In foregrounding this point, Ellison has tended to call less attention to the role of Negro authors who forged the integrated matrix of cultural meanings and literary legacy that informs his fiction. Certainly black folklore, particularly the tricksters and dupes represented by the figures of Brer Bear and Brer Rabbit, permeates *Invisible Man*, with the narrator not only serving as foil for each but also, at various points, from the opening episode at the battle royal on, assuming each of those archetypal roles. The battle royal—an entertainment at "a gathering of the town's leading white citizens" (*IM* 17) that involves ten blindfolded Negro teenagers fighting one another in a boxing ring—is coupled with an invitation for the invisible man to deliver an encore of his graduation speech that "showed that humility was the secret, indeed the very essence of progress" (*IM* 17).

When, prior to giving his speech, he is included among the ten boys in the boxing ring, the invisible man assumes the role of bear in that he is caught sleeping, that is, he is duped by the white citizens. He had come to the event as a "dignified" speaker only to discover that his entertainment value lies in the indignities that the event will put him through. At the same time, however, from the perspective of the other boys, he is the trickster rabbit, in that he displaces one of their friends; he had used his speech, in other words, to acquire additional money that would otherwise have gone to the regular performers. Once in the ring, moreover, he manages to trick the boys and the white citizens when he realizes he can see forms through his blindfold. Thus, he tells us, "I played one group against the other, slipping in and throwing a punch then stepping out of range while pushing the others into the melee to take blows blindly aimed at me" (*IM* 23). In failing to recognize that the battle royal is a performance, however, the invisible man once again becomes the dupe, tricked into remaining alone in the ring with the biggest of the other boys, who could then beat him up. Despite their having tricked the invisible man, however, all the boys become dupes when they are forced to dive for payment on an electrified carpet. When he finally delivers his speech, which he was duped into believing would restore his dignity, the white crowd's jeers and interruptions make clear that far from being more dignified, he has become the target of singular, additional humiliation. In the midst of the ordeal, however, the trickster in him resurfaces briefly when he substitutes the phrase "social equality" for "social responsibility," a subversive gesture that he is forced immediately to retract.

This pattern of oscillation between bear and rabbit pervades the novel, as the invisible man is repeatedly tricked into being the trickster. The initial trickster, of course, was the invisible man's grandfather, whose ambiguous deathbed words had tricked the invisible man into becoming the person invited to give a speech at the battle royal. Jim Trueblood, the vet at the Golden Day, Peter Wheatstraw, Lucius Brockway, the yam man, and Brother Tarp all echo to some degree the grandfather's encoded deceptions, each of which tricks or entices the invisible man to a new level of consciousness. At the same time that he is duped by each of them and, as well, by more nefarious figures, such as Dr. Bledsoe or Brother Jack (rabbit?), he also allows his naiveté to become a mask behind which he undermines the trick. By actually taking Mr. Norton at his word and showing him aspects of Negro life not consistent with the college's propaganda, the invisible man forces Norton to confront his own hypocrisy and helps undermine the duplicity with which Dr. Bledsoe exploits the trustees (and the college) for his own ends.

Ellison's intent focus on the place of Negroes in "white" history, literature, and culture, however, may distract readers away from the use of Negro literature in *Invisible Man*. Of particular importance are images from the autobiographical works of Frederick Douglass, Booker T. Washington, and W. E. B. Du Bois.

Douglass's autobiography, for example, is echoed in the invisible man's induction into the Brotherhood. Like Douglass, he is hurled into prominence by a spontaneous speech, in the invisible man's case made at the site of a Harlem eviction and in Douglass's at an abolitionist rally. In both cases, the men had no idea they would be making the speech. Douglass, an escaped slave living in New Bedford, Massachusetts, attended an 1841 antislavery convention with no expectation that he would take part in the proceedings. A prominent abolitionist, however, who had heard Douglass speaking to his "colored friends in the little schoolhouse on Second Street where we worshiped,"[3] sought him out in the crowd and induced him "to express the feelings inspired by the occasion, and the fresh recollection of the scenes through which [he] had passed as a slave" (215). Although Douglass remembered little of the speech itself, he reported that the "audience sympathized with me at once, and from having been remarkably quiet, became much excited" (215).

The same spontaneous ability to shake the audience from its complacency characterizes the invisible man's speech, which, in fact, foments a small riot. It too deals with a former slave, Primus Provo, freed in 1859 only to be evicted some eighty years later. In the same way that Douglass, at "the close of this great meeting . . . was duly waited on by Mr. John A. Collins, then the general agent of the Massachusetts Anti-Slavery Society, and urgently solicited by him to become an agent of the society and publicly advocate its principles" (216), the invisible man is enlisted in the Brotherhood. In both cases, moreover, the men embark on their new lives with the great enthusiasm typical of new converts, and in both cases they are placed under the mentorship of a white comrade, such that they become to some degree mindless puppets. "During the first three months," Douglass explained, "my speeches were almost exclusively made up of narrations of my own personal experience as a slave. 'Let us have the facts,' said the people. So said Friend George Foster [the Anti-Slavery Society agent with whom Douglass traveled]. . . . 'Give us the facts,' said Collins, 'we will take care of the philosophy'" (217). Similarly, the invisible man becomes the Negro spokesman of the Brotherhood, a representative Negro, whose opinions and philosophies are supplied by the organization. Although the respective narratives at this point take different turns, one can clearly see how Ellison is adopting Douglass's experience to demonstrate the problem of being taken merely for an example of someone else's philosophy rather than for an autonomous, thinking human being. Douglass succinctly pointed out a dilemma that remained true one hundred years later: "I could not always follow the injunction [simply to narrate my story], for I was now reading and thinking" (217).

More explicit and extensive are Ellison's references to Booker T. Washington's *Up from Slavery*. The "humility" manifest in the graduation speech that earned the invisible man his invitation to the battle royal clearly reflects the ethos that Washington projected, as does the word *responsibility*, which replaced in Washington's lexicon—as it does in the invisible man's (except when he slips)—the idea of equality. That speech, modeled on Washington's values, had motivated the white citizens to give the invisible man a scholarship "to the state college for Negroes" (*IM* 32), an institution that in its characteristics resembles Tuskegee, the school that Washington founded and that Ellison attended for three years. *Invisible Man*'s descriptions of Dr. Bledsoe, the president of the school, allude in many ways to Washington. Like Washington, Bledsoe is a subtle manipulator of the white trustees, particularly effective because of his ability to align the project of the school and, by implication, of Negro education in America, with maintaining a subordinate Negro class that viewed success not in terms of competing equally with white America but in terms of serving its needs.

The philosophy of Tuskegee was stated explicitly in Washington's 1895 Atlanta Exposition address, printed in its entirety in *Up from Slavery*. The unifying image of that speech is iterated frequently in the phrase "cast down your bucket where you are," by which Washington meant that rather than asking for help (much less for reparation or equality) from whites, Negroes should improve their lot by drawing on the resources already at their feet:

> Our greatest danger is that in the great leap from slavery to freedom we may overlook the fact that the masses of us are to

live by the production of our hands, and fail to keep in mind
that we shall prosper in proportion as we learn to dignify and
glorify common labour and put brains and skill into the common occupations of life. . . . No race can prosper until it
learns that there is as much dignity in tilling a field as in writing a poem. It is at the bottom of life that we must begin, and
not at the top. Nor should we permit our grievances to over-
shadow our opportunities.[4]

In this light, the numerous references in *Invisible Man* to Dr.
Bledsoe as "old bucket-head" seem clear attempts to associate
Bledsoe with Washington. Equally important is the emphasis
placed on "chapel" oratory by both Bledsoe and Washington.
Washington regularly had the students "meet [him] in the chapel
for a heart-to-heart talk about the conduct of the school" (121).
These meetings, he explained, "enable me to get at the very
heart of all that concerns the school" (121). Just prior to being expelled, the invisible man attends chapel, where he hears an oration in honor of the Founder and in praise of humility, an oration
that makes him feel that Bledsoe will not likely be sympathetic to
him. Bledsoe's actions (especially in conjunction with Norton's
Emersonian assurances that the invisible man is part of Norton's
"fate"), in the context of the Washington statement about the
chapel meetings, suggest an ironic commentary on the statement and its speaker.

The irony Ellison invokes resonates, moreover, through a
wide spectrum of Washington's remarks because Ellison presents the chapel as the site of oratory, a mode highly privileged in
Up from Slavery. Washington's book, in fact, is connected by a
string of oratorical occasions, clearly aimed at establishing Washington's importance as a (humble?) spokesperson for his race.
This is the position that the invisible man occupies too, from his
high school graduation speech through his employment as a
spokesperson by the Brotherhood. At one of the parties where
the invisible man is first being introduced to the (white) Brotherhood members, he is asked directly, "How would you like to
be the new Booker T. Washington?" (*IM* 305). Thus, as is typical
in Ellison's structuring in the novel, the ascent to the role of

spokesperson stands in relief, tensioned by two competing autobiographical models: Booker T. Washington and Frederick Douglass.

In moving away from slavery and, in the novel's symbology, from the South and the nineteenth century toward the North and the twentieth century, Ellison thus plays off two significant Negro autobiographies, qualified at least in one significant image by Washington's most prominent Negro contemporary, W. E. B. Du Bois. The invisible man remembers seeing, when he first arrived at the college, a statue of the college Founder, "his hands outstretched in the breathtaking gesture of lifting a veil that flutters in hard, metallic folds above the face of a kneeling slave; and I am standing puzzled, unable to decide whether the veil is really being lifted, or lowered more firmly in place; whether I am witnessing a revelation or a more efficient blinding" (*IM* 36).

The "veil," which, according to Du Bois, creates for Negro Americans a double-consciousness, forms an important motif in *The Souls of Black Folk*, introduced in the first chapter:

> After the Egyptian and Indian, the Greek and Roman, the Teuton and Mongolian, the Negro is a sort of seventh son, born with a veil and gifted with second-sight in this American world,—a world that yields him no true self-consciousness, but only lets him see through the revelation of the other world. It is a peculiar sensation, this double-consciousness, this sense of always looking at oneself through the eyes of others, of measuring one's soul by the tape of a world that looks on in amused contempt and pity.[5]

By identifying the Founder, the college, and, by extension, Washington with the veil, Ellison is suggesting exactly the critique Du Bois lodged against Washington's compromises.

Ellison also evokes this passage from Du Bois when Peter Wheatstraw, a trickster whom the invisible man encounters in Harlem, calls himself "aseventhsonofaseventhsonbornwithacauloverbotheyes" (*IM* 176). Operating with much the same purpose as Du Bois's book, Wheatstraw helps put the invisible man in touch with his heritage, his Negro identity. Similarly, the sense of sleepwalking that informs the invisible man's college experience and explains the deftness with which Bledsoe manipulates him, is very accurately suggested by Du Bois's statement that "there was among us but a half-awakened common consciousness, sprung from common joy or grief at burial, birth, or wedding; from a common hardship in poverty, poor land, and low wages; and, above all, from the sight of the Veil that hung between us and Opportunity" (102).

Invisible Man and *Autobiography of an Ex-Colored Man*

These autobiographical works of nonfiction, which represent some parameters of Negro American experience, also form a backdrop for James Weldon Johnson's fictional *Autobiography of an Ex-Colored Man*,[6] certainly one of *Invisible Man's* most significant precursors in Negro fiction. Both books present us with narrators who are simultaneously —and oxymoronically— anonymous and eponymous. Johnson's technique creates an autobiographical identity that epitomizes Du Bois's double-consciousness by combining the act of being entitled to one's life story with the experience of being nameless within it. In many ways, we can see Ellison as drawing on Johnson's exploration of that double-consciousness. Like Johnson's narrator, the invisible man finds his plans to attend college suddenly thrown into disarray. Both narrators as a result pass though a series of identities that are often less a function of any innate traits or of their personal histories or personalities than of the ways they affect the inner eyes of their beholders. Both narrators, moreover, receive special benefits because of their unique talents, the ex-colored man as a musician and the invisible man as an orator. But in both cases, these talents are not self-sufficient, in that they are symbiotically connected to a series of white benefactors. The double-consciousness, in this regard, arises out of both novels' constant recognition that for a Negro, talent, ability, and accomplishment are not self-sufficient guarantees of success or security. To the extent that identity is the composite of what one is able to do or be, identity itself for the Negro is thus revealed always to be potentially fragile, tenuous, illusory.

Ellison's variations on Johnson revisit the motifs set up by Johnson's structure from a different perspective. Whereas the ex-colored man comes to understand that fragility of identity because he can be taken for white, the invisible man comes to understand it because he is "taken" for black. If the Sambo doll in *Invisible Man* symbolizes every way that the black image is exploited by American culture, the invisible man, similarly, moves from one person or group's sense of him as image to another's. Bledsoe chose him as a representative Negro for Mr. Norton; the union members at the paint factory saw him as representative of Negro union busting, Brockway as a representative of the "New Negro," the Brotherhood as a spokesperson representing the black community, just to name a very few. In this way, the invisible man is very much the counterpart, the dark alternative to the ex-colored man, that is, the black image.

One scene in *Invisible Man* underscores this inversion. When the invisible man turns down the job he is offered to be the valet/companion to Emerson's son, he is turning down exactly the position that the ex-colored man accepts: to be the companion of a rich, white ne'er-do-well. In this moment, Ellison not only suggests the homoerotics repressed in the ex-colored man's relationship but, more important, makes clear that the companionship, no matter how the principals represent it, is a form of servitude. The ex-colored man may be spared the duties of a valet, and his color (or lack of color) may permit social opportunities verboten for the invisible man, but Ellison makes more explicit Johnson's point that whenever one depends on the generosity of another person for the stability of one's own identity, the relationship must be seen as a form of servitude. In this way, Ellison uses his modernist technique to build upon Johnson's innovations in speaking fictively from behind the veil of double-consciousness.

Invisible Man, Wright, and Dostoevski

More directly—and more problematically—Richard Wright stands as the Negro author who had the most profound impact on Elli-

son's work, a point Ellison conceded only with significant qualifi-
cation. Wright, as we have noted, pointed Ellison toward many
important texts and underscored the importance of technique:

> Having read Pound, Eliot, Shaw, and the criticism of Harriet
> Monroe and I. A. Richards—all available in Tuskegee's excel-
> lent little library—it was important that in Wright I had dis-
> covered a Negro American writer who possessed a working
> knowledge of modern literature, its techniques and theories.
> My approach to literature was by no means racial, but Wright
> was not only available, he was eager to share his interests, and
> it gave me something of that sense of self-discovery and exal-
> tation which is implicit in the Negro church and in good jazz.
> (CE 672)

Wright also encouraged Ellison, both by importation and by
example, to understand the need to establish himself within the
American, rather than Negro American, canon. "Like a good
Negro athlete," Ellison pointed out:

> he believed in his ability to compete. In 1940 he was well
> aware that Native Son was being published at a time when The
> Grapes of Wrath and For Whom the Bell Tolls would be his main
> competition. Nevertheless, he looked toward the publication
> day nervously but eagerly. He wished to be among the most
> advanced artists and was willing to run the risk required. (CE
> 733)

There is also no question that Wright was extremely influential
in getting Ellison to write fiction:

> As editor of New Challenge, Wright asked me to contribute a
> book review in its first issue. To one who had never attempted
> to write anything, this was the wildest of ideas. Still, pressed
> by his editorial needs and sustained by his belief that an un-
> tapped supply of free-floating literary talent existed in the
> Negro community, Wright kept after me, and I wrote a review
> and he published it. Then he went even further by suggesting
> that I write a short story! (CE 663)

By the same token, Ellison made clear that he did not include Wright among his direct influences. As he explained in his public written debate with Irving Howe:

> I *sought out* Wright because I had read Eliot, Pound, Gertrude Stein and Hemingway. . . . But perhaps you will understand when I say [Wright] did not influence me if I point out that while one can do nothing about choosing one's relatives, one can, as artist, choose one's "ancestors." . . . Eliot, whom I was to meet only many years later, and Malraux and Dostoevsky and Faulkner, were "ancestors"—if you please or don't please. (*CE* 185)

Nevertheless, elements of the battle royal can be connected to the scene in Wright's autobiography, *Black Boy*,[7] when the black youths are made to fight with each other for the entertainment of their white employers. In Ellison's version, however, the scene takes on mythic and surreal proportions that, in the Joycean mode, provide a symbolic template for the rest of the novel. Whereas Wright was using the scene metonymically—that is, as a small literal detail meant to suggest the larger body of experience from which it was extracted—Ellison used it metaphorically. The scene was to be read not only symbolically, but also as inextricably connected to the symbolic and archetypal structure of the novel.

Thus we can see the battle royal not as an allusion to or appropriation of Wright's autobiographical scene, but rather as a corrective enhancement of it. As he did throughout his work, Ellison rejected the naturalist/realist mode associated with the best of Wright's work in favor of a modernist/surrealist mode that had, as Ellison saw it, the potential to allow historical details to resonate with national, social, and canonical history. This understanding of the artist's social responsibility, which garnered some criticism, was something that Ellison came to, in part, because of works Wright encouraged him to read. Thus, even Ellison's revisions of Wright owe something to Wright, just as they do to the common ancestors whom he and Wright both chose.

This mode of appropriation and revision is even more evident in Ellison's use of Wright's short story "The Man Who Lived Underground" in conjunction with Dostoevski's *Notes from the Underground*. It is no coincidence that the opening sentence of *Invisible Man's* prologue—"I am an invisible man" (*IM* 3)—echoes Dostoevski's opening: "I am a sick man,"[8] nor that "It goes a long way back, some twenty years" (*IM* 15), the opening of *Invisible Man's* chapter 1, echoes the first sentence of *Notes from the Underground's* second paragraph: "I have been living like this for a long time—about twenty years" (2). As Ellison explained, when he first conceived the narrator of *Invisible Man*, "I associated him, ever so distantly, with the narrator of . . . *Notes from the Underground*" (*CE* 481). He came to this perspective because he decided that his narrator "would be one who had been forged in the underground of American experience and yet managed to emerge less angry than ironic" (*CE* 481). "As I tried to visualize the speaker," Ellison explained, "I came to relate him to those ongoing conflicts, tragic and comic, that had claimed my group's energies since the abandonment of the Reconstruction" (*CE* 481).

Ellison was forging the voice of an alternative historian, the only voice situated to tell the alternative history, the invisible history, the underground history of American life and culture. This is the history that Tod Clifton falls into when he falls outside of authorized history, be it the exceptionalist American history endorsed by mainstream historians or the "scientific" history advocated by the Brotherhood. It is the view of history that the invisible man imagines on the subway station when he staggers into the underground after Tod's shooting. Looking at three black boys on the platform, he thinks, "They were men outside of historical time" (*IM* 440). This leads him to wonder if they were "the saviors, the true leaders, the bearers of something precious? The stewards of something uncomfortable, burdensome, which they hated because, living outside of history, there was no one to applaud their value and they themselves failed to understand it" (*IM* 441). These thoughts in turn attribute to Ellison's alternative historian the voice of Dostoevski's narrator: "What if history was a gambler. . . . What if history was not a reasonable citizen, but a mad man full of paranoid guile?" (*IM* 441).

In this moment of epiphany, the invisible man is thus confronted, in the form of alternate historian, with the inspiration of his own voice. This need for psychological/philosophical perspective on the surreal experience of Negro America, which permeates the novel and blossoms in the epilogue, can clearly be connected to Dostoevski. The unique, surreal, underground topography of Ellison's narrative, however, resembles more strongly Wright's astonishing 1942 short story.[9] In many ways, in fact, the parallels are strong enough to view *Invisible Man* as a conscious—and very significant—revision of "The Man Who Lived Underground."

Like Ellison's protagonist, the man who lived underground finds his hideaway by fleeing into the sewer through an open manhole, which leads him to a set of secret unlit spaces, spaces that he, like the invisible man, must navigate by lighting his own way. Although Ellison broadens the symbolic dimension of this underground navigation by having the invisible man burn the papers in his briefcase, which comprise his "official" history, rather than just matches—à la Wright's underground man—the process of lighting one's own way through the uncharted underground of white American civilization informs both flights. In his progress, the man who lived underground finds subterranean entries into an array of sites that figure prominently in the invisible man's journey: the furnace room, the factory, the prize fight. In a church, the man who lived underground saw "black men and women dressed in white robes, singing, holding tattered songbooks in their black palms" (522), a scene similar to the moment in the subway car when the invisible man sees the two nuns, "a white nun in black telling her beads, and . . . another dressed completely in white, the exact duplicate of the other except that she was black and her black feet bare" (*IM* 441).

Both protagonists, moreover, find secluded spaces adjacent to a coal cellar, where they fall into a timeless sleep that turns into nightmare. Prior to the dream, the man who lived underground "stretched out full length on the ground and went to sleep" (531), and in his dream (rendered as one long modernist sentence) he is swept and buffeted by streams of water in which he starts to drown:

. . . his head touched sand at the bottom of the sea and his chest felt as though it would burst and he bent his knees and propelled himself upward and water rushed passed him and his head bobbed out . . . and he began to doubt that he could stand upon the water and then he was sinking and as he struggled the water rushed him downward spinning dizzily and he opened his mouth to call for help and water surged into his lungs and he choked . . . (531–32)

This dream journey resembles the invisible man's surreal passage through the dark underground: "But still whirling on in the blackness, knocking against the rough walls of a narrow passage, banging my head and cursing, I stumbled down and plunged against some kind of partition and sailed headlong, coughing and sneezing, into another dimensionless room" (*IM* 568). This immediately precedes the invisible man's dream, a dream that contains variations of the images in Wright's dream: "*But somehow the floor had turned to sand and the darkness to light, and I lay the prisoner of a group . . . who pressed around me as I lay beside a river of black water*" (*IM* 569). After the dream, the invisible man "awoke in the blackness" (570) and could "only lie on the floor, reliving the dream" (570–71). In an odd symbiosis of imagery, in other words, on the same underground floor where Wright's main character began his dream, Ellison's protagonist concludes his, only to relive it. There he decides to become a man who lives underground. "I would take up residence underground," the invisible man declares. "The end was in the beginning" (*IM* 571).

Living underground, both protagonists are able to divert electricity that provides them with lights and (radio) music. They both decorate their cells with inversions of the white society to which their secret space is parasitic. The man who lived underground covers the walls with money and gold rings, and he illuminates the floor by covering it with stolen gems that both literally and figuratively reflect their source. His decorations thereby parody white material values. The invisible man, on the other hand, uses his decorations—a ceiling covered with 1,369 lightbulbs and plans to wire the walls and the floors—as part of a "battle with Monopolated Light & Power" (*IM* 7), that is, as a symbolic assault on the conception of visibility and its attendant privilege, which illuminates white society.

The underground created by Wright is thus dramatically expanded and redefined through the rage and "paranoid guile" of Dostoevski's creation. Wright's surreal journey, rendered in primarily naturalistic terms, thus takes on, through Ellison, the symbolic and philosophic dimensions that remain, in Wright's rendition, at best a latent potential.

Invisible Man and Faulkner

If Wright was the Negro contemporary Ellison most needed to revise, Faulkner was the white contemporary he most needed to emulate. In Ellison's *Collected Essays*, Faulkner is the most frequently mentioned, and Wright and Faulkner are the most extensively discussed (although James, Twain, and Hemingway also get a great deal of attention). For Ellison, moreover, Faulkner occupies a unique place in the American canon, in that he is the only—or at least the most significantly successful—author to be influenced by the pervasive dynamics of Negro history in America and to engage those dynamics as central to any understanding of his own history and humanity, to any definition of himself as artist. As Ellison said in an interview published in 1967, "if you would find the imaginative equivalents of certain civil rights figures in American writing—Rosa Parks and James Meredith, say—you don't go to most fiction by Negroes, but to Faulkner" (*CE* 750). Faulkner's achievement, in Ellison's eyes, is that he focused the technical power of modernism on the task of articulating the moral imperative, especially in regard to race, that seemed to have disappeared from twentieth-century American fiction. "In Faulkner," Ellison wrote in 1946, "most of the relationships we have pointed out between the Negro and contemporary writing come to focus: the social and the personal, the moral and the technical, the nineteenth-century emphasis upon morality and the modern accent upon personal myth" (*CE* 97).

Particularly, Faulkner seemed to Ellison to have recognized

the ways in which—appearances to the contrary notwithstanding—American culture always had been integrated. As Ellison explained, speaking at West Point in 1969:

> Part of the music of the language, part of the folklore which informed our conscious American literature, came through the interaction of the slave and the white man, and particularly in the South. Mr. Faulkner . . . had no doubt about that, and some of our most meaningful insights into the experience of the South have come through his understanding of that complex relationship. (CE 528)

In light of Ellison's admiration for Faulkner, dating at least from the period just prior to his beginning *Invisible Man*, it is clear that Ellison drew some of his allusions from the Faulkner opus, especially given Ellison's stylistic commitment to creating a work that exposed the richly integrated heritage from which it emerged. Certainly Lucius Brockway, the old Negro man in charge of the furnace at the paint factory, bears a kinship to Faulkner's Lucas Beauchamp, the independent black man falsely accused of murder in *Intruder in the Dust*. The first thing that the invisible man is told about Brockway is "He's in charge" (IM 207). Although the statement ostensibly refers to the boiler room, the invisible man quickly sees that he is in charge of more than that. "No," the narrator tells us, "he was *making* something down here, something that had to do with paint, and probably something too filthy and dangerous for white men to be willing to do even for money" (CE 212). Like Lucas Beauchamp, Brockway is completely aware of his power and cannot be intimidated on the basis of race. Ellison considered Beauchamp to be one of Faulkner's most impressive characters:

> For all the racial and caste differences between [Lucas and the white boy Chick Mallison], Lucas holds the ascendancy in his mature dignity over the youthful Mallison and refuses to lower himself in the comic duel of status forced on him by the white boy whose life he has saved. Faulkner was free to reject the confusion between manhood and the Negro's caste status, which is sanctioned by white Southern tradition. (CE 105)

Indeed, for better or worse, and despite his apparent residence at the bottom of the factory's and society's caste system, Brockway is a very powerful man, suggestive of the power—with all its very real restrictions and ironies—that Faulkner saw the Negro as exerting over the white in the segregated South.

Joe Christmas in some ways serves as the complement in Faulkner's world to Beauchamp, Christmas's apparent whiteness disempowered by the specter of race. A (probably? possibly?) biracial child, Christmas grows up to be the enigmatic sacrificial figure of *Light in August*. Like the invisible man, he comes to associate his racial taint with a loss of social identity and often thinks of himself as "invisible." Given that Christmas's transgressions are primarily sexual—the arson and murder are the offshoots of his sexual relationship with Joanna Burden—Ellison may also have had Christmas in mind when the white woman Sybil asks the invisible man to play out her racial rape fantasy, and he writes in lipstick across her belly:

SYBIL, YOU WERE RAPED
BY
SANTA CLAUS
SURPRISE (*IM* 522)

In any case, as Cleanth Brooks points out, "Faulkner could hardly have stressed more emphatically that [Christmas's] status as a 'nigger' is a state of mind rather than a consequence of his possessing some Negro genes, nor could he have shown more persuasively that for Joe the notion that he is a Negro is part of his general alienation from the community."[10] Christmas is, in other words, a cogent touchstone for the relationship between perception and invisibility that informs *Invisible Man*.

Juneteenth

It is not surprising, therefore, that in *Juneteenth* Ellison returns once more to the figure of Joe Christmas, this time as a source for the central character and the novel's informing trauma, in order that he may revisit the traumatic moment of failed emancipation. *Juneteenth*, the more-or-less complete section of Ellison's more-or-less incomplete second novel, remains, nevertheless, an important work. In addition to Faulkner, Ellison drew heavily on Negro folklore and on *The Waste Land*.

If the monologue quality of *Notes from the Underground* inspired the narrative voice of *Invisible Man*, *Juneteenth* as a modernist dialogue seems more heavily indebted to the dialogic juxtaposition of voices that characterizes much of Faulkner's best work. The two principal voices in *Juneteenth* are those of Daddy Hickman, a southern Negro minister, and Sunraider/Bliss, a U.S. senator. Set in the 1950s, the novel begins at the intersection of two events: Hickman's leading a delegation to Washington to speak with Sunraider and Sunraider's being shot on the floor of the Senate by a would-be assassin. The gravely wounded Sunraider calls for Hickman, and the rest of the novel takes place with Hickman at Sunraider's bedside. Because Sunraider is rarely conscious, the two men rarely talk directly to one another. Instead each engages, for the most part, in interior monologues that often incorporate the other as addressee. The wounded, heavily medicated Sunraider, in an almost hallucinatory dream state, reviews the events of his life. He started out as Bliss, the white-skinned son of Hickman and the spiritual prodigy of Hickman's black church. As a young man, he ran away to become Mister Movie-Man, a director of silent pictures, and later he emerged in a new incarnation as Adam Sunraider, a white New Englander who became a senator with an explicitly racist agenda.

The grieving Hickman too oscillates through stages of consciousness, sometimes lapsing into dream or becoming lost in memory, sometimes speaking to a semiresponsive or unresponsive Sunraider. This medley of fragmented soliloquies, like the polyphonic *The Waste Land*, to which it heavily alludes, mixes memory and desire in the interest of effecting the resurrection— not of Sunraider but of the Bliss from whom he originated. Like *The Waste Land*, in other words, *Juneteenth* is very much an incomplete Easter story, one in which Bliss is both the Easter bunny and Brer Rabbit.

In one of the early chapters, this theme is acted out explicitly

as Bliss, who is supposed to reenact the Resurrection by spring-
ing from a coffin in his white suit, has to choose between taking
his Easter bunny or his teddy bear into the dark with him. As in
Invisible Man, the imagery oscillates between evocations of folkloric tricksterism and folkloric naiveté. In this case, however, the
images are explicitly linked to the cycles of death and resurrection, the movement from ritual to romance, upon which *The
Waste Land* is based. This secularization of Christian redemption
with racial difference as its original sin is, of course, at work in
Faulkner's conception of Joe Christmas, around whom Ellison
constructed one of the two central characters in *Juneteenth*.

Bliss is Joe Christmas, in that like Christmas, he is a Christ figure, sacrificed to the sins of racial difference, pigmentation, and
blindness. Like Christmas, he is an orphan with a complexion
that allows him to pass for white and a history that calls his skin
tone into question. Bliss, adopted by Hickman and raised as
Negro, does not know his parents. As it turns out, neither does
Hickman, who rescued the child from his white mother and
never learned the identity of Bliss's father. Bliss, a boy presumed
to be black although he may have no Negro blood, is thus the in-
verse of Christmas, who was raised white but with the belief that
he is actually Negro. For both characters, this creates an identity
crisis that leads them to oscillate between communities, reaping
the benefits and accumulating the guilt that accrues to each
incarnation.

In both cases, the stories are told from an alternating array of
perspectives, a technique typical of Faulkner, as it was of Eliot,
Pound, and Joyce. For Ellison, as for Faulkner, the multiplicity of
voices and points of view destabilizes the notion of authorized
truth or historical verity. And for both authors, destabilizing
those truths and verities seems essential to the task of unpacking
the historicity of race and its grip on American identity. "It
is worth remembering," Ellison pointed out, "that the past, as
William Faulkner warned, is never past" (*CE* 637).

Invoking *Light in August*, we can see that Sunraider / Bliss, like
Joe Christmas, is as haunted by—ultimately as destroyed by—the
race of which he is not a member as the race of which he is. And
for both men, the instrument of their destruction is the racism

that frames their vows and disavowals. "Sunraider knows that the question of his having Negro blood isn't important," Ellison states in his working notes:

> It is the fact that *he* himself can't be sure whether he has or not. Because he knows that many who think they don't, do. It is a matter flowing from the way society has been arranged, the power that flows from that arrangement. . . . The power was not biological or genetic, but man-made and political, economic . . . and immoral as far as the American ideal had a religious component. (*J* 361–62)

Although in the end Christmas is castrated, then killed, Sunraider/Bliss may yet survive, a possibility suggested by *Juneteenth*'s last chapter, a long, italicized dream in which, as Senator Sunraider, Bliss travels in a boxcar where he hears a tale of Brer Bear and Brer Rabbit, attends an elaborate bird hunt, and ends up walking down urban streets where he is threatened by three contemporary black men driving an outrageous, self-fashioned hot rod. The dream seems to unite Negro folklore with a version of the last section of Faulkner's *The Bear*, as if to suggest that the potential still exists for one more transmutation, for Bliss's conversion, figuratively, from Joe Christmas to Isaac McCaslin, the character through whom, according to Ellison:

> Faulkner comes most passionately to grips with the implications of slavery, the American land, progress and materialism, tradition and moral identity. . . . It is in the fourth section [of *The Bear*] that Faulkner makes his most extended effort to define the specific form of the American Negro's humanity and to get at the human values that were lost by both North and South during the Civil War. Even more important, it is here Isaac McCaslin demonstrates one way in which the individual American can assert his freedom from the bonds of history, tradition and things, and thus achieve moral identity. (*CE* 721–22)

Juneteenth thus poses the question: if Joe Christmas were raised as an anomaly of the Negro community, rather than of the white, could he have achieved the moral identity of Isaac McCaslin?

As *Juneteenth* demonstrates, in many ways Faulkner, as a high modernist obsessed by the mythic dimensions of his Americanism and, as well, the inherent role of race in both forging and destabilizing those dimensions, was Ellison's white artistic counterpart. And Ellison, as we have seen, was working to create an American literary identity reflective of its multiracial legacy commensurate with the American historical and regional identity that provided Faulkner's driving impetus, that is, one worthy of that "arduous task" of being an American.

NOTES

1. Throughout this essay I will use the word "Negro" instead of "black," "African American," and so on, to be consistent with the usage in the material quoted from Ellison's essays.

2. James Joyce, *A Portrait of the Artist as a Young Man* (New York: Viking, 1964), 8.

3. Frederick Douglass, *The Life and Times of Frederick Douglass, Written by Himself* (New York: Crowell-Collier, 1962), 215. Subsequent page citations will appear in the text.

4. Booker T. Washington, *Up from Slavery: An Autobiography* (New York: Bantam, 1956), 154. Subsequent page citations will appear in the text.

5. W. E. B. Du Bois, *The Souls of Black Folk* (New York: New American Library, 1969), 45. Subsequent page citations will appear in the text.

6. James Weldon Johnson, *Autobiography of an Ex-Colored Man* (1912; reprint New York: Hill and Wang, 1960).

7. Richard Wright, *Black Boy* (New York: Harper, 1945).

8. Fyodor Dostoevski, *Notes from the Underground*, translated by Mirra Ginsburg (New York: Bantam, 1974), 1. Subsequent page citations will appear in the text.

9. Richard Wright, "The Man Who Lived Underground," in *Richard Wright Reader*, edited by Ellen Wright and Michel Fabre (New York: Harper & Row, 1978), 517–76. Subsequent page citations will appear in the text.

10. Cleanth Brooks, introduction to William Faulkner's *Light in August* (New York: Modern Library, 1968), vii.

Ralph Ellison's Politics of Integration

Lawrence P. Jackson

In an essay called "'As White as Anybody': Race and the Politics of Counting as Black," the literary critic Ken Warren has asked "whether or not we ought to continue to count Ellison as a Negro or black writer" (714). Warren makes his claim unaudaciously and it is suggestive to consider that a significant—arguably *the* significant—professional achievement for black American writers is the suspension of their ethnicity.

Contemporary biology has dismissed the logic of racial essence, but social determinations of the racial situation continue to make the suspension or temporary erasure of blackness an achievement of consequence. While the goal here is not perhaps to become white (in fact, an argument could be made that transferring racial positions would make the result meaningless), the shift in basic assumptions that occurs when a "black" writer can shake off the burden of race and publish as a "writer" continues to afford important cultural power and legitimacy. William Faulkner bluntly recognized this process in 1955. He said to an audience in Japan, "Ellison has talent and so far he has managed to stay away from being first a Negro; he is still first a writer."[1] Faulkner's comment was considered an unambiguous measure of praise; it was used on Ellison's book jackets as advertisement.

Ellison's intellectual interests and his honesty never made

attractive the actual obsession with racial erasure that consumed a writer like Jean Toomer, who published the celebrated modernist prose work *Cane* in 1923. But Ellison's novel *Invisible Man* did move out of the limits of American mid–twentieth-century racial logic. He left the 1940s protest tradition of Richard Wright, Chester Himes, Ann Petry, Willard Motley, and J. Saunders Redding and attained a companionship and peerage with Saul Bellow, Ernest Hemingway, William Faulkner, John Cheever, Bernard Malamud, and Norman Mailer. Ellison's work transcended the ideology of protest and was suitable to examination by the New Critical method of literary analysis. His novel's epilogue, which originally had seemed to champion the scope of unlimited possibility available to the nameless black protagonist (which might destabilize the status quo), went on to be read as proposing the necessity of individual values (which kept the status quo in place). Contemporary interpretations of the book tended to stress the potential for shared human space that is echoed by the final phrase: "I speak for you." But before the end of the 1960s, the common ground of universally shared comity that Ellison tried to generate with the idea of an interracial or "mulatto" American democracy had blanched. Ellison's universal interracial space had become fairly indistinguishable from a universally standard "white" space. What is more, Ellison seemed to embrace the shift.

Ralph Ellison attained his moment of "racelessness," his stature as an American icon to a nonblack audience, during the roughly fifteen-year time span following the release of the novel *Invisible Man*. During those years in particular, Ellison painstakingly crafted his public career and, when he had arrived at the peak of professional respectability, he worked deliberately to maintain his position. The small industry publishing Ellison's works since the time of his 1994 death emphasizes the point that Ralph Ellison was able to establish a major career from a fairly small body of work, a fact of note when considering several of his contemporaries who barely receive academic scrutiny but who published regularly. This list would include writers like Redding, Petry, Willard Motley, William Gardner Smith, and John O. Killens. That Ellison was a writer of considerable power and unique eloquence is not a completely fulfilling answer to explain the magnitude of Ellison's career. To put it another way, and to use arguably another class of black writers, Toomer, Gwendolyn Brooks, William Demby, Melvin B. Tolson, William Melvin Kelley, Henry Dumas, Ishmael Reed, and Toni Cade Bambara have possessed power and eloquence, but they did not achieve a centrality to the American literary canon comparable to Ellison. In the main, the crucial difference centers around the fact that Ralph Ellison proposed and consistently developed a theory of American cultural life in his novel *Invisible Man* and then, more so than perhaps any other black writer in the twentieth century, he cultivated the legacy of his artistic contribution.

The novel *Invisible Man*'s celebration by American writers in the 1950s and 1960s occurred in part because of Ellison's vigilant enforcing of ways for the novel to be read and for his life as a public figure to be understood. During the two decades following its publication, *Invisible Man* moved from a tool designed to expose a distinctive kind of Negro humanity and to stimulate the conscience of white America into a novel that commented obliquely on politics and stressed chiefly individuality and self-definition. When he started the project in 1945, Ellison imagined that he was writing a book to break through the heavily defended white mind, which had protected itself from racial guilt by creating bizarre stereotypes of black life. Ellison allowed himself the use of semiotics, myth, ritual, and radical political philosophy to reveal not only black life, but also the process of white psychological repression that prevented whites from genuinely understanding or "seeing" blacks.[2] He also pondered in the book the vacuum of black leadership, the same problem that concerned authors like Redding and Himes. But critics rarely interpreted the novel in terms of Ellison's early concerns, and Ellison, who had at one point wanted to have sour cream oozing from the vagina of the white paramour of his hero, caught their drift.

Underlying this transformation in the meaning of the novel *Invisible Man* was the widespread adaptation of the New Criticism in American colleges and universities, a doctrine that greatly advocated the scrutiny of the literary artifact in a purportedly "nonideological" manner. The New Criticism tended to ground itself in the literary essays of T. S. Eliot and strove to

work outside of the influence of the Freudian, Marxist, and historicist terminologies that had preceded it and vied with it for
dominance in the field of humanistic inquiry. In the place of the
"ideological" criticism that the movement's proponents tended
to associate with leading critics like New Yorkers Lionel Trilling
or Philip Rahv, New Critical methods investigated tropes of paradox, irony, and ambiguity and exclusively confined their analyses
to the printed artifact.[3]

Ellison, a conservatory-trained musician who had become a
literary radical on the Left in the 1930s and 1940s, assisted in this
shift in the understanding of his text. He had the fortune to write
his novel during a period of literary change, and as a result his
work tended to carry valences of significance for a broad constituency, including the Marxists, the Freudians, and the symbol-
hunting New Critics. One of Ellison's earliest goals was to produce a work that would find a home among a wide range of
readers. But perhaps his greatest reason after the 1950s to enno-
ble *Invisible Man*, a book that he had originally called modestly a
"not quite fully achieved attempt at a major novel" (*SA* 102), was
his inability to publish another full-length work of fiction within
ten years of his first success and, ultimately, for the rest of his life.
Instead, in 1964 Ellison published *Shadow and Act*, a retrospective
collection of essays that reflected his literary sensibility and cultural tastes over a period of roughly twenty years. The essays, especially "Hidden Name and Complex Fate," served as a counter-
point and a statement of position for Ellison against his two main
literary rivals during the late 1950s and 1960s (when the country
had not arrived at the moment of racelessness): James Baldwin
and LeRoi Jones. Both men, in different but profound forms, fundamentally challenged the value of an American identity. In public statements, Ellison scoffed at the notion that his race in any
way diminished or attenuated his national identity.

Part of the work that was accomplished during the transition
in meaning of Ellison's novel had to do with its transportation
into the realm of American fable, and for that to occur, Ellison's
own life had to adapt to the contour of myth. American critics
rarely situate the pages of *Invisible Man* in a context of the 1940s
and 1950s, to better read the novel as a fable extolling the 1950s as

a kind of prelapsarian and unique moment in the drama of American life, preceding the still-unresolved dilemmas of value and coherence revealed by the tumult of the 1960s. But ten years following its release, the novel was taken increasingly as a triumph in a line of American triumphs, less an example of risk and daring, and far more a decision by the author to embrace a tradition of freedom that was habitually available. The contending portions of his work were eased from scrutiny. The complexity of his own identity and talent as an American writer received a similar gloss. On its book flaps and in its press releases, Random House perfected fully the mystique of a novel written by a black by helping to create an author who was an authentic Negro—a former shoeshine boy and jazz musician, both proletariat and hipster. With his solitary working-man's credentials in place, Ellison was then imagined to have simply struck gold with his first book, a stunning proof of the native genius rife throughout, if not indicative of, postwar America. The somber intellectual trials and costly political engagements of a highly experimental modernist writer ran counter to the creation of an authentically black yet competent artist.

But the novelist who wrote *Invisible Man* did not publish the book out of complete obscurity, or even out of the Negro version of the Franklinian catalog of odd jobs that evoked for the book-buying public such an image of stirring authenticity. Before he was the first Negro to win the National Book Award, Ellison had been the first Negro to serve as a regular critic for the Communist party's literary journal *New Masses*, from 1939 until 1942.[4] He had been the first Negro to publish a piece of literary criticism in *Antioch Review*,[5] one of a handful, which would have included W. E. B. Du Bois, Langston Hughes, Richard Wright, and J. Saunders Redding, to have written a review published by the *New York Times*; and a member of another handful that been invited to the writer's colony at Yaddo. He was probably the only Negro to have ever published in the British journal *Horizon*, and he had been the first Negro to publish fiction in *Partisan Review*. His steps leading up to *Invisible Man* had taken more than ten years. Ellison did not emerge ex nihilo.

When Ellison's book first appeared, readers—all of them—

recognized that it was a literary event, and yet they were unprepared to accord lasting significance to the work of a first-time novelist. Many of the reviews included lengthy and sweeping criticisms, counseling advice that would have eliminated glaring flaws; chiefly, the brass of the advice grew out of the explicit understanding that Ellison had many, a great many, more novels in him. Perhaps the treatment that Ellison received from the magazines that one might imagine really shape the book-buying public explains the first year's book sales of about 12,000 copies.[6] Writing for the *Atlantic*, Charles Rolo found himself in the decided rearguard of the literary elite when he said, "My admiration for the book is qualified, which puts me in a dissident minority." Rolo praised the work but steadily pointed to gaffes: "overwriting, stretches of fuzzy thinking, and a tendency to waver, confusingly, between realism and surrealism" (Rolo 94). In lengthier treatment in the *New Yorker*, the critic Anthony West thought, "Few writers can have made a more commanding first appearance," and called Ellison's book "exceptionally good" (West 96, 93). West, however, was even stronger in his condemnation than Rolo. He decided that the novel's prologue, which had been published separately in *Partisan Review*'s January 1952 edition, the epilogue, and everything that had been written in italics ought to be skipped by the reader.

The classy conservative academic reviews, homes of the New Criticism, were among Ellison's more vigorous supporters. R. W. B. Lewis, writing for the *Hudson Review*, said, "*Invisible Man* is the most impressive work of fiction in a number of years" (148), and Richard Chase in *Kenyon Review* thought the novel exemplary of "sheer richness of invention" (681). The creative writers Saul Bellow and Delmore Schwartz were ecstatic over the book. (It might also be remembered that they could not but have been pleased by the challenge to the Anglo-American literary aristocracy that the book represented.) Bellow liked the fact that Ellison was not bred by the American literary institutions that had been broadcasting the death of the novel since the end of World War II: "It is commonly felt that there is no strength to match the strength of those powers which attack and cripple modern mankind. . . . But what a great thing it is when a brilliant individual victory occurs, like Mr. Ellison's, proving that a truly heroic quality exists among our contemporaries" (608). Schwartz flattered the book enough to suggest that he couldn't really offer it a competent review; only William Faulkner was capable. What Ellison's peers interpreted him as doing was striking a blow against the naysayers of art, who, laying the groundwork for the ideas that became postmodernism, began to argue that art had little ability to improve or even influence the caliber of human relationships and interactions in the era of the atomic bomb, genocide, and the totalitarian state. Ellison was seen by some camps as an extremely valuable optimist, whose faith in the tradition of lyrical eloquence and whose heavy attention to the emotive life of the individual celebrated the resilience of the human being. And in terms of American literary politics, Ellison's talkative, analytical, and self-conscious Invisible Man swung out defiantly against both the emotionally and psychologically terse novels of Hemingway and the hard-boiled naturalists touting environmental determinism.

During the year of publication and the year following, when he was the prize-winning author, Ellison predictably bristled from the criticism and thought some of the praise fulsome, and he kept a certain sort of psychological distance from the community of literary celebrity makers. At first he thought it was an example of old-fashioned racial attitudes, but later he grew to see it as a vivid example of American literary parochialism. He wrote to Albert Murray in February 1954 about Saul Bellow's receipt of the National Book Award:

> He's getting some of the same shit I received last year: the envy, the snobbery, the general display of lousiness, which some of the bright boys tried to pass on to me. He's shamed them by winning something that they want and by writing about them as they really are, without love, without generosity, sans talent, sans life. I thought they were simply reacting to my being a mose [American Negro]. (*TT* 67)

And yet, the sometimes ambivalent praise and attention from the commercial, academic, and artistic camps was the typical literary reception granted Ellison. The African-American press hedged its support of the prize-winning novel (save Langston Hughes, a lifelong Ellison supporter). J. Saunders Redding reviewed the novel in his regular column at the *Baltimore Afro-American* and put on the table the consistent disappointment voiced by black critics. Powerful though the writer's technique and intelligence might be, Ellison's scope was tragically foreshortened. Redding spanked the first-time novelist: "The book's fault is that a writer of power has put all his power into describing the diurnal life of gnats" (10). There was more to the criticism than a squabble over the theme. In 1950, Redding, a Hampton University professor, had published an ugly novel called *Stranger and Alone*, which revealed the traitorous and cynical heart in the bosom of the southern black leadership class. When he broke onto the pages of the *New York Times* with his review, Ellison spared a book he thought second-rate by calling it "sociologically important" ("Collaborator" 4). Redding obviously had not failed to notice and responded with the biting review in his column for the *Afro-American*. Ellison was supposed to learn a lesson from the exchange with the highly placed literary critic, but instead it confirmed for him the durability of Booker T. Washington's favorite metaphor for Negro Americans: a barrel of crabs, pulling one another back into the pit.

Black newspaper reviewers expressed confusion, not as Aristotelians objecting to the novel's dramatic scope, but rather looking a bit suspiciously at the novel's characters and their preoccupations: incestuous farmers, bitter and cynical college presidents, and young men blindly aping Booker T. For writers who held regular posts in urban interracial organizations and who were members of the National Association for the Advancement of Colored People (NAACP), the novel hardly reflected their existence. If the protest novels of Richard Wright, Ann Petry, and Chester Himes had examined the depravity of black life with a kind of moral fervor, Ellison seemed amused by it. Writing for the *Chicago Sunday Tribune*, Roi Ottley offered the worn observation that summed up the black middle class's prescrip-tive approach to the novel-as-public-relations: "I doubt that every Negro's life is only an endless series of defeats and frustrations" (4).

Straightforward animus to Ellison's book came predictably from his old home, New York's black communists and fellow travelers. The young writer Lloyd Brown, who had drawn off a stint in jail to create his gripping *Iron City* (1951), was writing for *Masses and Mainstream* and angrily dismissed the novel: "The firstborn of a talented young Negro writer enters the world with no other life than its maggots" (62). John O. Killens, on the verge of success with *Youngblood* in 1954, wrote an equally damning review. And Communist party member Abner Berry, with whom Ellison had debated dialectics and art theory in the late 1930s, rejected the novel as a work of cynicism. He claimed that the book was "a maze of corruption, brutality, anti-communist slander, sex perversion and the sundry inhumanities upon which a dying social system feeds": "good business, but nauseating as art" (Berry 7). The black Left thought Ellison was trying to earn bourgeois success by way of abstract symbolism, Freudian psychoanalysis, and anticommunism, the coin of the day. In effect, the radicals accused him of being an Uncle Tom and a sellout, draped in the tinsel of existential neuroses.

And it wasn't just embittered Reds making the charge. Shortly before he died in 1960, Richard Wright spoke about the challenges facing African-American writers and intellectuals, and used as an example a confrontation reputed to have taken place between Chester Himes and Ralph Ellison. At one point, the writers had been close friends. But in Wright's vivid description, the two men nearly came to violence sometime in the mid-1950s after Himes persisted in the accusation that, far from a pure and diligent exercise of talent, Ellison had merely taken advantage of an understood literary conceit that would appeal to both whites and blacks and secure fame. Wright produced a dramatic version of the events replete with a dialogue-based interaction between Ellison and his well-respected black peer that apparently was not unique:

> "Your combination really worked."
> Ellison rose, his hands gripping his glass.
> "What in hell are you talking about?" Ellison demanded.
> "You know what I mean, son," Chester Himes egged Elli-

son on. "You added it all up and produced the right kind of book."

There was now no escaping the meaning of Chester Himes' remarks. He was saying that, within the narrow racial limits allowed Ellison by the white race, Ellison had found a way of writing a novel that would please both whites and blacks,—a statement that carried with its meaning a stinging insult. (Wright 25)

Ellison and Himes had been good friends, and, though different accounts of this event appear in Ellison's letter to Wright in 1953 and in Himes's book *The End of a Primitive*, Wright captured a crucial aspect of how Ellison's new celebrity restructured the bases of his relationships even with friends. Understandably, Ellison responded to insults in kind (in Wright's anecdote, Ellison goes on to draw a knife on Himes). Before the end of the 1950s, Ellison's elevated national standing made complicated and difficult his relationships with other black writers.

After Ellison had received the National Book Award for fiction, black writers were uneasy about his place as an organic part of the black community, in part undoubtedly because they could not match the recognition accorded Ellison from top-tier white colleges and universities, foundations, media organs, and award-granting bodies. At Margaret Walker's black writers' jubilee at Jackson State College in Mississippi in 1953, most of the significant working black modernist poets and critics attended: Langston Hughes, Gwendolyn Brooks, Robert Hayden, William Demby, Melvin Tolson, J. Saunders Redding, Arna Bontemps, and Sterling Brown. Walker confided to Hughes that she had hoped to have Ellison participate, but, though she had known him since the 1930s, she was beginning to see him in another league. Her comments to Hughes about the possibility of Ellison participating suggest the complexity of Ellison's relationships with other black writers after he had achieved a degree of fame: "I would very much like to have invited Ralph Ellison to come down also, but our money has run out and we are operating on a much smaller budget than originally expected. Of course, he may not have accepted" (Walker). His peers were beginning to see Ellison as apart from them; they may have felt lingering resentment at the white publishing industry that had catapulted Ellison into fame and, powerless to influence the press and literary journals, they sniped at Ellison for being the favorite. Arna Bontemps' comment to Langston Hughes in October of the same year suggests what many talented and productive black artists felt when *Invisible Man* climbed into the literary stratosphere:

> Why don't you (as a suggestion) pick out a few of the *ideas* previously used, ideas which seemed to catch the fancy of ofays who read or reviewed the books, and work up new treatments or new situations in which to air them. For example, the idea of elevating one Negro (like Ralph [Ellison]) while neglecting or closing the eyes to the millions. (Bontemps and Hughes 315)

Despite Ellison's receipt of the National Book Award in 1953 and his subsequent television appearances and radio interviews, black critics were still slow to embrace his literary style. Alain Locke included *Invisible Man* in a 1953 essay published in Atlanta University's *Phylon*, the leading black academic journal. Locke liked the novel well enough to place it among three peaks of black narrative fiction, with Toomer's *Cane* and Wright's *Native Son*. And yet, Locke lamented the unnecessary language; the book was "smothered with verbosity and hyperbole" (34). Mainly he intended to invest in Ellison's future: "For once, too, here is a Negro writer capable of real and sustained irony. *Invisible Man*, evidently years in the making, must not be Ralph Ellison's last novel" (34). The rumors describing the seven-year ordeal that had made the near-masterpiece stimulated a chorus of well-placed pleas. America's premiere literary voices applauded the book but hoped earnestly that Ellison's future work would be genuinely distinguished.

The rosy prediction for his future novels did not prevent black American critics from continuing to voice a degree of confusion over what they read, perhaps because of the unflattering mirror that the novel upheld. In 1954, the Morgan State College literary critic Nick Aaron Ford published an essay in *Phylon* comparing the bestselling well-known male novelists of the time: Wright, Willard Motley, Frank Yerby, and Ellison. Unsurprisingly, he had some serious problems with the style and approach of *Invisible Man*, specifically the novel's conclusion: "The only avenue open to the Negro who wants to keep his self-respect is complete withdrawal. This seems to be the meaning of the final episode" (35). Ford echoed early criticisms that the novel was uneven, and that the tensions between comedy and tragedy and realism and surrealism were quite strained: "Another fault in the book, as I see it, is the very noticeable unevenness of style, which may be due to the author's inability to decide whether he wanted to be serious or comical in his personal attitude toward his material" (36). In 1956, Langston Hughes, who claimed he could never finish reading *Invisible Man*,[7] described Ellison's personality as a fitting counterpart to the kind of alienation that piqued Nick Aaron Ford about the narrator of *Invisible Man*:

> I have known a great many writers in my time, and some of them were very much like [Arthur] Koestler—always something not quite right in the world around them. Even on the brightest days, no matter where they are. Richard Wright seemed like that in Chicago . . . and Ralph Ellison in New York—all friends of mine whom I liked for one quality or another, and certainly for their talent—seemed unhappy fellows. No matter where, under what conditions, or when, something was always wrong. (Hughes 120)

While Ellison may not have felt repudiated by these kinds of remarks, he was confident that he had developed a literary style that built upon the other key experiments with the twentieth-century American modernist idiom, especially the approaches of Eliot and Faulkner. The arguments from the black critics seemed evidence to him of willful neglect or backwardness. Ellison's insight and aesthetic sensibility were different from the black Americans in the segregated college system, differences that were confirmed for him during a 1954 tour of black colleges. On 12 April of that year, he wrote to Albert Murray, his old Tuskegee classmate and literary peer, about his putrid discoveries. The black educators who comprised the middle class and staffed the schools put up stout resistance to modern literature and to threatening ideas. Southern University's teachers, serving one of the largest black schools in the country, were among the worst: "One night at a party at the dean's home the Negroes started needling me and I started asking questions and soon had everybody yelling at me, defending the right to be second-rate! . . . One Negro even drew his Caddy on me!" (*TT* 74). Howard University, the "capstone" of Negro education, was no better. Ellison found the scene "depressing": "[Sterling] Brown, [E. Franklin] Frazier, [Arthur P.] Davis, [John] Lovel [*sic*] and others were there but none of them would say a mumbling word—not even when I attacked some of their assumptions concerning Mose and America and culture" (*TT* 74–75). Later on during the Washington visit, an old friend politely suggested that Ellison behave more like Matthew Arnold. He was disgusted by the inactivity and fawning Victorianism of the black intelligentsia, a dislike of certain black scholars that he had had, it is worth noting, as early as 1942.[8] Irritated and dismayed, Ellison found himself taking on the role of antagonist.

While the African-American print media and colleges were not engaging his work as a participant in the formal modern experiments with narrative fiction, in an era when Paul Robeson had his passport revoked and his means of earning a living denied, Ellison began to receive steady invitations to participate in the most exclusive regions of American society. In the summer of his receipt of the National Book Award, Ellison was invited to Harvard as one of a small number of creative artists to participate in a symposium with critics on the indelicate but favorite topic of the moment: the "death" of the novel. Perhaps as a testament to the gravity of the discussion, two thousand people attended. Few could have been prepared for Ellison's sincerity concerning the power of art, his erudition, or his iconoclasm. At the "Harvard Symposium on the Contemporary Novel," Ellison countered the expectations of literary critics at one point by saying, "We don't expect novels—even great novels—to stay fashionable." He did his best to advance the ideas of experimentation and change, of which he was the walking personification. Ellison found these gatherings exciting, and the former League of American Writers seminar leader apparently excelled at them. Frank O'Connor, the Irish short story writer, wrote the conference up for the *New York Times Book Review* and excluded Ellison completely from his thoroughly negative review of the proceedings ("Conferences, I am convinced, do not promote understanding" [O'Connor 5]). But O'Connor's exclusion of the lone black writer probably comes more from Ellison's determination to use the conference as an avenue for intellectual debate and his determination to take on the public role of the novelist and critic with an almost religious seriousness. At one point Ellison had cause to embarrass and scold the well-regarded Irish writer O'Connor. Ellison wrote to Albert Murray in September, after the conference, the details of the fracas: "I told him [O'Connor]—over the air, though I didn't realize it at the time—that jokes were all very well, but that I hadn't realized that we had been asked to Harvard as entertainers" (*TT* 58). He had not overplayed his hand. Ellison expressed his ideas at the conference well enough to be asked by Harvard's Henry Kissinger, then editor of *Confluence*, to contribute to a forthcoming edition of the journal devoted to "Tradition in Culture and Politics: The Problem of Minorities."

In a move that in some ways signaled the significant departure Ellison felt from his earliest political leanings in the late 1930s and early 1940s, he published an essay that was at that time his principal statement on the idea of the Negro in American literature and culture. Ellison had begun the essay in 1946 when the journalist Thomas Sancton was assembling a special issue of *Survey Graphic* entitled "Segregation." Sancton thought Ellison's work too ambitious and had declined to publish it. Ellison revised portions of the essay, originally entitled "Imprisoned in Words," then submitted to Kissinger a header note distancing him from the essay's mildly radical conclusion: that white American writers had been unable to depict black Americans as complex human characters. Kissinger complied and placed at the article's head the following caveat:

> When I started rewriting this essay it occurred to me that its value might be somewhat increased if it remained very much

as I wrote it during 1946. For in that form it is what a young member of a minority felt about much of our writing. Thus I've left in much of the bias and shortsightedness, for it says as much about me as a member of a minority as it does about literature. I hope you still find the essay useful, and I'd like to see an editorial note stating that this was an unpublished piece written not long after the Second World War. (*SA* 24)

While he certainly retained the ideas and thrust of the original, Ellison rewrote much of the essay. He had been thirty-three when he put together "Imprisoned in Words," and his 1953 effort both to couch his ideas in a form that would find favor and yet to remain true to his compelling observation of the American scene shows the bind that he accepted. From the brief correspondence around the event between editor and writer, Kissinger showed no reluctance concerning the article.[9] In fact, what emerged in their letters refracting the essay was Ellison's earnest commitment and sincere desire to demonstrate a mastery of a complex range of ideas and perspectives from literature to social theory. And underneath that seems to be Ellison's nearly pious belief that his unique perspective and channeling of information would have an important bearing on American culture. Obviously, by late 1953 and the successive lower-court decisions leading to the 1954 Supreme Court decision to overturn racial segregation, Ellison sought to emphasize the unity of American experience. But his sensitivity toward *Confluence*'s readers, his new caution, his desire to write truthfully of the near-rancor he had experienced from America's most esteemed writers handling the Negro, and yet his passionate hope to escape the fate of the ranting ideologue, afforded him a very small margin for operation. Nor is it clear for what sort of "bias" and "shortsightedness" Ellison wanted readers to forgive him.

The most radical supposition in the essay was contained in a footnote:

Perhaps the ideal approach to a work of literature would be one allowing for insight into the deepest psychological motives of the writer at the same time that it examined all external sociological factors operating within a given milieu. For while objectively a social reality, the work of art is, in its genesis, a projection of a deeply personal process, and any approach that ignores the personal at the expense of the social is necessarily incomplete. (*SA* 27)

Although his phrase "at the expense of" lends itself to a couple of interpretations (is it synonymous with "for the sake of"? or does it really mean the elimination of *both* the psychological and the social?), it is difficult to imagine that Ellison had completely abandoned his interest in an author's psychology, a pursuit which was losing favor with the rise of Wimsatt and Beardsley's theory of the "intentional fallacy." Concerns with milieu and society might have been understood as more properly Marxist, an approach which had declining significance for Ellison as the conclusion of the era of McCarthyism had by then made certain intellectual positions automatic, such as the recognition of the Soviet Union as a totalitarian regime.

Ellison's decision to publish work that reflected areas of his intellectual past suggests the bind he felt by the early 1950s. Kissinger had asked for a piece dealing with a "minority" problem, and Ellison felt he had a responsibility to present one with a sharp critical sensibility, even if it didn't represent his most current view. Plainly, Ellison wanted to operate at the level of prestige that the National Book Award had shown him was available and that the invitation from the Harvard journal confirmed. However, Ellison also seems to have been a bit skeptical concerning his readiness to produce a cogent statement of his literary and cultural attitudes on the fly. His response was to split his career into halves: the young writer who had edited *Negro Quarterly* and held radical views in the 1940s, and the mature writer who had won the National Book Award in 1953.

In 1955, Ellison moved into a regular relationship with the reigning American literati when he participated in a symposium published in *American Scholar*. Ivy League graduates Alain Locke and J. Saunders Redding had served, not simultaneously, on the journal's editorial board; their posts confirmed the journal's liberal views. But Ellison's position on a panel with other celebrated writers (Jean Stafford and William Styron) and the cream of the publishing world's editors (Albert Erskine, Simon Bessie, and Hiram Haydn) showed the newly available participation, more or less, for which there was no previous model in American society. In the 1940s, Ellison had been an occasional gadfly in this world, an unknown quantity, free to speak his mind because he was black and unrecognized. But in the 1950s, his duties and responsibilities took on enormous significance. He faced now the pressure of appearing regularly and in public on the dais surrounded by the recipients of the country's finest endowments and most elaborate primping. Necessity and good taste required him both to comport himself with intelligence and never to show public bitterness at the system of racial injustice that previously had peremptorily excluded blacks from similar opportunities of encouragement and support. Ellison chose to look at these groupings in the most enabling manner he knew: they were exceedingly rare opportunities for whites as well. In these forums, it would have been more acceptable to demonstrate unintelligence than to show bitterness, and the effort of principled dissent combined with affability was exhausting.

Symposia like *American Scholar's* needed a black voice. Ellison's residency in New York City enabled his own professional visibility, especially during the years after Wright's permanent departure from the United States and while James Baldwin spent most of his time abroad. But if he was becoming a literary spokesman, it was as an intellectual, not as a "race" man. For the *American Scholar* symposium, Ellison tended to endorse the traditions of American vernacular language and pluralist democracy, another way of challenging traditional divisions of social status and rank. He also faulted American writers for resisting the evidence of considerable social change. He concluded that "for much too long, American novelists have set up certain aesthetic ideals . . . national values, which very often have gotten in the way of the novelist's sense of reality." In shorthand, he pointed to a "snobbery of style" that had removed the writer's vision from the plane of reality. And he believed that the great responsibility of the writer was to remain in relation to the audience, while keeping in mind the tradition of artistic excellence: "My task is to reach them, doing the least violence to what I think are the great artistic achievements of the craft" ("What's Wrong" 36). His emphasis on vernacular language as well as his mandate to infuse the writer's vision with the freshly changing and fluid world made his views radically egalitarian. And he had achieved them without the appearance of any resentment or spikiness on account of racism.

Curiously, one of the final points of discussion presented to the panelists dealt with pecking order. How did the writers determine a "first-rate novelist"? *American Scholar* editor Hiram Haydn suggested that "one test of a really first-rate novelist, I should say, as against a writer of a first-rate novel, is that he should produce more than one first-rate novel" ("What's Wrong" 48). Ellison responded easily to the sickness that ultimately jaundiced his own career. Writers failed to produce a series of excellent books because of the same condition he'd challenged his peers to document: "the extreme fluidity of our society." Ellison told them, "Reality changes fast and if you don't keep up with it, you are apt to fall into writing the same book—I mean, writing the book that is expected of you" ("What's Wrong" 49). Ellison was proud of his original view of life as a chaotic world of possibility in need of a formal structure to offer it meaning. He resisted cheapening his imagination by returning to a vision of the world similar to the one he had immortalized in his novel. Though in 1963 he did publish "Out of the Hospital and under the Bar," one of the excised fragments from *Invisible Man*, for his future work he strove to produce an entirely new fictive conception of reality. And yet his increasingly urgent value as a public figure in the 1950s made it impossible for him to make use of anonymity and to take intellectual and artistic risks in order to renew his vision. His career was on notice.

Ellison's participation in symposia and at conferences introduced him to new and influential people. He connected himself to critics and writers like Robert Penn Warren and R. W. B. Lewis, who wrote for reviews like *Kenyon* and *Sewanee*, of which Ellison remained suspicious. These men had been champions of the New Criticism, and their technical approach promised to continue to glean important nuggets from his novel even after the slow process of racial integration appeared to make his book obsolete by ending the social conditions which had generated it and upon which it had satirized with such acuity.[10] Black writers resisted the New Criticism (beyond merely the crude examples of color prejudice written early by Allen Tate, Donald Davidson, and Warren) principally because of their discomfort with the intrinsic value of the text or literary artifact. They remained suspicious of the ideas that meaning could be certified objectively inside of a text and that the external circumstances producing literature and the determinations of communities reading literature had limited influence on the creation of fine art.

Ellison lived in Rome between 1955 and 1957 as a fellow of the American Academy of Arts and Letters. While in Europe, he attended the first African Writers Conference in Paris and worked steadily on the main segment of the novel published in 1999 as *Juneteenth*. He had been propositioned by American magazines to lend his critical intelligence to the problem of desegregation, and he undertook these sorts of tasks with an increasing degree of frustration, not only because the requests took him away from his fiction, but because the topics always implied that he was black before he was a writer. The assumptions of a society eagerly looking for and appointing racial spokesmen wearied Ellison, as he revealed in a letter to Albert Murray in 1956: "I'm simply not interested in racial approaches to culture. . . . Dick Wright, he's on that kick, not me" (*TT* 143). Indeed, for his part, Ellison sought to reconstruct his earlier political radicalism by making himself into a fiction writer and literary critic.

During the later 1950s, after he published "'Twentieth-Century Fiction and the Black Mask of Humanity" in Kissinger's *Confluence*, Ellison made distinct the separation between his earlier and later years. His publications were mini-events, and in them he sought elegant distinction. On the other side of his literary education, he wrote a long essay called "Society, Morality, and the Novel" for a Granville Hicks anthology called *The Living Novel* (1957). In the essay, Ellison tried to resolve the dilemma of the contemporary novelist who had been informed by a generation of critics that the novel as a form had lost its importance, its meaning as a literary genre. In sweeping language, Ellison made a passionate defense for the novel's high moral purpose and rewrote nineteenth-century Western literary history, connecting issues of ethical justice and the development of the craft of novel writing. His essay made the tradition of American narrative fiction completely serviceable and indebted to the descendants of African slaves, whose nineteenth-century struggle against slavery had richly shaped the American definition of social, moral, and political freedom.

In 1958 he rebutted critic and "literary" folklorist Stanley Edgar Hyman, who had been instrumental in the creation of *Invisible Man*, in an essay called "Change the Joke and Slip the Yoke." The essay, placed in *Partisan Review*, opposed Hyman's notion of the folk trickster as a dominant archetype explaining African-American culture. Ellison's broader cultural enemy was the sweeping generalizations concerning black life that began to appear as public racial integration took shape, including Norman Mailer's sensational 1957 article "The White Negro." Ellison defended himself by refocusing Hyman's assertion that the narrator of *Invisible Man* was a trickster figure: "He gets his restless mobility not so much from the blues or from sociology but because he appears in a literary form which has time and social change as its special province. Besides, restlessness of the spirit is an American condition that transcends geography, sociology and past conditions of servitude" (*SA* 57–58).

Whenever his public critics draped him in a shroud of "blackness," Ellison deliberately draped his work and his life in twin flags of authority: "literary form" and the "American condition." The point that he stressed most clearly was the inherently domestic nature of his own artistic creations and their relationship with an Anglo-American lineage. Obviously such claims were designed to resist the notion that Americans lived in isolated and exclusive spheres corresponding to race. Six years later, he would claim as ancestors in his own literary genealogy Faulkner, Eliot, Dostoevski, Malraux, and Hemingway.

James Baldwin, too, in essays from the early 1950s like "Many Thousands Gone," had believed that it was ignorant and deceitful to suggest that racial "segregation" had ever been more than a cruel ideal, and never realized. But, after a rebuttal to William

Faulkner in 1956 called "Faulkner and Desegregation," followed by a trip to the South in 1958 that produced the essays "The Hard Kind of Courage" (reprinted as "Fly in the Buttermilk") and "Nobody Knows My Name: A Letter from the South," Baldwin and other black writers found it increasingly difficult to endorse faithfully "the American condition" and "literary form" as sources of optimism. Since the pace of change seemed to demand another kind of active and more satisfying response, many of the most vigorous writers and intellectuals believed it a serious obligation to demystify sacrosanct terms that guarded American literary and cultural ideals.

While he was abroad in 1956, Ellison joined the American Committee for Cultural Freedom (the sociologist and Fisk University president Charles Johnson was the other black member), an affiliate of the Congress for Cultural Freedom.[11] The group, which included most of the prominent American anticommunists and much of the editorial board of the influential journal *Partisan Review*, was the domestic cultural arm of the broader congress that assisted American foreign policy abroad.[12] Ellison was no longer just a writer with his own conscience to guard, but rather was acting in an international capacity in coordination with the efforts of the "neoliberal" intellectuals of his era. He had officially begun to take seriously the idea of patriotism— undeniably crafted in his own vernacular ideal—and he resented increasingly the assumption that as a Negro he must automatically feel excluded from his homeland.

His visibility as a black writer, however, caused him to appear in the ranks of the dissident expatriates. *Time* magazine's "Amid the Alien Corn" included Ellison alongside William Demby and Ben Johnson in a black group that the writer Richard Gibson described as living in Rome "because of social and political causes which everyone knows" (28). The article spent most of its description on Ellison's sometime-friend Chester Himes, but it was Richard Wright, the "dean of Negro writers abroad," who delivered the pronouncement that grated against, if not Ellison's deepest personal feelings, then certainly his public career. Wright said, "The Negro problem in America has not changed in 300 years." Ellison smarted at having to justify living abroad, and it became imperative for him to clarify the public record. He persisted in having a rebuttal published, although it took three months for his correction to appear.

Ellison's dogged response in *Time's* February 1959 issue made clear that he had not voluntarily exiled himself in Rome from late 1955 until late 1957 to escape the race problem. Instead of imposing upon himself "self-exile," Ellison felt it important to robe himself in the garment of American success:

> I returned to the U.S. a year and three months ago—not from voluntary exile, "for social and political causes," as Richard Gibson's rhetoric would have it, but from a stay at the American Academy in Rome, which was my privilege as winner of the 1955 Fellowship in Literature granted by the American Academy of Arts and Letters. Admittedly, two years may seem a long time in this swiftly changing country even for purposes of broadening one's personal culture—which is the aim of fellowship—but exile is, fortunately (and even for Negro Americans) largely a state of mind. ("At Home" 2)

Ellison disliked being lumped into groups by the likes of Gibson, an ardent commentator on Negro art but certainly not a well-known writer himself.[13] But the argument that "exile is . . . a state of mind" was perhaps a bit disingenuous, or at least flaringly ambivalent. He suggested that while racism and inequality could be resisted mentally without the necessity of physical departure, one could also suffer the alienating pain of exile domestically, hinting that he himself was not immune to the effects of exile in his living room and study in Washington Heights, New York City.[14] Also of importance, a new group of exiles was preparing to depart the colonies, and Europe was no longer necessarily the destination; writers were leaving for the Caribbean, especially Cuba, and West Africa. Also, the famous exiles of this period—Richard Wright, James Baldwin, Frantz Fanon, Julian Mayfield, W. E. B. Du Bois, Chinua Achebe, and Wole Soyinka—were able to continue to produce their work under the condition of physical alienation from a homeland, and Ellison's apparent rejection of the power of the political and social conditions that necessitated exile did not seem to prove effective in the case of his own artistic production. While he successfully drafted large segments of the work that ultimately became *Juneteenth* during his Roman sojourn, the environment of the United States proved quite challenging to composing serious fiction. Ellison perhaps underestimated the degree to which problems of alienation and exile "of mind" lay at the core of his own struggle to complete his fiction.

Ellison's confidence in America rested upon the fact that race relations had changed, and quite remarkably. While abroad and at the American Academy, he jousted intellectually with American writers like R. P. Blackmur, Archibald MacLeish, Van Wyck Brooks, and especially Robert Penn Warren, with whom Ellison developed a close friendship beginning in 1956.[15] Ellison believed that Warren had evolved greatly from his days as the writer of "The Briar Patch," the southern agrarian critic's manifesto on race, an infamous document from the 1920s supporting racial segregation. Ellison wrote to Murray in April 1957 and justified his new friendship: "Warren is a man who's lived and thought his way free of a lot of irrational illusions" (*TT* 158). In 1964, Warren and MacLeish successfully petitioned for Ralph Ellison to become the first African-American member of the Century Club, one of America's most exclusive literary fraternities. Again in 1964, Warren helped Ellison to win a Rockefeller grant, an award that prevented him from having to take a teaching job, prior to the publication of *Shadow and Act*. The headiness of his success apparently caused Ellison occasionally to misgauge the extent of support for his opinions and his stylistic approaches to literary study. When interviewing in 1961 at the University of Chicago, in the form of offering the distinguished Alexander White Lecture series, Ellison, to his sponsor Richard Stern's chagrin, decided to lecture extemporaneously.[16] Ellison was disappointed when Chicago offered Saul Bellow a faculty position the next year. Despite his setbacks, Ellison was still lauded heartily by new supporters, some of them people he could not have set oars with in the 1940s.

The publication of *Shadow and Act* in 1964 turned into an event for Ellison that consolidated his critical reputation and presented most vigorously the standpoint of black and white cultural and racial mutuality. Two things are interesting about the collection. First, he wrote no new material for it, rather collecting the better and more temperate materials from his files since he had begun a career as a professional critic in 1938.[17] Two of the pieces were previously unpublished, the essay "Harlem Is Nowhere," written for 48 *Magazine of the Year*, and a review of Gunnar Myrdal's *American Dilemma*. Both of the essays had been contracted in the 1940s and were for a variety of reasons neglected. Second, the best of the essays of *Shadow and Act* were written with short deadlines and other political and critical pressures, an important key to Ellison's creative process. This seems to be the situation where Ellison's critical intelligence worked best. Scholarly consensus seems to regard the essay "The World and the Jug" as the most significant that Ellison ever wrote. In the essay, Ellison felt compelled to stake out an independent position distinct from the post-Stalinist leftist radicalism of *Dissent* editor Irving Howe. Ellison wrote the two sections, published in the *New Leader* in December 1963 and February 1964, in a matter of weeks.

"The World and the Jug" was Ellison's art-versus-ideology dispute with Howe, a Jewish socialist who had published a 1957 study called *Politics and the Novel*. (Ellison, who liked attending the Gauss seminars at Princeton where Howe had developed his early ideas for the confluence between politics and art, would not have missed the fact that Howe, a passionate advocate of Richard Wright, had completely neglected race in *Politics and the Novel*.) Despite the fact that Ellison was, essentially, rebuking the liberal Jewish intelligentsia whose support was crucial to the Civil Rights movement, the essay became nearly a creed for future black writers and intellectuals and many liberal whites who advanced the cause of racial integration. Howe had nervily suggested that Baldwin and Ellison were able to pursue their finished prose styles over literary expressions of black rage because Richard Wright had already accepted the burden of exposing the sordid problem of racial injustice at the expense of his art. Ellison dissented heartily. He believed in a plurality of effects, and he took pains to show how even the formation of racial oppositions like "white" and "black" not only were inaccurate, but also were hiding a more dangerous erasure of long histories of American ethnic conflict, compromise, and solution. The essay touted Ellison's maverick rodeo style by ridiculing the age-old tactic of appealing to white guilt, whether to press for social justice or merely to win debate. Ellison out of hand rejected what he took to be Howe's expression of empathy and, instead, undercut the theoretical ground from which Howe's generous empathic offer had been born: his membership in the race of whites:

> Thus I feel uncomfortable whenever I discover Jewish intel-
> lectuals writing as though *they* were guilty of enslaving my
> grandparents, or as though *Jews* were responsible for the sys-
> tem of segregation. . . .
>   The real guilt of such Jewish intellectuals lies in their facile,
> perhaps unconscious, but certainly unrealistic, identification
> with what is called the "power structure." Negroes call that
> "passing for white." (*SA* 126)

The criticism here is a stiff jab at Jewish pretension, when it achieves a measure of assimilation by expressing pity at the African-American plight. The level of commentary throughout *Shadow and Act* persisted in this manner: a friendly, jovial even, series of jabs at the regular pieties and shibboleths which passed for reasoned observation and analysis of the racial and dynamic American cultural scene. Ellison did not use the book to identify forces deliberately opposing racial justice. He chose to focus his talents on revealing the native richness and diversity of African-American life, discriminating among degrees of opposition, and clarifying the effects of well-meaning but misguided friends.

Shadow and Act served to anoint Ellison, especially to a new readership, as a voice of moderation during the time that the nonviolent Civil Rights movement attained its most tangible goals of legal reform, and then began splintering into factions of black nationalism, socialism, and mytho-romanticism. The book was reviewed well by his friends, and the *New York Times* titled its appraisal as if he were a combination of Emerson and James Joyce wrapped in one African-American package: "Portrait of a

Man on His Own." In the hands of the influential writer and personal friend Robert Penn Warren, the collection was talked about in sacrosanct terms, almost completely apart from any of the essays' actual subject matter. Ellison was being placed beyond the reality of Negro experience and instead had become the standard-bearer of truth: "The moral effort to see and recognize the truth of the self and of the world, and the artistic effort to say the truth are regarded as aspects of the same process," Warren reverently concluded his review ("Unity" 92). Ellison's work was being moved into a category of the morally and artistically just, whereas writers like James Baldwin and LeRoi Jones would be defined increasingly as "ideologically expedient" and embittered malcontents. In contrast to the despoilers of America, there was Ellison, effusively praised in *Sewanee*:

> [Ellison] emerges as clearly one of the most intelligent and wise authors of our time. Widely and deeply educated, very observant, aloof from pat assumptions, capable of using ideas without becoming their victim, he is able to perceive and explain the paradoxes of American experience and the Negro's relation to it, ready to debunk any theories whose explanations are demonstrably false, and unwilling to let any biases get in the way of his perception of reality or his mission to write novels. (Kostelanetz 171)

At fifty-one, Ellison had gained a reputation of infallibility, a stature that normally makes impossible the pursuit of risk and uncertainty, an artist's doorway to possibility and truth.

The political ramifications of *Shadow and Act* did not go unnoticed. Liberal journals like the *Nation* warned, "One effect of Ellison's work may be to dissipate the general guilt that the [Civil Rights] movement must exploit to progress" (Lissovoy 335). The Yale University critic R. W. B. Lewis was probably the most perceptive when he admitted the incredible pressure under which black American writers tried to thrive: "For even those among us who consent to Negroes being accepted as human beings, don't really want them to be writers. We want them to be warriors, and wounded warriors at that; with their creative talents enlisted in the (great and real) struggle for racial justice." As to Ellison's concerns with mastery of his craft during an era characterized by antiblack terrorism and black rioting, Lewis noted that a preoccupation with literary standards was likely to be understood as "mere aestheticism, or worse, as a kind of betrayal" ("Ellison's Essays" 19). But for himself, Lewis saw the book as an important marker of the boundaries of racial identity that might enable the dialogue between black and white in America to begin. By 1964, Ellison's oeuvre had significant relevance for chiefly the academic and literary establishment, which, in the era prior to the emergence of a black professoriat on white American university campuses or black writers on the staffs of major magazines and journals, amounted to a form of tokenism.

Today, Ellison's famous response to Irving Howe rings a bit hollow. In "The World and the Jug" Ellison had begged off participating in the evolving political, cultural, and critical dynamics of the United States on the grounds that he was too busy writing fiction. Any subsequent cradling of Ellison's reputation seems dubious, because Ellison was unable economically to carry out the function that he established for himself: to write novels. Furthermore, this inability seems connected to his critical facility, which, after *Shadow and Act*, became repeatedly focused upon nostalgic recoveries of the era prior to legal integration and the "vanished tribe" of American Negroes, whom Ellison thought had begun to disappear in earnest after the legal defeat of segregation in 1954. Ellison's public reluctance to weigh in on the great issue among American intellectuals in the second half of the 1950s—the initially nonviolent resistance to the customs of racial segregation and the legacy of American slavery—indicated the increasingly limited role he imagined for the artist, as much as it indicated his distrust of sloganeers and propagandists. The measure of the void left by Ellison's absence can be gauged by the influence of the essay "The White Negro," Norman Mailer's 1957 nose thumbing to both southern paternalism and Negro propriety.

Ellison's quietude in the late 1950s and early 1960s reflects his finally narrow perception of the role and possibility of an artist. Part of this had to do with neutralizing the contradiction in his

novel that had afforded it such theoretical power. The novel's culmination had always retained a tension between twin ideals. In
the coal cellar, the Invisible Man concludes his narrative with two
important observations: "My world has become one of infinite
possibilities" (*IM* 576); and "Who knows but that, on the lower
frequencies, I speak for you?" (*IM* 581). The twin mantras offer interesting solutions to the dilemma of American identity in an age
of transition: synecdoche and mimesis. With "possibility" as its
keyword, the book could be comfortably read as advancing the
trope of synecdoche as the key to the character of American
identity. The metaphor of synecdoche, a part representing the
whole, allows for any one of the infinite facets of American possibility to describe or to stand in for the gemstone body of the
democratic polity. But the reality of integration after 1954 introduced a series of new concerns for Ellison, who grew less interested in the possibility of, say, an individual Negro characterizing
the indelible values of American society, than in living up to the
idealized values and norms that the society's laws guaranteed.
The contradiction's tension was eased, and the novel became
read as an endorsement of mimetic standards, the concept of
artistic value based on a faithful reproduction of reality that exists outside of or unmediated by discourse. Instead of the tension
between manifold possibility and transcendental standards, Ellison attributed increasing importance to the notion of universal
standards. The growing significance of "speaking for you" in the
conclusion indicates the necessity of blacks being able to occupy
white spaces. (Whites already had a vigorous tradition of occu-
pying black literal and figurative spaces, from minstrel shows to
Elvis Presley.) This shift was predicated on the ability of the black
social inferior to reproduce the thoughts, desires, and speech of
the socially esteemed, a form of racial obtrusion, but one imagined to occur without tumultuous shifts in the social order.

To highlight the point, one of the most remarkable anecdotes
that Ellison enjoyed sharing entailed the long tradition of American blacks disguising themselves as foreign ethnics to skirt the
regulations of Jim Crow during the first half of the twentieth
century (or during slavery in the nineteenth century). Blacks
would adopt languages of gibberish, colorful turbans, and out-

landish mannerisms to masquerade as foreign ethnics. It is important to understand that Ellison never emphasized this behavior as a form of cowardice—a fear-ridden unwillingness to face injustice. Nor did he see the masquerade as buffoonery, an act that whites might have tolerated or encouraged had they recognized it because it would have confirmed so many of their assumptions about innate black incapacity. However, in the 1960s and 1970s, Ellison seemed personally insulted when he encountered young blacks adopting non-Western names, behaviors, and forms of dress. Large portions of the black political and aesthetic movement of the 1960s understood their behavior as a critical act of self-definition, taken from a vast sea of possibility, as well as a form of resistance to a racist episteme. But Ellison believed that he was witnessing a cowardly, facile, and near-schizophrenic determination to reject a stable and empirically grounded identity. He faulted young blacks for misinterpreting the fixed conditions of their existence, chiefly that they were heirs to equal and irreducible portions of black and white racial ancestry and culture. He became a public spokesman who reminded black people who had come of age in the wake of the *Brown* decision that they had their origins in North America, and consequently, his work increasingly had at its center the motif of black and white interchangeability and indistinction.

In 1969 Ellison wrote a blurb in support of James Alan McPherson's first book, *Hue and Cry*. His ringing endorsement revealed not only the resentment that had built up, but also his increasingly fixed perception of an acceptable code of social behavior:

With this collection of stories, McPherson promises to move right past those talented but misguided writers of Negro American cultural background who take being black as a privilege for being obscenely second-rate and who read their social predicament as Negroes as exempting them from the necessity of mastering the craft and forms of fiction. Indeed, as he makes his "hue and cry" over the dead-ends, the confusions of value and failures of sympathy and insight of those who inhabit his fictional world, McPherson's stories are in themselves a hue and cry against the dead, publicity-sustained writing which has come increasingly to stand for what is called "black writing." (Ellison, *Hue and Cry* book jacket)

Ellison's point is limited by a glaring misperception. The job of the second-rate writer, black or white, is to write and, it is hoped, to improve. If offered the opportunity for publication, it isn't the second-rate writer's job to limit or withhold his own opportunities, rather that is the job of the public and the critic, who have the choice to embrace or repudiate the work. (There is also the historical point of Grub Street creating the market for eighteenth-century novelists Samuel Richardson and Laurence Sterne.) Ellison was dismayed by the profound emotional need of American audiences and critics for what he called the "obscenely second-rate" black writer. But he neither continued to investigate that problem, nor did he publish additional novels to compete for the public's attention. Ellison reverted to a rationale that both pitted black writers against one another and blemished the black expert because of the foibles of the black novice. If the works of Malcolm X, Nikki Giovanni, Eldridge Cleaver, or Amiri Baraka were popular, he believed it diminished the audience for McPherson and himself. Since Ellison published only occasional pieces of short fiction, he did not relieve the lack of available imaginative representations. Rather, he insisted on the value of the artistic achievement residing in the representational relationship of art to a true empirical reality, an ideal mimesis, and, on another level, the existence of that ideal outside the mediation of critical discourse. The frustrating irony of his career, then, was that he concluded it as a critic, at a time when he seemed most to doubt the value of shaping the artist's reality.

NOTES

1. William Faulkner, jacket notes, from *Faulkner at Nagano, Shadow and Act* (New York: Random House, 1964).

2. The best available examples of Ellison's early intent for the novel are his letter to Kenneth Burke of 23 Nov. 1945, Kenneth Burke Papers, Pennsylvania State Library; and his drafted notes to his first

publisher, Reynal and Hitchcock, Ralph Ellison, draft letter to Peggy Hitchcock, n.d., Ralph Ellison Papers, box 52, folder *"Invisible Man* Drafts Notes #19," Library of Congress. Portions of the Burke letter are in Timothy L. Parrish, "Ralph Ellison, Kenneth Burke, and the Form of Democracy," *Arizona Quarterly* 52 (Fall 1995): 117–43. For a broader treatment of Ellison's concerns during the mid-1940s, see Lawrence P. Jackson, *Ralph Ellison: Emergence of Genius* (New York: Wiley, 2002), 304–431. Ellison wrote of the white American psyche in his 1940s essays "Beating that Boy," "Richard Wright's Blues," and "Twentieth-Century Fiction and the Black Mask of Humanity."

3. Gerald Graff, *Professing Literature* (Chicago, Ill.: University of Chicago Press, 1987): 183–208.

4. Barbara Foley, "Ralph Ellison as Proletarian Journalist," *Science and Society* 62, no. 4 (Winter 1998–1999): 537–56. Foley's essay describes in significant detail and places in context Ellison's body of published criticism from 1938 to 1944. She convincingly shows Ellison's often-buried left-wing commitments.

5. Ralph Ellison, "Richard Wright's Blues," *Antioch Review* 5 (Summer 1945): 198–211. J. Saunders Redding preceded Ellison in *Antioch Review* with a piece of critical journalism in 1943. See Redding, "The Black Man's Burden," *Antioch Review* 3 (Winter 1943): 587–95.

6. Jackson, *Ralph Ellison*, 440.

7. Arnold Rampersad, *The Life of Langston Hughes*, vol. 2, *1941–1967: I Dream a World* (New York: Oxford University Press, 1988), 201.

8. Jackson, *Ralph Ellison*, 268.

9. See Ralph Ellison, letter to Henry Kissinger, 3 Nov. 1953, Ralph Ellison Papers, box 172 "Speeches, Lectures," folder "Harvard 1953," Manuscripts and Special Collections, Library of Congress.

10. Robert Penn Warren, *Who Speaks for the Negro* (New York: Random House, 1966), 354. Warren thought the book still determined black human subjectivity in his bestselling book of 1966: "No one has made more unrelenting statements of the dehumanizing pressures that have been put upon the Negro. And *Invisible Man* is, I should say, the most powerful artistic representation we have of the Negro under these dehumanizing conditions; and, at the same time, it is a statement of the human triumph over those conditions."

11. Diana Trilling, letters to Ralph Ellison, 19 Sept. 1956 and 28 Nov. 1956, Ralph Ellison Papers, box 81, folder "American Commit-

tee," Manuscript Division, Library of Congress. The committee sponsored symposia and marshaled American writers and critics to present their views. A November 1956 program called "The North American Image in Latin America" is suggestive of their concerns during the mid-1950s.

12. It has lately been revealed that the Congress for Cultural Freedom was financed and offered direction from the Central Intelligence Agency. See Frances S. Saunders, *The Cultural Cold War* (New York: New Press, 1999). Morris Dickstein's *Leopards in the Temple* (Cambridge, Mass.: Harvard University Press, 2002), 14–15, reminds us that much of the art exported and touted by the CIA-funded committee blatantly ran counter to the narrow aims of U.S. government officials.

13. Gibson, a product of Kenyon College, appeared on the literary scene in 1951 with an essay disparaging black writers. He moved abroad and became known in the black expatriate community. Gibson's novel *A Mirror for Magistrates* was published in London in the late 1950s and was not reviewed in the United States.

14. An example from the late 1960s is illustrative. The writer James Alan McPherson began an interview essay by noting Ellison's steady observation of the outside black world through high-powered binoculars. McPherson, "Indivisible Man" (1969), in *Conversations with Ralph Ellison*, ed. Maryemma Graham and Amritjit Singh (Jackson: University Press of Mississippi, 1995), 173.

15. Ralph Ellison, letter to Nathan Scott, 17 July 1989, in Joseph Blotner, *Robert Penn Warren* (New York: Random House, 1997), 536. In his letter to his long-time friend Scott, Ellison reminisces about his early friendship with Warren in Rome: "It was through such pleasurable roaming that any bars to our friendship that might have been imposed by Southern manners and history went down the drain and left the well-known Fugitive poet and the fledgling writer and grandson of Freedmen marvelously free to enjoy themselves as human beings."

16. Richard Stern, "Ralph Ellison," *Callaloo* 18, no. 2 (1995): 284–87. Stern recalled, "To my surprise, he arrived without anything on paper. His model was jazz: inspiration would arrive as needed, and, therefore, the lectures would be more powerful, fresh, and true. They weren't. They were a disaster. Ralph said a few good things, but he stumbled, repeated himself, went off on tangents, and then

the tangents of tangents. After the first one, I hinted it might be easier to put something down on paper. He wouldn't; he thought the lecture had gone well" (285).

17. Ellison, for example, chose not to revive his antiwar pieces written prior to the American involvement in the Second World War, such as "Negro Soldier" or "Let Us Consider the Harlem Crime Wave," Ralph Ellison Papers, box 35, folder "Let Us Consider the Harlem Crime Wave," Library of Congress.

WORKS CITED

Bellow, Saul. "Man Underground." *Commentary* 13 (1952): 608–10.

Berry, Abner W. "Ralph Ellison's Novel *Invisible Man* Shows Snobbery, Contempt for Negro People." *Worker*, 1 June 1952, 7.

Blotner, Joseph. *Robert Penn Warren: A Biography*. New York: Random House, 1997.

Bontemps, Arna, and Langston Hughes. *Arna Bontemps–Langston Hughes Letters 1925–1967*. Edited by Charles Nichols. New York: Paragon, 1990.

Brown, Lloyd. "The Deep Pit." *Masses and Mainstream* (June 1952): 62.

Chase, Richard. "A Novel Is a Novel." *Kenyon Review* 14 (1952): 678–84.

Elliott, George P. "Portrait of a Man on His Own." *New York Times Book Review*, 25 Oct. 1964, 4–5.

Ellison, Ralph. "At Home." *Time*, 9 Feb. 1959, 2.

———. Book jacket endorsement of James Alan McPherson's *Hue and Cry*. Boston: Little, Brown, 1969.

———. "Collaborator with His Own Enemy." *New York Times Book Review*, 19 Feb. 1950, 4.

———. "Remarks." "Harvard Symposium on the Contemporary Novel." [n.p.]. [1953]. Box 172, folder "Speeches and Lectures Harvard 1953." Ralph Ellison Papers. Manuscripts and Archives, Library of Congress.

———. "What's Wrong with the American Novel?" (1955). In *Conversations with Ralph Ellison*. Edited by Maryemma Graham and Amritjit Singh, 20–62. Jackson: University Press of Mississippi, 1995.

Foley, Barbara. "Ralph Ellison as Proletarian Journalist." *Science and Society* 62 (1998–1999): 537–56.

Ford, Nick Aaron. "Four Popular Negro Novelists." *Phylon* 15, no. 1 (1954): 29–39.

Gibson, Richard. "Amid the Alien Corn." *Time,* 17 Nov. 1958, 28.

Graff, Gerald. *Professing Literature.* Chicago, Ill.: University of Chicago Press, 1987.

Himes, Chester. *The End of a Primitive.* New York: Norton, 1997.

Howe, Irving. "Black Boys and Native Sons." *Dissent* 4 (1963). Reprinted in *A World More Attractive.* New York: Horizon Press, 1963.

———. *Politics and the Novel.* New York: Horizon, 1957.

———. "A Reply to Ralph Ellison." *New Leader,* 3 Feb. 1964, 10–14.

Hughes, Langston. *I Wonder as I Wander.* 1956. Reprint. New York: Thunder's Mouth, 1989.

Jackson, Lawrence. *Ralph Ellison: Emergence of Genius.* New York: Wiley, 2002.

Kostelanetz, Richard. "Ellison's Essays." *Sewanee Review* 73, no. 1 (1965): 171–72.

Lewis, Richard W. B. "Eccentric's Pilgrimage." *Hudson Review* 6, no. 1 (1953): 144–50.

———. "Ellison's Essays." *New York Review of Books,* 28 Jan. 1965, 19–20.

Lissovoy, Peter de. "The Visible Ellison." *Nation,* 9 Nov. 1964, 334–36.

Locke, Alain. "From *Native Son* to *Invisible Man*: A Review of Literature of the Negro for 1952." *Phylon* 14, no. 1 (1953): 34–44.

Mailer, Norman. "The White Negro." *The Long Patrol: 25 Years of Writing from the Work of Norman Mailer,* 209–28. New York: World Publishing, 1971.

O'Connor, Frank. "The Novel Approach." *New York Times Book Review,* 23 Aug. 1953, 5, 24.

Ottley, Roi. "Blazing Novel Relates a Negro's Frustrations." *Chicago Sunday Tribune,* 11 May 1952, 4.

Redding, J. Saunders. "Invisible Man." *Baltimore Afro-American,* 10 May 1952, 10.

Rolo, Charles. "Candide in Harlem: Ralph Ellison's *Invisible Man.*" *Atlantic* 190, no. 1 (1952): 83.

Schwartz, Delmore. "Fiction Chronicle: The Wrongs of Innocence and Experience." *Partisan Review* 19 (1952): 354–59.

Walker, Margaret. Letter to Langston Hughes, 22 July 1952. Langston Hughes Papers, box 107, folder 1667, James Weldon Johnson Collection, Beinecke Rare Manuscript Library, Yale University.

Warren, Kenneth. "'As White as Anybody': Race and the Politics of Counting as Black." *New Literary History* 31 (2000): 709–26.

Warren, Robert Penn. "The Unity of Experience." *Commentary* 39 (1965): 91–96.

———. *Who Speaks for the Negro?* New York: Random House, 1965.

West, Anthony. "Black Man's Burden." *New Yorker*, 31 May 1952, 93–96.

Wright, Richard. "The Position of the Negro Artist and Intellectual in American Society" (1960). Richard Wright Papers, box 3, folder 41, James Weldon Johnson Collection, Beinecke Rare Manuscript Library, Yale University.

ILLUSTRATED
CHRONOLOGY

Ellison's Life

1913   Ralph Waldo Ellison born
(1 March) in Oklahoma City,
Oklahoma, to Lewis Ellison and Ida
Millsap Ellison.

1916   Ida takes on added
employment to support herself and
two sons after Lewis Ellison dies on
19 July.

1919   Enters Oklahoma City's
Frederick Douglass School; Paul
Laurence Dunbar Library becomes
the scene of voracious reading by
the young Ellison throughout the
1920s.

Historical Events

1913   D. H. Lawrence publishes
Sons and Lovers; Armory
Show in New York introduces
cubism and postimpressionism;
premiere of Igor Stravinsky's
controversial *Le Sacre du
Printemps*; Niels Bohr
generates theory of atomic
structure; death of Harriet
Tubman.

1914   Vachel Lindsay publishes *The
Congo*; James Joyce publishes
Dubliners; Robert Goddard initiates
rocketry experiments; World War I
breaks out.

*Niels Bohr generated his theory of atomic structure the year Ellison was born, just
ten years before Ellison's jazz hero Louis Armstrong made his first recordings.
Courtesy Niels Bohr Archive, Copenhagen.*

Joel E. Spingarn, chairman of the Board of Directors of the NAACP, in 1914 instituted the Spingarn Medal for outstanding achievement by an African American. Courtesy Special Collections and Archives, W. E. B. Du Bois Library, University of Massachusetts, Amherst.

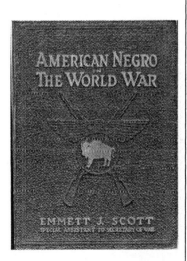

The participation of African Americans in World War I, documented by Emmett J. Scott, did not guarantee full citizenship rights at home, as the violence of the "Red Summer" of 1919 demonstrated. Photo by Steven C. Tracy.

1915   Marcel Duchamp generates the first dadaist paintings; D. W. Griffith's film *Birth of a Nation* premieres; Einstein postulates his general theory of relativity; Alexander Graham Bell places the first transcontinental telephone call; Ku Klux Klan receives charter from Fulton County (Georgia) Superior Court; Carter G. Woodson establishes the Association for the Study of Negro Life and History and *Journal of Negro History*; fifty-six African Americans are reported lynched.

1916   Angelina Weld Grimké publishes *Rachel*; Carl Sandburg publishes *Chicago Poems*; first birth control clinic opens in the United States; Marcus Garvey arrives in the United States and establishes the Universal Negro Improvement Association (UNIA).

1917   C. G. Jung publishes *Psychology of the Unconscious*; first jazz recordings made by the white Original Dixieland Jazz Band; Woodrow Wilson inaugurated president; United States enters World War I; T. S. Eliot publishes *Prufrock and Other Observations*; 10,000 people march down New York's Fifth Avenue to protest lynchings and racial injustice; thirty-six African Americans are reported lynched.

Blues singer Bessie Smith was the best of the female blues singers of the 1920s, an icon in the black community, and a figure mentioned by Ellison in a number of his works. Photo by Steven C. Tracy and William L. Taylor.

Scholars and folklorists began collecting slave narratives from slavery's survivors in the 1920s, culminating in the systematic work done for the Federal Writers Project. According to legend, Aunt Polly Jackson used a kettle of hot water and a butcher knife to battle slave catchers. Courtesy Ohio Historical Society.

1918   Oswald Spengler publishes *The Decline of the West*; Max Planck introduces quantum theory; race riots continue to break out; sixty African Americans are reported lynched.

1919   Sherwood Anderson publishes *Winesburg, Ohio*; W. E. B. Du Bois organizes the first Pan-African Congress; *Gospel Pearls* published by the National Baptist Convention; American Communist party established; Prohibition enacted; eighty-three African Americans are reported lynched in the "Red Summer of Hate."

1920   Eugene O'Neill publishes *The Emperor Jones*; Nineteenth Amendment grants woman suffrage; Mamie Smith records first commercial African-American blues songs; Mahatma Gandhi becomes leader in India's struggle for independence.

1921   KKK activities become brazenly violent across the South; *Shuffle Along* opens in New York City; Warren G. Harding inaugurated president; fifty-nine African Americans are reported lynched.

Recordings marketed to African Americans beginning in the 1920s were termed "race records" and sometimes carried ludicrous or racist illustrations. Photo by Steven C. Tracy and William L. Taylor.

A blues song folio from 1921 illustrates the craze for blues that helped to bring certain elements of African-American music into mainstream American culture. Photo by Steven C. Tracy and William L. Taylor.

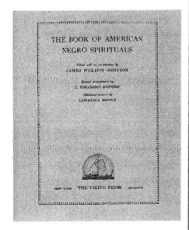

James Weldon Johnson's The Book of American Negro Spirituals (1925) was an important collection and discussion of the genre. Photo by Steven C. Tracy.

1922 James Joyce publishes *Ulysses*; T. S. Eliot publishes *The Waste Land*; Sinclair Lewis publishes *Babbitt*; James Weldon Johnson edits *The Book of American Negro Poetry*; Meta Vaux Warrick Fuller's *Ethiopia Awakening* exhibited in New York; Dyer antilynching bill passed in the House but filibustered in the Senate; discovery of the tomb of Tutankhamen; fifty-one African Americans are reported lynched.

Black nationalist Marcus Garvey promised repatriation to Africa aboard his Black Star steamship line, galvanizing the masses in the black community in a way similar to Ras the Exhorter in Invisible Man. *Photo courtesy Steven C. Tracy.*

1924   Ida marries James Ammons, who teaches Ellison how to hunt; Ammons dies within a year.

1926   Ellison joins Zelia Breaux's Junior and Senior High School Band; he and his friends adopt the ideal of the fifteenth-century Renaissance man as model for their behavior.

1929   Ida marries John Bell.

1930   Ellison begins taking trumpet lessons from Ludwig Hebestreit; familiarizes himself with local night spots and prominent jazz musicians, including the Blue Devils, which eventually evolve into the Count Basie Band with Jimmy Rushing and Lester Young.

1923   Jean Toomer publishes *Cane*; Wallace Stevens publishes *Harmonium*; *Runnin' Wild* introduces and popularizes the Charleston; George Gershwin premieres *Rhapsody in Blue*; Calvin Coolidge succeeds Harding as president.

1924   Ida Cox records "Wild Women Don't Have the Blues"; James Van Der Zee begins a photographic series dealing with Marcus Garvey and the UNIA; Lenin dies (b. 1870).

1925   F. Scott Fitzgerald publishes *The Great Gatsby*; Alain Locke edits *The New Negro*; Howard W. Odum and Guy B. Johnson publish *The Negro and His Songs*; Bessie Smith and Louis Armstrong record W. C. Handy's "St. Louis Blues"; Calvin Coolidge inaugurated president; Scopes "Monkey Trial" takes place.

1926   Ernest Hemingway publishes *The Sun Also Rises*; Carl Van Vechten publishes *Nigger Heaven*; Blind Lemon Jefferson records his first blues for Paramount Records; Aaron Douglas embarks on the Emperor Jones series of illustrations; twenty-three African Americans are reported lynched.

The short-lived Fire!! (1926) was an independent journal outlet for the more incendiary works of some Harlem Renaissance writers. Photo by Steven C. Tracy.

1932 Graduates from segregated Frederick Douglass High School, where he performed jazz and light classical music on soprano saxophone, trumpet, and other instruments in the school band and served as first-chair trumpeter and student conductor.

1933 Exits Oklahoma City via freight train and enters Alabama's Tuskegee Institute on a music scholarship under the direction of William L. Dawson; studies sculpture with Eva Hamlin.

1927 James Weldon Johnson publishes *God's Trombones*; Duke Ellington takes up residence at the Cotton Club; the first talking motion picture, *The Jazz Singer*, premieres; Charles Lindbergh flies the "Spirit of St. Louis" nonstop from New York to Paris; the Harlem Globetrotters are formed; Sacco and Vanzetti executed.

1935 Initiates an intensive study of modern literature, influenced by his reading of T. S. Eliot's *The Waste Land* and "Tradition and the Individual Talent," James Joyce's fiction, Jessie L. Weston's *From Ritual to Romance*, and George Frazer's *The Golden Bough*.

1936 Departs Tuskegee and arrives in New York City on 4 July; meets Langston Hughes; studies sculpture with Augusta Savage and Richmond Barthé; earns money to continue his studies at Tuskegee. He never returns, finding his meager wages from working as a food bar server, receptionist, file clerk, and factory worker insufficient to meet his tuition needs; initiates interest in leftist politics and radical literature; lives in Harlem.

1937 Ida dies in Cincinnati on 16 October, and Ellison remains for seven months in Dayton, Ohio; writes his first short story, "Hymie's Bull."

1938 Returns to New York; Hughes introduces Ellison to Richard Wright, who edits *New Challenge*, which publishes Ellison's first book review; establishes ties with musician Walter Riegger and immerses himself in the Harlem jazz scene; finds employment with Wright's assistance; collects and studies children's, urban, and industrial folklore for the Federal Writers Project in New York City (through 1942); marries Rose Poindexter on 17 September.

1928 Claude McKay publishes *Home to Harlem*; Nella Larsen publishes *Quicksand*; Stephen Vincent Benet publishes *John Brown's Body*; Ravel's *Bolero* premieres; Oscar DePriest elected first African-American congressman from a northern state; Archive of American Folk Songs established.

1929 Virginia Woolf publishes *A Room of One's Own*; William Faulkner publishes *The Sound and the Fury*; Archibald Motley paints *Blues*; Einstein propounds the unified field theory; "Black Friday" stock market crash; Herbert Hoover inaugurated president.

1930 Hart Crane publishes *The Bridge*; Augusta Savage sculpture *Gamin* completed; Grant Wood paints *American Gothic*; Pluto discovered; Nation of Islam founded by W. D. Fard.

1931 George S. Schuyler publishes *Black No More*; James Weldon Johnson publishes *Black Manhattan*; Edgar Varèse premieres *Ionisation*; Scottsboro Boys convicted of raping two white women in Alabama.

1932 Aldous Huxley publishes *Brave New World*; Sterling Brown publishes *Southern Road*; Wallace Thurman publishes *Infants of the Spring*; Amelia Earhart becomes first woman to fly solo across the Atlantic.

Death certificate for Ida Bell, listing her son Ralph Ellison as informant. Photo by Steven C. Tracy.

1939 His first published short story, "Slick Gotta Learn," appears in the September issue of *Direction*; begins publishing (through 1942) reviews and essays in leftist periodicals such as *New Masses*.

1940 Differing artistic sensibilities cause Ellison to cease showing his work to Wright; short story "The Birthmark" appears in *The Best Stories of 1940*.

1941 Short story "Mister Toussan" published in *New Masses*.

1942 Appointed *Negro Quarterly's* managing editor.

1933 W. B. Yeats publishes *Collected Poems*; James Weldon Johnson publishes *Along This Way*; Nathaniel West publishes *Miss Lonelyhearts*; Leadbelly makes his first recordings for the Library of Congress; Franklin Delano Roosevelt inaugurated president; Adolf Hitler appointed German chancellor; Roosevelt's New Deal programs initiated.

1934 Nancy Cunard edits *Negro: An Anthology*; Aaron Douglas paints *Aspects of Negro Life*; Du Bois resigns position at NAACP.

Miles Davis was one of the bop musicians of the 1940s who interested Ellison and who continued to develop over his varied career. Photo by Ed Tracy.

1943 *New York Post* publishes his coverage of the Harlem race riot; becomes cook in the U.S. Merchant Marines (through 1945); short story "That I Had the Wings" published in *Common Ground*.

1944 Encouraged to write a novel through a Rosenwald Foundation Fellowship; short stories "King of the Bingo Game," "In a Strange Country," and "Flying Home" published.

1945 In summer, in a barn in Waitsfield, Vermont, on sick leave from the merchant marines, begins *Invisible Man*; "Richard Wright's Blues," a critique of *Black Boy* published in the *Antioch Review*, solidifies Ellison's reputation as a literary critic.

1935 Clifford Odets publishes *Waiting for Lefty*; Zora Neale Hurston publishes *Mules and Men*; George Gershwin premieres *Porgy and Bess*; Roosevelt signs Social Security Act; Mary McLeod Bethune founds the National Council of Negro Women; Federal Writers Project established (1935–1939); Harlem riots.

1936 William Faulkner publishes *Absalom, Absalom!*; Archibald Motley paints *Saturday Night Street Scene*; Jesse Owens wins four gold medals at the Berlin Olympics; Mary McLeod Bethune receives the first major appointment of an African-American woman in the federal government, director of Negro Affairs of the National Youth Administration; Federal Theatre Project established (1936–1939).

1937 Zora Neale Hurston publishes *Their Eyes Were Watching God*; Pablo Picasso completes *Guernica*; Jacob Lawrence begins Toussaint L'Ouverture series; Frank Whittle builds first jet engine; William H. Hastie becomes first African-American federal judge; Joe Louis becomes world heavyweight boxing champion.

Ellison acknowledged that the personality of William Bunch, who recorded from 1930 to 1941 under the name Peetie Wheatstraw, influenced his portrayal of the blueprint man in Invisible Man. *Photo courtesy Paul Garon.*

1946   Marries Fanny McConnell Buford, at the time executive director of the American Center for Burma; continues writing *Invisible Man* while freelancing as a writer, photographer, and electronics technician; becomes interested in existentialist philosophy.

1947   Opening chapter of *Invisible Man* published as a short story in British journal *Horizon*.

1938   Thornton Wilder publishes *Our Town*; Richard Wright publishes *Uncle Tom's Children*; first "From Spirituals to Swing" concerts at Carnegie Hall; Supreme Court rules that University of Missouri Law School must admit African Americans due to lack of other facilities in area; establishment of the forty-hour work week in the United States.

1939   John Steinbeck publishes *The Grapes of Wrath*; World War II begins (1939–1945).

The house where Harriet Beecher Stowe first began to collect information for her controversial Uncle Tom's Cabin, *a novel which was vilified in James Baldwin's "Everybody's Protest Novel" in 1949, still stands as a historical monument in Cincinnati. Photo by Steven C. Tracy.*

1951   Completes first full draft of *Invisible Man* at the home of friends Stanley Edgar Hyman and Shirley Jackson in Westport, Connecticut; Langston Hughes dedicates *Montage of a Dream Deferred* to Ralph and Fanny Ellison.

1952   *Invisible Man* published.

1953   Wins National Book Award, Russwurm Award of the National Newspaper Publishers, and the Certificate of Award from the *Chicago Defender*; publishes the essay "Twentieth-Century Fiction and the Black Mask of Humanity."

1954   Wins Rockefeller Foundation Award; embarks on a lecture tour in Germany and lectures in Austria at the Salzburg Seminar; publishes short story "Did You Ever Dream Lucky?"

1940   Ezra Pound publishes *Cantos*; Richard Wright publishes *Native Son*; Eugene O'Neill publishes *Long Day's Journey into Night*; Robert Hayden publishes *Heart-Shape in the Dust*; Lascaux caves with prehistoric wall paintings discovered in France; troop integration ruled out for morale reasons by FDR; Benjamin O. Davis appointed first African-American general in the U.S. armed forces.

1941   Supreme Court rules that separate railroad car facilities must be substantially equal; United States enters World War II after attack on Pearl Harbor; threat of protest march by African Americans prompts FDR to issue Executive Order 8802, prohibiting discrimination in defense industries.

1955 Receives the Prix de Rome Fellowship from the American Academy of Arts and Letters to work on his second novel; tours and lectures for two years in Italy.

1957 Becomes vice president of the National Institute of Arts and Letters.

1958 Employed at Bard College as instructor of Russian and American literature (through 1961); initiates work on the Hickman stories.

1960 "And Hickman Arrives" published; with this, Ellison's much-anticipated second novel begins appearing in periodicals, though he never completes it.

1962 Serves as Alexander White Visiting Professor at the University of Chicago; visiting professor at Rutgers, teaching creative writing (through 1969); visiting fellow, American Studies, Yale University (through 1964).

1963 Receives Russwurm National Newspaper Publishers Award and honorary doctorate of humane letters from Tuskegee Institute; responds to Irving Howe's criticism of his work by publishing the first part of "The World and the Jug" in the *New Leader*.

1942 Margaret Walker publishes *For My People*; Albert Camus publishes *L'Etranger*; first issue of *Negro Digest* published; development of the first automatic computer in the United States; Congress of Racial Equality (CORE) organized in Chicago.

1943 First one-man show by Jackson Pollock; Paul Robeson stars in Theatre Guild production of *Othello* on Broadway; singer-saxophonist Louis Jordan dominates rhythm-and-blues charts for the next eight years; race riots break out in Mobile, Beaumont, Detroit, and Harlem; zoot suits and jitterbugging gain widespread popularity.

1944 Lillian Smith publishes *Strange Fruit*; Melvin B. Tolson publishes *Rendezvous with America*; Aaron Copland writes *Appalachian Spring*; Supreme Court rules that "white primaries" excluding African Americans are unconstitutional; Adam Clayton Powell elected first African-American congressman from the East; Rayford Logan publishes *What the Negro Wants*; Gunnar Myrdal publishes *An American Dilemma*.

1964   *Shadow and Act* published; delivers Gertrude Clark Whittall Lecture at the Library of Congress and Ewing Lectures at the University of California.

1965   Book Week poll names *Invisible Man* the most distinguished American novel published since World War II; declines opportunity to participate in New School for Social Research Black Writers Conference; publishes the short story "Juneteenth."

1966   Receives honorary doctorate from Rutgers; lectures at Yale University and the Library of Congress.

1967   Much of the 368-page manuscript of Ellison's second novel is destroyed by a fire on 29 November at Ellison's summer home in the Berkshires near Pittsfield, Massachusetts; receives honorary doctorates from the University of Michigan and Grinnell College; at the awards ceremony for an honorary doctorate from Grinnell College, student accosts Ellison, calling him an "Uncle Tom."

1945   George Orwell publishes *Animal Farm*; Richard Wright publishes *Black Boy*; Gwendolyn Brooks publishes *A Street in Bronzeville*; Guggenheim Museum designed by Frank Lloyd Wright; FDR dies and is succeeded by Harry Truman; United States drops atomic bombs on Hiroshima and Nagasaki; end of World War II; Charlie Parker's Reboppers record for the Savoy label.

1946   William Carlos Williams publishes *Paterson I*; Ann Petry publishes *The Street*; Mahalia Jackson does the first of her recordings for the Apollo label; Supreme Court bans segregation in interstate bus travel; Truman creates Committee on Civil Rights; first session of UN General Assembly held in London.

1947   Jean-Paul Sartre publishes *No Exit*; Alan Lomax tapes interview/discussion with Big Bill Broonzy, Memphis Slim, and Sonny Boy Williamson in New York City; discovery of the Dead Sea Scrolls; transistor invented by scientists at Bell Laboratories; Jackie Robinson becomes the first African-American major league baseball player in modern times.

James Brown's 1968 anthem "Say It Loud—I'm Black and I'm Proud" made Brown one of the "right on" people for some in the 1960s, while Ellison's cultural assimilationist stance put him on the bad foot with black militants. Photo courtesy Steven C. Tracy.

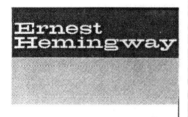

Ellison identified the prose of Hemingway as an important influence on his style, though by the time of this pirated edition of Hemingway's poems, the lionized Hemingway was on the brink of suicide. Photo by Steven C. Tracy.

1948   Norman Mailer publishes *The Naked and the Dead*; Theodore Roethke publishes *The Lost Son and Other Poems*; Dorothy West publishes *The Living Is Easy*; Alan Paton publishes *Cry, the Beloved Country*; World Council of Churches organized; Alfred C. Kinsey publishes *Sexual Behavior in the American Male*; equal treatment in the armed forces mandated by Truman in Executive Order 9981.

1949   George Orwell publishes *1984*; Truman inaugurated president.

1950   Gwendolyn Brooks is first African American to win Pulitzer Prize (for *Annie Allen*, 1949); Ralph Bunche is first African American to receive Nobel Peace Prize; emergence of anticommunist demagogue Joseph McCarthy; anti-apartheid riots in Johannesburg; outbreak of Korean War (1950–1953).

1951   J. D. Salinger publishes *Catcher in the Rye*; Benjamin Britten publishes *Billy Budd*; Ralph Bunche appointed undersecretary to the United Nations.

Two major political activists in the black community, singer-actor Paul Robeson and scholar-writer W. E. B. Du Bois, in 1949. They belonged to the anticolonial Council of African Affairs and associated themselves with leftist causes, which resulted in their being blacklisted and harassed. Courtesy Special Collections and Archives, W. E. B. Du Bois Library, University of Massachusetts, Amherst.

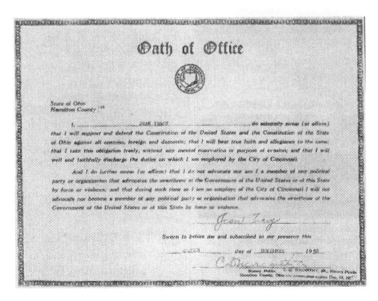

U.S. citizens sometimes signed oaths of fidelity to the government in the wake of the "red scare" of the McCarthy era. Photo by Steven C. Tracy.

1968 Anthology *Black Fire*, edited by Larry Neal and Amiri Baraka, published without selections from Ellison's works.

1969 On a visit to Oberlin College, Ellison is criticized by black students for his political, social, and artistic stances; President Johnson awards Ellison the Presidential Medal of Freedom.

1970 Begins a decade-long stint as Albert Schweitzer Professor of Humanities at NYU; awarded the Chevalier de l'Ordre des Artes et Lettres by French cultural affairs minister André Malraux; awarded honorary doctorate from Williams College.

1971 Appointed trustee of the Colonial Williamsburg Foundation; receives honorary doctorates from Adelphi University and Long Island University.

1972 Awarded honorary doctorate from the College of William and Mary.

1973 Publishes "Cadillac Flambé."

1974 Awarded honorary doctorates from the University of Maryland, Wake Forest University, and Harvard University.

1952 Ralph Ellison publishes *Invisible Man*; Ernest Hemingway publishes *The Old Man and the Sea*; Marianne Moore publishes *Collected Poems*; Samuel Beckett publishes *Waiting for Godot*; Revised Standard Version of the Bible published; according to a Tuskegee report, for the first time in seventy-one years, no lynchings occur in the United States.

1953 Arthur Miller publishes *The Crucible*; Melvin B. Tolson publishes *Libretto for the Republic of Liberia*; Gwendolyn Brooks publishes *Maud Martha*; James Baldwin publishes *Go Tell It on the Mountain*; execution of the Rosenbergs as spies; Simone de Beauvoir publishes *The Second Sex*; segregation banned in Washington, D.C., restaurants by Supreme Court; Dwight D. Eisenhower inaugurated president.

1954 Tennessee Williams publishes *Cat on a Hot Tin Roof*; segregated schools declared unconstitutional in *Brown v. Board of Education* decision; first annual Newport Jazz Festival held; Elvis Presley cuts his first commercial sessions for Sun Records.

Rhythm and blues of the 1940s–1960s was marketed to the white crossover market as rock and roll, complete with incongruous cover illustrations to attract consumers. Photo by Steven C. Tracy.

Scholar-activist W. E. B. Du Bois and Chinese Communist party chairman Mao Zedong greet each other at Mao's Wuhan villa in 1959. Courtesy Special Collections and Archives, W. E. B. Du Bois Library, University of Massachusetts, Amherst.

1955   James Baldwin publishes *Notes of a Native Son*; Flannery O'Connor publishes *A Good Man Is Hard to Find*; Marian Anderson debuts at the Metropolitan Opera House; Supreme Court orders school integration "with all deliberate speed"; Rosa Parks refuses to give up her seat on a Montgomery, Alabama, bus and triggers a 382-day-long bus boycott.

1956   Eugene O'Neill publishes *A Long Day's Journey into Night*; Allen Ginsberg publishes *Howl and Other Poems*; Montgomery bus boycott leader Martin Luther King, Jr.'s home is bombed; African-American artists and writers attend first international conference at the Sorbonne; Sudan becomes an independent state.

1975 Becomes member of the American Academy of Arts and Letters; Ralph Ellison Public Library opens in Oklahoma City.

1977 Publishes "Backwhacking: A Plea to the Senator."

1978 Echoing the *Book Week* poll of 1965, professors of American literature, in a *Wilson Quarterly* poll, designate *Invisible Man* the most important novel published in the United States since World War II; awarded honorary doctorate from Bard College.

Tennessee blues singer-guitarist Sleepy John Estes, who first recorded in 1929, would never have expected at that time that an African-American blues artist would tour Europe and release recordings on four-track tape, as he did during the 1960s blues revival. Photo by Steven C. Tracy.

1957 Jack Kerouac publishes *On the Road*; Dr. Seuss publishes *The Cat in the Hat*; Leonard Bernstein produces *West Side Story*; Southern Christian Leadership Conference organized; Ghana becomes an independent state; Civil Rights Act of 1957 establishes Civil Rights Commission and a division in the Justice Department; Arkansas governor Orval Faubus orders the National Guard to turn away African-American students from a Little Rock high school, prompting Eisenhower to send in federal troops to enforce desegregation orders.

1958 John Barth publishes *The End of the Road*; Archibald MacLeish publishes *J.B.*; bluesman Muddy Waters tours England and influences British musicians whose work will help feed American blues into the pop music mainstream in the 1960s and 1970s; first moon rocket launched by United States.

1959 Lorraine Hansberry publishes *A Raisin in the Sun*; Eugene Ionesco publishes *The Rhinoceros*; Newport Folk Festival influences generations of folk music performers by introducing such artists as Sonny Terry and Brownie McGhee, Lightnin' Hopkins, John Lee Hooker, Son House, Mississippi John Hurt, Skip James, Sleepy John Estes, and others on stage over the next eight years; Miles Davis records *Kind of Blue*; Berry Gordy, Jr., establishes Motown Records; Fidel Castro becomes premier of Cuba.

1980   Awarded honorary doctorate from Wesleyan and Brown universities.

1982   Publication of the thirtieth-anniversary edition of *Invisible Man*, including an introduction by Ellison; named Professor Emeritus at NYU.

1985   Awarded the National Medal of Arts.

1986   Publishes collection of reviews, addresses, and essays in *Going to the Territory*.

1994   Dies on 16 April of pancreatic cancer and is buried in Washington Heights; he and his wife had been residents on Riverside Drive in Harlem for more than forty years.

1995   *The Collected Essays of Ralph Ellison* published.

1996   *Flying Home and Other Stories* published.

1999   John Callahan's editing of the manuscripts for Ellison's second novel, *Juneteenth*, published.

1960   Harper Lee publishes *To Kill a Mockingbird*; sit-in movement initiated at Woolworth lunch counter in North Carolina; Student Non-Violent Coordinating Committee (SNCC) organized; Civil Rights Act of 1960 passed by Congress; numerous sections of Africa proclaimed independent.

1961   Joseph Heller publishes *Catch-22*; LeRoi Jones publishes *Preface to a Twenty-Volume Suicide Note* and *Dutchman*; James Baldwin publishes *Nobody Knows My Name*; Ornette Coleman records *Free Jazz*; John F. Kennedy inaugurated president; Bay of Pigs affair; Berlin Wall erected; Freedom Riders harassed and attacked in Alabama and Mississippi.

1962   Edward Albee publishes *Who's Afraid of Virginia Woolf*; Robert Hayden publishes *A Ballad of Remembrance*; James Baldwin publishes *Another Country*; John Glenn orbits the earth in a spacecraft; Telstar launched; Rachel Carson publishes *Silent Spring*; Supreme Court rules that the University of Mississippi must admit James Meredith; executive order issued by JFK bars discrimination in federally financed housing.

1963   LeRoi Jones publishes *Blues People*; Martin Luther King, Jr., writes "Letter from Birmingham Jail"; pop art exhibition at the Guggenheim; Medgar Evers assassinated; JFK assassinated; March on Washington culminates in a series of speeches at the Lincoln Memorial, including King's "I Have a Dream" speech.

1964   Saul Bellow publishes *Herzog*; Melvin B. Tolson publishes *Harlem Gallery*; Ralph Ellison publishes *Shadow and Act*; B. B. King records *Live at the Regal*; Organization of Afro-American Unity founded by Malcolm X; Civil Rights Act of 1964 includes public accommodations and fair employment sections; race riots widespread; Martin Luther King, Jr., wins the Nobel Peace Prize; Cassius Clay / Muhammad Ali becomes world heavyweight boxing champion; the Beatles initiate the "British invasion" of musical groups; Nelson Mandela sentenced to life in prison.

1965   Malcolm X and Alex Haley publish *The Autobiography of Malcolm X*; John Berryman publishes *77 Dream Songs*; Black Arts movement initiated by LeRoi Jones / Amiri Baraka and others in Harlem; Lyndon Baines Johnson inaugurated president; Malcolm X assassinated; LBJ signs Voting Rights Bill; United States sends troops to prevent South Vietnamese government from collapsing.

The Georgia-based Thunderbolt *magazine, organ of the National States' Rights party, vowed to "fight communism and race mixing" in the 1970s. Photo by Steven C. Tracy and William L. Taylor.*

1966   Sylvia Plath's *Ariel* is published; Thomas Pynchon publishes *The Crying of Lot 49*; Indira Gandhi becomes prime minister of India; Dakar, Senegal, hosts first world festival of African art; Stokely Carmichael named chairman of SNCC; Black Panther party and National Organization for Women established; CORE and SNCC espouse Black Power concept.

1967   William Styron publishes *Confessions of Nat Turner*; Ishmael Reed publishes *The Freelance Pallbearers*; Dr. Christiaan R. Barnard performs first human heart transplant; major race riots take place in Detroit, Newark, and Chicago; LBJ nominates first African-American Supreme Court justice, Thurgood Marshall.

1968   Martin Luther King, Jr., assassinated; Robert F. Kennedy assassinated.

1969   Richard M. Nixon inaugurated president; Duke Ellington presented with the Medal of Freedom; Apollo 11 astronaut Neil Armstrong walks on the moon.

1970   Four students killed by National Guard at Kent State University in Ohio during an antiwar demonstration.

1971   Louis Armstrong and Igor Stravinsky die; Lt. William L. Calley, Jr., convicted of premeditated murder at the My Lai massacre in Vietnam.

1972 Mahalia Jackson, Kwame Nkrumah, and Jackie Robinson die; the Watergate break-in and cover-up dominate the American political scene.

1973 Pablo Picasso and Arna Bontemps die; five original Watergate defendants plead guilty; Vice President Spiro T. Agnew resigns; beginning of the Arab oil embargo causes gas shortages in the United States.

1974 Duke Ellington and Darius Milhaud die; Nixon resigns and is later pardoned by President Gerald Ford.

1975 Josephine Baker dies; United States ends involvement in Vietnam War.

1976 Paul Robeson and Roland Hayes die; Saul Bellow receives Nobel Prize for literature; U.S. Air Force Academy breaks all-male tradition at U.S. military academies; anti-apartheid rioting in South Africa.

1977 Jimmy Carter inaugurated president; Steven Biko dies; British scientists identify a living organism's complete genetic structure.

1978 Jomo Kenyatta and William Grant Still die; Bakke "reverse discrimination" case.

1981   Ronald Reagan inaugurated president.

1982   Equal Rights Amendment fails to garner enough state ratifications after ten years.

1983   Alice Walker wins Pulitzer Prize for *The Color Purple*.

1984   The Reverend Jesse Jackson mounts serious campaign for U.S. presidency; Ronald Reagan visits China; Count Basie dies.

1985   Scientists collect evidence of a huge black hole in the middle of the galaxy.

1986   Federal holiday established for Martin Luther King's birthday; Desmond Tutu becomes first African-American archbishop of Cape Town; space shuttle *Challenger* explodes, killing crew; Wole Soyinka receives Nobel Prize for literature.

1987   James Baldwin dies; South Africa bans African National Congress (ANC) activities; surrogate mother loses case in Baby M trial.

1989   Massive pro-choice rally in Washington, D.C.; L. Douglas Wilder becomes first elected African-American governor; George H. W. Bush inaugurated president; Oliver North found guilty in Iran-Contra scandal.

1990 One in four Americans
claim non-European ancestry in
Census Bureau statistics; Nelson
Mandela is freed.

1991 Persian Gulf War;
confirmation of Clarence Thomas
as Supreme Court justice despite
Anita Hill's allegations of sexual
harassment.

1992 Acquittal of police in
Rodney King beating sets off riots
in Los Angeles; first African-
American woman, Carol Moseley
Braun, elected to U.S. Senate.

1993 Nobel Prize for literature
awarded for first time to an African
American, Toni Morrison; drawing
of congressional districts to
increase African-American
representation struck down by
Supreme Court; William Clinton
inaugurated president.

1994 National African-American
Leadership Summit meets in
Baltimore; Republican candidates
for House sign conservative reform
proposal "Contract with America."

Bibliographical Essay

Probing the Lower Frequencies:
Fifty Years of Ellison Criticism

Robert J. Butler

Who knows but that, on the lower
frequencies, I speak for you?
—Ralph Ellison, *Invisible Man*

Like most important American writers of the twentieth century, Ralph Ellison had a healthy suspicion of critics and critical schools, occasionally doing spirited battle with them but often simply ignoring them. In "Society, Morality, and the Novel," he declared that he had "for the most part, been content to keep out of the critics' domain," sensing that his work as a novelist was by its very nature opposed to the activity of the critics. While they were intent on developing "systems of thought," which resulted in a "formula" to "analyze" and "classify" reality as if it were a "pre-mixed apple pie" (GT 240), he regarded the writer's task as the recreation of life in its full density, richness, and complexity. Envisioning the writer's vocation in Promethean terms as "play[ing] with the fires of chaos" so that they could be rearranged "to the patterns of imagination" (GT 239), he was deeply suspicious of any critic, theory, or school which would cool down these fires (or extinguish them altogether) as a way of simplifying reality and thus making it more manageable. To use the metaphor which concludes his great novel, *Invisible Man*, Ellison usually saw critics as working on the "higher frequencies" of

233

reality, which would enable them to make clear but shallow statements *about* life while true writers focus their attention on the "lower frequencies" of life, which enables them to distill a more complex and disturbing truth from human experience.

Despite Ellison's long-term doubts about modern criticism and his occasional clashes with individual critics and schools, his work has been highly praised for more than fifty years by a wide variety of perceptive critics, writers, and scholars who have been remarkably well attuned to the lower frequencies of both his fiction and nonfiction. Since the publication of *Invisible Man* in 1952 to the appearance of several posthumously published writings in recent years, Ellison has been generally regarded as a major American writer who has made enormously important contributions to American, African-American, and modernist traditions. Early reviewers such as Saul Bellow, R. W. B. Lewis, and Alain Locke immediately sensed that *Invisible Man* was a seminal work which would provide many fruitful new directions for an entire generation of post–World War II writers. And novels such as Ken Kesey's *One Flew over the Cuckoo's Nest*, Joseph Heller's *Catch-22*, and Sylvia Plath's *The Bell Jar*, each of which was deeply influenced by Ellison's novel, certainly offer impressive evidence of the rightness of these claims. Over the years, Ellison's fiction and essays have continued to draw high critical praise while influencing a broad spectrum of important writers such as Ernest Gaines, Ishmael Reed, Clarence Major, Charles Johnson, and Toni Morrison. Ellison's writing surely has inspired, fascinated, and sometimes angered several generations of writers, scholars, and critics, but its literary and cultural importance are firmly established.

The critical response to Ellison's work should be understood in terms of the historical milieu in which it was produced since all of Ellison's writing speaks to very specific cultural circumstances, even while transcending them. Although Ellison often reminded his readers that he wanted to distill universal meanings while capturing "the basic unity of human experience" (*SA* 129), he never tired of reminding us that this could only be done by fully exploring the historical times and specific cultural circumstances which he experienced as a modern African-American writer. Likewise, the critical reception of all of Ellison's work is heavily conditioned by some of the main historical trends and crises of modern American culture, most notably the Cold War, the Civil Rights movement, the Black Power movement, and the feminist movement.

The critical response to Ellison's work can thus be roughly divided into four main time periods: (1) the early reviews of *Invisible Man*, (2) scholarly articles and chapters in books written from the mid-1950s to the late 1960s, (3) commentary produced from the late 1960s to the late 1970s, and (4) critical and scholarly work from the early 1980s to the present. As is always the case, these periods should be seen as helpful but somewhat arbitrary markers which can help us to detect main trends in Ellison scholarship. But they are not by any means objective and empirically reliable boundaries which can allow us to categorize the critical responses into absolutely neat but artificial patterns. (Those constructing a history of Ellison scholarship must be mindful of the author's deep mistrust of abstract formulae, what he characterized as "the pre-mixed apple pie.") Certain continuities clearly do cohere in all phases of Ellison criticism, and overlapping of critical interests and judgments are more the rule than the exception. As the narrator of *Invisible Man* reminds us, the end can be found in the beginning, and reality moves more like a boomerang than an arrow. Nevertheless, the critical response to Ellison's work has developed in roughly discernible phases, producing revealing patterns which, however shifting and blurry, still have meaning.

Ellison's career as a writer began in the late 1930s with reviews published in leftist journals such as *New Masses* and *New Challenge* and continued throughout the 1940s as he published ten stories and thirty-seven essays on literature, music, culture, and politics. None of this literary activity drew any critical attention, but when *Invisible Man* appeared in 1952 it generated an extraordinary outpouring of largely positive responses from a wide variety of influential critics, who hailed Ellison as a fresh voice who was destined to make important contributions to American, African-American, and modernist traditions.

Saul Bellow, for example, characterized *Invisible Man* as "a book of the first order," which "is immensely moving and has greatness" (608). Bellow argued that Ellison's book reinvigorated the modern novel by providing a new voice which connected African-American experiences to universal themes in Western literature. R. W. B. Lewis observed that *Invisible Man* equaled Faulkner's best work and, like Bellow, praised the book for transcending narrowly racial and political concerns in favor of exploring broadly American and modernist themes. Richard Chase was deeply impressed by the novel's "sheer richness of invention" (683) and placed Ellison's writing firmly in the main tradition of the American, British, and European novel. Alain Locke examined *Invisible Man* in the context of African-American literature, ranking it, along with Richard Wright's *Native Son* and Jean Toomer's *Cane*, as one of the three high points of achievement in black fiction. Sensing *Invisible Man* as a "great novel" (34), Locke predicted it would change the course of African-American literature. William Barrett welcomed *Invisible Man* as a novel which was deeply rooted in the masterworks of European modernism, such as Céline's *Journey to the End of Night*. Characterizing the novel as "a book that just misses greatness," he envisioned a bright future for its author: "I do not see that we can set any limits now to how far Ellison may yet go in the novel" (104).

There were some dissenting reports in the early reviews of *Invisible Man*, but these negative assessments were relatively few in number and came mainly from two sources: ideologically driven critics and critics who were not sufficiently aware of the fresh techniques which Ellison employed to capture some of the new features of post–World War II American life, especially as that life affected a younger generation of African Americans. Marxist critics, for example, faulted the novel for straying from and even attacking the assumptions of leftist criticism and politics which had informed Ellison's earlier work. Abner Berry and Irving Howe complained that the novel presented a crudely stereotyped view of the Communist party. Lloyd Brown, a black novelist writing for the leftist journal *Masses and Mainstream*, objected to what he felt was a negative view of the black working classes, characterizing Ellison as a "Judas" (64) who had betrayed his people. Several other black reviewers also made serious criticisms of the novel, claiming that it failed to express African Americans adequately. John O. Killens, for instance, regarded the novel as a "vicious distortion of Negro life" and concluded that "the Negro people need Ralph Ellison's *Invisible Man* like we need a hole in the head or a stab in the back" (12). Marguerite D. Cartwright's *Amsterdam News* review, similarly, accused Ellison of defaming black people by providing an essentially hopeless portrait of the African-American condition.

Reviewers who accused Ellison of providing a negative vision of black life failed to grasp how Ellison was breaking new ground in using African-American music and folk materials to actually celebrate black culture in impressively affirmative ways. Langston Hughes was one of the few reviewers sensitive to this important aspect of Ellison's art. In his *New York Age* review of *Invisible Man* he enthusiastically praised the book as a "deep, beautifully written, provocative and moving" (13) portrait of African-American experience.

The reviews of *Invisible Man* emphatically ended the virtual anonymity of Ellison's first fifteen years as a writer and established a framework for the lively critical debate about Ellison's work which continues to the present day. Taken as a whole, they raise the following questions, which have driven much of Ellison scholarship over the past fifty years. To what extent is *Invisible Man* a seminal work which has reinvigorated American, African-American, and modernist traditions? How successfully has Ellison represented the cultural life and historical experience of black people in America? Has he been able to connect fruitfully black life with the life of other cultures, thus universalizing it? Or has Ellison's attempt to broaden his vision of black experience by perceiving its connections to other traditions had the opposite effect of diluting it and thus led him to a betrayal of his responsibilities as a black writer? Is Ellison's deep suspicion of organized politics a strength or a weakness? Has it resulted in an irresponsible withdrawal from public life, as Marxist critics have alleged, or has it provided us with a tough-minded critique of the political

failures and betrayals which have characterized so much of twentieth-century history? Is Ellison an antipolitical writer, or does
he provide a positive answer to the question posed so powerfully
in *Invisible Man*: "Could politics ever be an expression of love?"
(452).

The next phase of Ellison scholarship, which extended from
the mid-1950s to the end of the Civil Rights movement in the late
1960s, provided largely positive answers to the above questions.
For the most part, Ellison's reputation rose during this period as
a large number of articles in journals and chapters in books
praised Ellison for both his formal artistry and the subtlety and
amplitude of his vision. A few negative estimates appeared during this time, but they were clearly a minority viewpoint and
were overshadowed greatly by the positive assessments and prestigious awards which began to pour in. *Invisible Man* won the National Book Award for fiction in 1953, and a national poll sponsored by *Book Week* in 1965 selected *Invisible Man* as the most
important American novel to appear since 1945. Ellison won several other significant awards during this period, including a
Rockefeller Foundation Award in 1954 and the Presidential Medal
of Freedom in 1969.

Some of the most important critical studies of the American
novel published from the mid-1950s to the late 1960s devoted
significant space and extravagant praise to *Invisible Man*. R. W. B.
Lewis's 1955 seminal study of classic American literature, *The
American Adam*, ranked *Invisible Man* with Bellow's *The Adventures
of Augie March* and Salinger's *Catcher in the Rye* as the three most
outstanding American novels produced after World War II. Leslie
Fiedler's *Love and Death in the American Novel* five years later
praised the book for its technical artistry and argued that its vision
of American life surpassed the achievement of previous black
novelists. Robert Bone's groundbreaking *The Negro Novel in
America* characterized Ellison as a major American writer and
cited *Invisible Man* as a pivotal work in African-American literature. Jonathan Baumbach's 1965 study of contemporary American
fiction compared Ellison favorably with writers in the absurdist
tradition such as Kafka, West, Camus, and Faulkner, assessing *Invisible Man* as one of the four best novels written since 1945.

This period produced a growing number of scholarly articles which began laying the groundwork for the book-length studies which would emerge in later decades by connecting *Invisible Man* to a number of important traditions. Esther Merle Jackson's "The American Negro and the Image of the Absurd" placed the novel in the existential tradition and made particularly apt comparisons with Faulkner's *Light in August* and Wright's *Native Son*. Gene Bluestein's "The Blues as Literary Theme" examined Ellison's literary use of blues themes and techniques. Two other influential studies focused on how Ellison drew from two closely related comic traditions. Earl Rovit's 1960 essay "Ralph Ellison and the American Comic Tradition" described *Invisible Man* as a comic work growing out of comic masterpieces such as Melville's *The Confidence Man* and Whitman's "Song of Myself." Floyd Horowitz's "Ralph Ellison's Modern Version of Brer Brer and Brer Rabbit in *Invisible Man*" appeared three years later and carefully analyzed Ellison's roots in African-American folklore. For Horowitz, Invisible Man is a descendant from a long line of black trickster heroes dating back to the oral literature of the slaves.

Ellison's literary stock, therefore, rose steadily in the ten years following the publication of *Invisible Man*, but in 1963 Irving Howe published "Black Boys and Native Sons," which made a serious attack on Ellison's art and vision of American life. Howe chided Ellison for abandoning the tradition of black protest literature brought to a culmination by Richard Wright in favor of a mode of writing which was excessively literary and self-indulgently individualistic. Howe's essay therefore echoed the objections made in early reviews of *Invisible Man* by leftists such as Killens, Berry, and Brown, who alleged that Ellison had reneged upon his responsibilities as a black writer by aligning himself with mainstream modernists who valorized a stance of alienation which justified their abandoning social and political commitments.

Ellison was quick to respond to Howe in two masterfully argued essays published in the *New Leader*, which were later included in *Shadow and Act* as a single essay entitled "The World and the Jug." He reminded Howe that black writers, like all writers, have literary options which include but extend beyond the limits of protest fiction. Ellison stressed that black life in America is too richly varied and complex to be contained in a single literary mode. Sharply contesting Howe's claim that unrelieved suffering is the only "real" Negro experience, Ellison pointed out that there is a long tradition in African-American culture of mastering pain by transforming it into genuine art. Such art, which Ellison found not only in black musical forms such as the spirituals, blues, and jazz but also in black religious expression and folk art, produces a "fullness" and "richness" of Negro life which eloquently demonstrates the "humanity" (*SA* 119) of black people which rarely gets expressed in protest fiction.

In thus freeing himself from what he believed was an obsolete naturalistic tradition of protest literature which was inadequate to express the complexities and possibilities of the post–World War II American world, Ellison also stressed emphatically that he was not abandoning his political and social responsibilities as an African-American writer. He made it clear in his response to Howe that he was not rejecting protest in his art but was instead intent on not *limiting* his art to protest. He did insist that art can indeed "reject" and "destroy" what is unjust in a given society, and he emphasized his lifelong battle against American racism and his endorsement of the freedom movement. But he strongly emphasized that genuine art must be as many-faceted as life itself and declared that the black writer must have the artistic freedom to explore life in all of its dimensions. Ellison finally claimed that protest may be an important element in art but art itself can never be reduced to simple protest. Instead, art arises "out of an impulse to celebrate human life," and it therefore must "preserve" as it "destroys," "affirm" as it "rejects" (*SA* 121).

In the next phase of Ellison scholarship, which ran roughly from the late 1960s to the late 1970s, the sort of objections made by Howe became more prominent. The reasons for this can be found by examining the enormous cultural shifts that took place during the thirty-five years following World War II. The early years of the Cold War, with its deep suspicion in the academic community of mass culture and its recoil from the organized politics of the McCarthy era, clearly produced a favorable environment to receive an existentially centered novel such as *Invisible Man*. And the Civil Rights movement, which moved into high gear just a few years after Ellison's novel was published, also created the kind of moral and intellectual climate which would favor Ellison's work. Clearly, *Invisible Man* is closely in tune with the core values of the freedom movement, emphatically rejecting violence and celebrating the ideal of a fully integrated America where all people would be "visible" and responsible to each other since, on the lower frequencies, they had similar needs and drives. Then too, the novel's extended meditation on the central importance of love and its wish that politics could somehow be transformed so that it could be "an expression of love" (*IM* 452) was also solidly in harmony with the freedom movement.

But by 1966 and for many years thereafter, a major shift occurred in black cultural and political life which led to a negative reassessment of Ellison's writing, especially among a younger generation of African-American militants, writers, and intellectuals. Politically, this resulted in the Black Power movement, with its emphasis on black nationalism and revolutionary violence, both of which Ellison emphatically rejected. Culturally, this resulted in the Black Arts movement, which envisioned art as a weapon that must be put to the service of producing revolutionary changes in American society—ideals for which Ellison had little enthusiasm. Neither movement, of course, was likely to produce an environment where Ellison's work could get a fair hearing and, in fact, both movements produced a number of strong attacks on Ellison's writing.

Perhaps the clearest example of this hostile response is a 1967 piece by Ernest Kaiser entitled "Negro Images in American Writing." Kaiser faults Ellison for being "an establishment writer" (152) who has positioned his work in the mainstream of American culture and who therefore has both denied his vital roots as a black person and turned a cold shoulder to African-American protest literature. Another vivid sign of this shift in the critical response to Ellison's work can be found in a poll taken in 1968 by

Negro Digest which asked young black writers to characterize their relationship to African-American writers of previous generations. Although some of them expressed admiration for Ellison and cited *Invisible Man* as a work which strongly influenced their own fiction, the majority were critical of Ellison and saw themselves as influenced by politically engaged figures such as Richard Wright. According to John Reilly, these younger writers "did not speak of Ellison as an author to be emulated," and several regarded him as "irrelevant" (8).

It is important to realize, however, that not all black writers and critics of this period shared this negative assessment. Novelist James Alan McPherson in 1970 voiced deep admiration for Ellison's ability to recreate black American experience in a broad, nuanced, and balanced way, emphasizing both its unique characteristics and its relationship to American culture in general. McPherson noted that a growing number of young black writers, including Michael Harper, Ernest Gaines, Ishmael Reed, and Al Young, were strongly influenced by Ellison's work. Larry Neal, who in 1968 characterized Ellison's fiction as outdated because it was mired in mainstream angst, two years later dramatically reversed this view in an influential article published in *Black World*. Arguing that much of the criticism directed against Ellison was either "personal or oversimplified" or rooted in "a specific body of Marxian or Black Neo-Marxist thought," he emphatically rejected the "ideological sources" of his earlier criticism of Ellison and characterized *Invisible Man* as "one of the world's greatest novels" (31, 50).

Two other influential black critics, George Kent and Houston Baker, also had high praise for Ellison during this period. In a special *College Language Association Journal* number devoted to Ellison in 1970, Kent supported the author's rejection of narrowly political conceptions of race and his transcending the thinly "rhetorical" racial ideas of the many young "radical" writers of the period. Although Kent expressed reservations about Ellison's refusal to acknowledge the African roots of black American experience, he nevertheless honored him as a writer who expressed "a deep sense of the beauty as well as the terror of Black tradition" (268). Indeed, Kent ascribed an "almost god-like knowledge of

Blackness" (275) to Ellison. Baker in 1974 likewise viewed *Invisible Man* as a rich and complex work of art which had deep roots in black literary and folk traditions dating back to the spirituals and slave narratives. Far from being a conservative text arising out of a decadent white modernism, Ellison's novel was for Baker a pivotal work in African-American literature which portrays both "the spirit of black culture and the liberation of its citizens" (*Singers* 30).

If the critical response to Ellison's writing by black critics during this period was a complex mixture of conflicting attitudes, the reactions by other writers during this time was nearly unanimous in its praise. William Schafer and Thomas Vogler wrote influential articles exploring the formal artistry and thematic complexities of *Invisible Man*. Tony Tanner's 1971 study of contemporary American fiction, *City of Words*, devoted an important chapter to Ellison's novel, claiming that it was "the most profound novel about American identity written since the war" (51). Many other studies emerging at this time focused sharply on a matter which would continue to fascinate Ellison scholars for many years to come: his skillful artistic uses of modernist, American, Afro-American, and European literary traditions. Archie Sanders examined the parallels between *The Odyssey* and *Invisible Man*; Charles Scruggs explored Ellison's self-conscious use of *The Aeneid*; and Marcia Lieberman probed connections between Ellison's novel and *Candide*. Other critics produced valuable source studies connecting Ellison with various American writers. Leonard Deutsch argued that Ellison's moral vision was rooted in Emerson's essays while Martin Bucco examined the author's Oklahoma background, discussing how western images and symbols are used in *Invisible Man*. Valerie Bonita Gray's 1978 book provided an in-depth analysis of Melville's pervasive influence on Ellison's vision.

Work done in the 1950s, 1960s, and 1970s therefore provided a solid foundation for the more elaborate and detailed studies which emerged in later decades. By the late 1970s, it was clear that reviews, articles, chapters from books, and special issues of journals were not sufficient to capture the full scope of Ellison's art. Book-length studies were needed to bring Ellison scholarship closer to maturity.

Robert O'Meally's *The Craft of Ralph Ellison* was published in 1980 and became one of the foundational blocks upon which much subsequent scholarship was based. Containing a wealth of previously undisclosed biographical information, it was a balanced and incisive examination of Ellison's writing from apprentice pieces published in the late 1930s to works in progress of the late 1970s. O'Meally argued persuasively that Ellison's greatest achievement was his masterful fusion of black folk expression with the sophisticated techniques of high modernist art. The book's superb central chapter, a close reading of *Invisible Man*, explored how "an intricate pattern of folk forms," including the blues, gospel music, sermons, and toasts, are "woven through the fabric" (79) of the novel to produce a richly textured celebration of African-American experience. The book also contained sensitive analyses of Ellison's short fiction and essays while making astute observations on the "big" novel, on which Ellison continued to work for the remainder of his life.

Several other important books on Ellison were published in the last two decades of the twentieth century. Robert List's *Dedalus in Harlem* (1982) was an extremely valuable study which traced Joyce's influence on Ellison's fiction, particularly in terms of how both writers made brilliant use of folk materials and how they had similar conceptions of the hero as trickster and artist. Rudolf Dietze's *Ralph Ellison: The Genesis of an Artist* (1982) examined a variety of literary influences but was particularly strong in demonstrating how Ellison was powerfully affected by Malraux's conception of the modern artist. Alan Nadel's *Invisible Criticism* (1988) investigated Ellison's writing in the light of postmodern critical theory, arguing that it redefined the American canon in ways that created new space for black writers. Mark Busby's *Ralph Ellison* (1991) also made a cogent argument for Ellison as an important shaping influence on American literary tradition, claiming that "Ellison charted new frontiers in American literature" (144) by integrating a wide range of literary and folk traditions. Busby's book offered a particularly valuable discussion of

Ellison's careful use of the comic techniques of American frontier humor and also offered useful analyses of Ellison's short fiction and essays.

Some critics in the 1990s continued to fault Ellison for drawing
too heavily on mainstream traditions and, as a result, failing to
give an adequate representation of African-American experience.
For example, Jerry Gafio Watts's *Heroism and the Black Intellectual:
Ralph Ellison, Politics, and Afro-American Intellectual Life* (1994) reit-
erated many of the complaints of black militants of the 1960s
and 1970s, arguing that Ellison's admiration for masterworks of
white modernism resulted in him recoiling into an elitist alienation which cut him off from the realities of contemporary black
experience. But many other black writers and critics of this period aligned themselves with Ellison, regarding him as a seminal
influence. Charles Johnson regarded *Invisible Man* as "something
of the modern Ur-text for black fiction" (*Being* 15), which has,
along with the Black Arts movement, defined one of the two
major directions for contemporary black writing. Leon Forrest,
Clarence Major, and Toni Morrison have also expressed considerable admiration for Ellison's fiction and have seen him as a model
for younger black writers as they search for alternatives to
mimetic fiction.

This period also witnessed a number of books on African-
American literature which featured important chapters on Ellison. Keith Byerman's *Fingering the Jagged Grain* (1985) provided an
in-depth analysis of the dialectical nature of Ellison's art, using
an open narrative as a means of generating a ceaseless flow of
new ideas which become the basis of a protean conception of
self. Valerie Smith's *Self-Discovery and Authority in Afro-American
Literature* (1987) came to a similar conclusion, offering a subtle
discussion of how first-person narration is used in *Invisible Man*
to dissolve fixed, stereotyped notions so that the central character can finally be liberated by an open, indeterminate identity
which he creates with his own consciousness and will. Melvin
Dixon's *Ride Out the Wilderness* (1987) explored how Ellison uses
underground settings and images of flight to express themes
which go to the heart of African-American tradition.

John F. Callahan's *In the African-American Grain* (1988) took issue with those who accused Ellison of grounding his art in a white aesthetic which valorizes excessive individualism. Callahan instead argued convincingly that Ellison's work is centered in a distinctively African-American tradition of call-and-response, which harmonizes individual expression with the voice and values of the community. Such a narrative strategy, which is firmly grounded in black religious and musical discourse dating back to the time of slavery, generates a powerful conversation between the self and the public world which is essential to the life of a healthy democracy. Linking the individual with a meaningful social world, this "narrative discourse of democratic possibility" (257) endows Ellison's writing with an energy, coherence, and resonance often missing in mainstream fiction.

Since the 1980s, Ellison studies also benefited from some of the theoretical approaches to literature which became prominent during this time. The chapter on Ellison in Houston Baker's *Blues, Ideology, and Afro-American Literature* (1984) applied post-structuralist methods to a close reading of the Trueblood episode in *Invisible Man*, finding that Trueblood's extraordinary artistic abilities enable him to deconstruct the "systems of signs" (176) which the dominant culture uses to imprison him. For Baker, Trueblood becomes a "cosmic creator" (183) who can serve as a liberating model for the novel's central character. Henry Louis Gates's *Figures in Black* (1987) used *Invisible Man* as a vivid illustration of the concept of "signifying," a mode of discourse at the heart of black literary and musical traditions which both repeats and artfully revises previous discourse, thereby creating fresh meanings which are distinctively black. Gates saw Ellison as "our Great Signifier" (244), someone who made use of previous texts such as *The Odyssey*, *Up from Slavery*, and *Native Son* as a means of creating a new African-American art of extraordinary power.

Feminist scholars also responded to Ellison's fiction, sometimes celebrating it and at other times criticizing it. In 1989, Hortense Spillers complained that Ellison's female characters are crudely stereotyped because his narratives are filtered through a male consciousness which is insensitive to the experiences of women. Mary Rohrberger, in a similar way, faulted Ellison for portraying female characters as "one-dimensional figures playing roles in a drama written by men" (130). Claudia Tate, on the other hand, found that a careful reading of *Invisible Man* revealed that Ellison's women play roles which are surprisingly more important than at first seems to be the case. For Tate, these characters usually are introduced as simplified types but eventually are endowed with an individualized humanity which enables them to become teachers who inspire the novel's central character to liberating forms of awareness and action.

The last two decades of the twentieth century were also significant for a wide variety of studies of how Ellison's art arose from a wide range of cultural forces and circumstances. Thomas Schaub's new historicist study of post–World War II fiction, *American Fiction in the Cold War* (1991), devoted a chapter to *Invisible Man* and *Shadow and Act* which claimed that Ellison's theory and practice arose out of a disillusionment with leftist politics of the 1930s and a desire to formulate a new vision of African-American life which was consistent with post–World War II realities and possibilities. Berndt Ostendorf's "Ralph Waldo Ellison: Anthropology, Modernism, and Jazz" envisioned Ellison's art as grounded in three factors: modernist theory, African-American folklore, and jazz. Whereas Ellison's commitments to highly individualistic theory and the essentially communal practice of folklore were a source of possible artistic conflict, jazz supplied him with a richly satisfying synthesis of these two extremes, mediating as it does between high art and popular art. For Ostendorf, jazz is a musical form which enabled Ellison to "square the circle of intellectual excellence and group loyalty" (117).

Several other superb studies of Ellison's sophisticated use of black music also appeared in this period. Thomas Marvin's 1996 article "Children of Legba: Musicians at the Crossroads in Ellison's *Invisible Man*" focused on Ellison's use of a motif which has great importance in African-American folklore and music, a crossroads setting which is presided over by a wise *griot* named Papa Legba, who dispenses wisdom and special powers to young persons at pivotal moments in their lives. Identifying characters such as Trueblood and the yam vendor as well as historical figures such as Louis Armstrong and Frederick Douglass as people who performed the role of Papa Legba, Marvin concluded that Invisible Man is able to negotiate successfully the various crossroads of his life by finally understanding and acting upon the folk wisdom given to him by these liminal figures.

Steven Tracy also penetrated deeply into Ellison's vision of African-American life by accessing it through the rich complexities of the blues tradition. Drawing revealing parallels between a historical figure named Peetie Wheatstraw, who was a prominent East St. Louis blues singer of the 1930s, and the fictional character who sings a blues song at the beginning of chapter 9 in *Invisible Man*, Tracy made a convincing argument for viewing this episode as especially important because it telescopes many of the novel's core themes as well as dramatizing in a lucid way what Invisible Man must do in order to achieve genuine identity. The fictional Wheatstraw became for Ellison a mythic figure who distills the wisdom of the blues experience by combining "individual freedom" and "group traditions" (63), neither of which the novel's protagonist understands by chapter 9 but which he finally realizes, in the epilogue, hold the keys to his identity. Both a bad-man figure who rebels against a repressive society and a trickster figure who "used the system to defeat the system" (55), Wheatstraw became for Ellison the kind of existential hero which Invisible Man must ultimately aspire to be.

Several fresh directions in Ellison scholarship were created following the author's death in 1994. The most important new development was John Callahan's editing of three books and his co-editing, with Albert Murray, Ellison's long correspondence with Murray. *The Collected Essays of Ralph Ellison* (1995) conflated *Shadow and Act* and *Going to the Territory*, while including eleven previously published but uncollected essays and nine significant pieces that appeared in print for the first time. *Flying Home and Other Stories* (1996) included recently uncovered apprentice pieces such as "A Party Down at the Square," "Boy on a Train," and "I Did Not Learn Their Names," as well as masterworks like "Flying Home" and "King of the Bingo Game." Ellison's long-awaited second novel, *Juneteenth*, appeared in 1999, and *Trading*

Twelves: The Selected Letters of Ralph Ellison and Albert Murray was published in 2000.

These four important books provided scholars with a rich storehouse of valuable materials and contain much new knowledge that will generate fresh readings of Ellison's work as well as significant insights into his life. To date, *Juneteenth* has drawn the most vigorous critical attention, sparking a debate which should continue for many years. Louis Menand complained that the book was lacking in coherence, a "Frankenstein monster" (4) created by a literary executor who stitched together an assortment of manuscript fragments from a projected three-volume novel which Ellison could never complete. Max Brzezinski described *Juneteenth* as a "rather powerful, captivating fragment" (119). But several important critics hailed the novel as an impressive literary achievement which would occupy a significant place in American and African-American letters. For example, Robert O'Meally, in "How Can the Light Deny the Dark?" praised *Juneteenth* not only for its "Ellisonian zest, depth, and resonance" but also for its formal control, arguing that "the work holds together as a complete, aesthetically satisfying, and at times, thrilling whole" (89). In his preface to the novel, Charles Johnson, likewise, had high praise for the book, which he described as a "many splendored" (xv) novel that adds to Ellison's "literary legacy" (xv) by extending and deepening the meanings of *Invisible Man*. For Johnson, *Juneteenth* is an especially significant work for twenty-first-century readers; he regards its deeply multicultural vision as precisely the kind of literature "we have needed for decades to refine our discourse on race" (xv).

The past fifty years of Ellison scholarship have produced an enormous body of criticism which has firmly established Ellison as a major writer who has made lasting contributions to American, African-American, and modernist traditions. But much serious work needs to be done if we are to gain a truly comprehensive understanding of Ellison's remarkable achievement. As John Callahan has observed, "There's work to be done, facts to be tracked, stories to be gathered and preserved, connections to be made, interpretations to be offered" ("American Scholar(s)" 12). Now that they have been expertly gathered and edited, Ellison's short stories and essays await the sustained critical analysis and evaluation which they have long deserved but not received. Critics have barely scratched the surface of Ellison's extraordinary second novel, *Juneteenth*, and other significant fiction could be forthcoming from the materials now cataloged in the Library of Congress. Moreover, *Invisible Man*, as closely as it has been studied, is far from exhausted. Certainly much more needs to be said about Ellison's envisioning of female experience and how feminine values are a crucial aspect of this vision. Postmodern critical approaches, such as new historicism and reader-response criticism, provide promising but as yet underutilized perspectives on Ellison's many-layered and historically situated fiction. Lawrence Jackson's *Ralph Ellison: Emergence of Genius* (2002) is the first biography of Ellison, but this impressive study calls out for more biographical investigation into Ellison's life from other perspectives and after 1953.

Ellison, who always regarded himself as the product of a western upbringing and who never tired of reminding us that America was a place of limitless possibilities, once remarked that "the territory ahead is an ideal place—ever to be sought, ever to be missed, but always there" (Callahan, "American Scholar(s)," 12). In the same way, the literary frontier he opened up and explored in his remarkable career is still a wide open space awaiting our careful attention, not a dusty museum in need of cataloging.

SELECTED BIBLIOGRAPHY

Collections of Essays

Benston, Kimberly W., ed. *Speaking for You: The Vision of Ralph Ellison*. Washington, D.C.: Howard University Press, 1987.

Bloom, Harold, ed. *Ralph Ellison*. New York: Chelsea House, 1986.

Butler, Robert J. *The Critical Response to Ralph Ellison*. Westport, Conn.: Greenwood, 2000.

Gottesman, Ronald, ed. *The Merrill Studies in* Invisible Man. Columbus, Ohio: Merrill, 1971.

Hersey, John, ed. *Ralph Ellison: A Collection of Critical Essays*. Englewood Cliffs, N.J.: Prentice Hall, 1970.

O'Meally, Robert G., ed. *New Essays on* Invisible Man. New York: Cambridge University Press, 1988.

Parr, Susan Resneck, and Pancho Savery, eds. *Approaches to Teaching Ellison's* Invisible Man. New York: Modern Language Association, 1989.

Reilly, John M., ed. *Twentieth-Century Interpretations of* Invisible Man. Englewood Cliffs, N.J.: Prentice Hall, 1970.

Trimmer, Joseph, ed. *A Casebook on Ralph Ellison's* Invisible Man. New York: Crowell, 1972.

Special Issues of Journals

Carleton Miscellany 18 (1980).
CLA Journal 13 (Mar. 1970).
Delta (Montpellier, France) 18 (1984).
Oklahoma City Law Review 26 (Fall 2001).

Parts of Books and Chapters in Books

Baker, Houston A., Jr. *Blues, Ideology, and Afro-American Literature: A Vernacular Theory.* Chicago, Ill.: University of Chicago Press, 1984.

———. *The Journey Back: Issues in Black Literature and Criticism.* Chicago, Ill.: University of Chicago Press, 1980.

———. *Singers at Daybreak.* Washington, D.C.: Howard University Press, 1974.

Baumbach, Jonathan. *The Landscape of Nightmare: Studies in the Contemporary American Novel.* New York: New York University Press, 1965.

Bone, Robert. *The Negro Novel in America.* New Haven, Conn.: Yale University Press, 1965.

———. "Ralph Ellison and the Uses of the Imagination." In *Anger and Beyond*, edited by Herbert Hill, 86–111. New York: Harper and Row, 1966.

Bryant, Jerry. *The Open Decision: The Contemporary American Novel and Its Intellectual Background.* New York: Free Press, 1969.

Butler, Robert. "The City as Psychological Frontier in Ralph Ellison's *Invisible Man* and Charles Johnson's *Faith and the Good Thing.*" In *The City in African-American Literature*, edited by

Yoshinobu Hakutani and Robert Butler. Teaneck, N.J.: Fairleigh Dickinson University Press, 1995.

Byerman, Keith. *Fingering the Jagged Grain: Tradition and Form in Recent Black Fiction*. Athens: University of Georgia Press, 1985.

Callahan, John F. "Frequencies of Eloquence: The Performance of Composition of *Invisible Man*." In *New Essays on Invisible Man*, edited by Robert O'Meally, 54–94. New York: Cambridge University Press, 1988.

———. *In the African-American Grain: The Pursuit of Voice in Twentieth-Century Black Fiction*. Urbana: University of Illinois Press, 1988.

Christian, Barbara. "Ralph Ellison: A Critical Study." In *Black Expression*, edited by Addison Gayle, Jr., 353–65. New York: Weybright and Tally, 1969.

Cooke, Michael G. *Afro-American Literature in the Twentieth Century: The Achievement of Literacy*. New Haven, Conn.: Yale University Press, 1984.

Dietze, Rudolf F. "Ralph Ellison and the Literary Tradition." In *History and Tradition in African-American Culture*, edited by Gunter H. Lenz, 18–29. Frankfurt: Campus Verlag, 1984.

Dixon, Melvin. *Ride Out the Wilderness*. Urbana: University of Illinois Press, 1987.

Fiedler, Leslie A. *Love and Death in the American Novel*. New York: Stein and Day, 1960.

Gates, Henry Louis, Jr. *The Signifying Monkey: A Theory of African-American Literary Criticism*. New York: Oxford University Press, 1988.

———. *Figures in Black: Words, Signs, and the Racial Self*. New York: Oxford University Press, 1987.

Harper, Michael S., and Robert B. Stepto, eds. *Chant of Saints: A Gathering of Afro-American Literature, Art, and Scholarship*. Urbana: University of Illinois Press, 1979.

Hassan, Ihab. *Radical Innocence: Studies in the Contemporary American Novel*. Princeton, N.J.: Princeton University Press, 1961.

Howe, Irving. "Black Boys and Native Sons." In *A World More Attractive*, 98–122. New York: Horizon, 1963.

Johnson, Charles. *Being and Race: Black Writing since 1970*. Bloomington: Indiana University Press, 1990.

———. Preface to Ralph Ellison, *Juneteenth*. New York: Vintage, 2000.

Jones, LeRoi, and Larry Neal, eds. *Black Fire: An Anthology of Afro-American Writing*. New York: William Morrow and Son, 1968.

Klein, Marcus. *After Alienation*. Cleveland, Ohio: World, 1965.

Klotman, Phyllis Rauch. *Another Man Gone: The Black Runner in Contemporary Afro-American Fiction*. Port Washington, N.Y.: Kennikat, 1977.

Lewis, R. W. B. *The American Adam*. Chicago: University of Chicago Press, 1955.

Margolies, Edward. *Native Sons: A Critical Study of Twentieth-Century Negro American Authors*. Philadelphia, Pa.: Lippincott, 1968.

Murray, Albert. *The Omni-Americans*. New York: Avon, 1971.

Ostendorf, Berndt. "Ralph Waldo Ellison: Anthropology, Modernism, and Jazz." In *New Essays on Invisible Man*, edited by Robert O'Meally, 95–122. Cambridge: Cambridge University Press, 1988.

Petesch, Donald A. *A Spy in the Enemy's Country*. Iowa City: University of Iowa Press, 1989.

Reilly, John M. "The Testament of Ralph Ellison." In *Speaking for You: The Vision of Ralph Ellison*, edited by Kimberly W. Benston, 49–62. Washington, D.C.: Howard University Press, 1987.

Rogers, Lawrence R. *Canaan Bound: The African-American Great Migration Novel*. Urbana: University of Illinois Press, 1997.

Rohrberger, Mary. "'Ball the Jack': Surreality, Sexuality, and the Role of Women in *Invisible Man*." In *Approaches to Teaching Ellison's* Invisible Man, edited by Susan Resneck Parr and Pancho Savery. New York: Modern Language Association, 1989.

Rosenblatt, Roger. *Black Fiction*. Cambridge, Mass.: Harvard University Press, 1974.

Schaub, Thomas. *American Fiction in the Cold War*. Madison: University of Wisconsin Press, 1991.

———. "Ellison's Masks and the Novel of Reality." In *New Essays on Invisible Man*, edited by Robert O'Meally, 123–56. New York: Cambridge University Press, 1988.

Scruggs, Charles. *Sweet Home: Invisible Cities in the Afro-American Novel*. Baltimore, Md.: Johns Hopkins University Press, 1993.

Smith, Valerie. "The Meaning of Narration in *Invisible Man*." In *New Essays on Invisible Man*, edited by Robert O'Meally, 25–54. New York: Cambridge University Press, 1988.

――――. *Self-Discovery and Authority in Afro-American Literature.* Cambridge, Mass.: Harvard University Press, 1987.

Spillers, Hortense. "'The Permanent Obliquity of an In(pha)llibly Straight': In the Time of the Daughters and the Fathers." *Changing Our Own Words: Essays on Criticism, Theory, and Writing by Black Women,* edited by Cheryl A. Wall, 127–49. New Brunswick, N.J.: Rutgers University Press, 1989.

Stepto, Robert B. *From behind the Veil: A Study of Afro-American Narrative.* Urbana: University of Illinois Press, 1979.

Tanner, Tony. *City of Words: American Fiction, 1959–1970.* New York: Harper and Row, 1971.

Tate, Claudia. "Notes on the Invisible Woman in Ralph Ellison's *Invisible Man.*" In *Speaking for You: The Vision of Ralph Ellison,* edited by Kimberly W. Benston, 163–72. Washington, D.C.: Howard University Press, 1987.

Tracy, Steven. "Ellison's Molotov Cocktail Party and All that Modernist Jazz." In *T. S. Eliot and the Heritage of Africa,* edited by Robert F. Fleissner, 178–86. New York: Peter Lang, 1992.

Wright, John. "The Conscious Hero and the Rites of Man." In *New Essays on Invisible Man,* edited by Robert O'Meally, 157–86. New York: Cambridge University Press, 1988.

Books

Busby, Mark. *Ralph Ellison.* Boston: Twayne, 1991.

Dietze, Rudolf F. *Ralph Ellison: The Genesis of an Artist.* Nuremberg: Verlag Hans Carl, 1982.

Gray, Valerie Bonita. Invisible Man*'s Literary Heritage:* Benito Cereno *and* Moby-Dick. Amsterdam: Rodopi, 1978.

Jackson, Lawrence Patrick. *Ralph Ellison: Emergence of Genius.* New York: Wiley, 2002.

List, Robert N. *Dedalus in Harlem: The Joyce-Ellison Connection.* Washington, D.C.: University Press of America, 1982.

McSweeney, Kerry. Invisible Man: *A Student's Companion to the Novel.* Boston: Twayne, 1988.

Nadel, Alan. *Invisible Criticism: Ralph Ellison and the American Canon.* Iowa City: University of Iowa Press, 1988.

O'Meally, Robert. *The Craft of Ralph Ellison.* Cambridge, Mass.: Harvard University Press, 1980.

Reilly, John M. *Twentieth-Century Interpretations of* Invisible Man. Englewood Cliffs, N.J.: Prentice Hall, 1970.

Schor, Edith. *Visible Ellison: A Study of Ralph Ellison's Fiction*. Westport, Conn.: Greenwood, 1993.

Sundquist, Eric. *Cultural Contexts for* Invisible Man. Boston: St. Martin's, 1995.

Watts, Jerry Gafio. *Heroism and the Black Intellectual: Ralph Ellison, Politics, and Afro-American Intellectual Life*. Chapel Hill: University of North Carolina Press, 1994.

Articles

Abrams, Robert E. "The Ambiguities of Dreaming in Ellison's *Invisible Man*." *American Literature* 49 (Jan. 1978): 592–603.

Anderson, Jervis. "Going to the Territory." *New Yorker* 22 (22 Nov. 1976): 55–108.

Baker, Houston. "To Move without Moving: An Analysis of Creativity and Commerce in Ralph Ellison's Trueblood Episode." *PMLA* 98 (Oct. 1983): 828–45.

Barrett, William. "Black and Blue: A Negro Céline." *American Mercury* 74, no. 342 (June 1952): 100–104.

Bellow, Saul. "Man Underground." *Commentary* 13 (June 1952): 608–10.

Benston, Kimberly. "Ellison, Baraka, and the Faces of Tradition." *Boundary* 2, no. 6 (Winter 1978): 333–54.

Blake, Susan L. "Ritual and Rationalization: Black Folklore in the Works of Ralph Ellison." *PMLA* 94 (1979): 121–36.

Bluestein, Gene. "The Blues as Literary Theme." *Massachusetts Review* 8 (1967): 593–617.

Brown, Lloyd. "The Deep Pit." *Masses and Mainstream* 5 (June 1952): 62–64.

Brzezinski, Max. "Juneteenth." *Antioch Review* 58 (Winter 2000): 119.

Bucco, Martin. "Ellison's Invisible West." *Western American Literature* 10 (1975): 237–38.

Butler, Robert. "Dante's *Inferno* and Ellison's *Invisible Man*: A Study in Literary Continuity." *CLA Journal* 28, no. 1 (Sept. 1984): 54–77.

———. "Down from Slavery: Invisible Man's Descent into the City and the Discovery of Self." *American Studies* 29, no. 2 (Fall 1988): 57–67.

————. "Patterns of Movement in Ellison's *Invisible Man.*" *American Studies* 31, no. 1 (Spring 1980): 5–21.

————. "The Plunge into Pure Duration: Bergsonian Visions of Time in Ellison's *Invisible Man.*" *CLA Journal* 33, no. 3 (Mar. 1990): 260–79.

Callahan, John F. "The American Scholar(s): Inaugural Address of the Morgan C. Odell Professorship in the Humanities," 14 March 1995, Lewis and Clark College, Portland, Ore.

————. "Democracy and the Pursuit of Narration." *Carleton Miscellany* 18, no. 3 (Winter 1980): 51–69.

————. "Piecing Together Ralph Ellison's Unfinished Work." *Chronicle of Higher Education* 43 (1996): B3–B4.

Cartwright, Marguerite. "Review of *Invisible Man.*" *Amsterdam News*, 7 Mar. 1953, 20.

Chase, Richard. "A Novel Is a Novel." *Kenyon Review* 14 (Autumn 1952): 678–84.

Chisholm, Lawrence. "Signifying Everything." *Yale Review* 54, no. 3 (Spring 1965): 450–54.

Clipper, Lawrence J. "Folklore and Mythic Elements in *Invisible Man.*" *CLA Journal* 13 (Mar. 1979): 239–54.

Cohn, Deborah. "To See or Not to See: Invisibility, Clairvoyance and Revisions of History in *Invisible Man* and *La casa de les espiritus.*" *Comparative Literature Studies* 33, no. 4 (1996): 372–95.

Collier, Eugenia. "The Nightmare Truth of an Invisible Man." *Black World* 20 (Dec.1970): 12–19.

Deutsch, Leonard. "Ellison's Early Fiction." *Negro American Literature Forum* 7 (Summer 1973): 53–59.

————. "Ralph Waldo Ellison and Ralph Waldo Emerson: A Shared Moral Vision." *CLA Journal* 16 (1972): 160–73.

Dixon, Melvin. "O Mary Rambo, Don't You Weep." *Carleton Miscellany* 78 (Winter 1980): 98–104.

Doyle, Mary Ellen. "In Need of Folk: The Alienated Protagonists of Ralph Ellison's Short Fiction." *CLA Journal* 20, no. 2 (Dec. 1975): 165–72.

Dupre, F. W. "On *Invisible Man.*" *Book Week (Washington Post)* 26 (Sept. 1965): 4.

Fass, Barbara. "Rejection of Paternalism: Hawthorne's 'My Kinsman, Major Molineux' and Ellison's *Invisible Man.*" *CLA Journal* 14 (1971): 317–23.

Forrest, Leon. "Luminosity from the Lower Frequencies." *Carleton Miscellany* 18, no. 3 (Winter 1980): 82–97.

Frank, Joseph. "Ralph Ellison and a Literary 'Ancestor': Dostoevski." *New Criterion* (Sept. 1983): 140–52.

Goede, William. "On Lower Frequencies: The Buried Men in Wright and Ellison." *Modern Fiction Studies* 15 (1969): 483–501.

Gordon, Gerald T. "Rhetorical Strategies in Ralph Ellison's *Invisible Man*." *Rocky Mountain Review* 41 (1987): 199–209.

Harding, James M. "Adorno, Ellison, and the Critique of Jazz." *Cultural Critique* 31 (Fall 1995): 129–58.

Harris, Trudier. "Ellison's Peter Wheatstraw: His Basis in Folk Tradition." *Mississippi Folklore Register* 6 (1975): 117–26.

Herman, David. "Ellison's 'King of the Bingo Game': Finding Naturalism's Trap Door." *English Language Notes* 29, no. 1 (Sept. 1991): 71–74.

Horowitz, Floyd. "The Enigma of Ellison's Intellectual Man." *CLA Journal* 7 (Dec. 1963): 126–32.

———. "Ralph Ellison's Modern Version of Brer Bear and Brer Rabbit in *Invisible Man*." *Midcontinent American Studies Journal* 4 (1963): 21–27.

Hughes, Langston. "Review of *Invisible Man*." *New York Age* 28 (28 Feb. 1953): 12–13.

Hyman, Stanley Edgar. "Ralph Ellison in Our Time." *New Leader* 47, no. 22 (26 Oct. 1964): 21–22.

Jackson, Esther Merle. "The American Negro and the Image of the Absurd." *Phylon* 23 (Winter 1962): 359–71.

Kaiser, Ernest. "A Critical Look at Ellison's Fiction and at Social and Literary Criticism by and about the Author." *Black World* 20, no. 2 (Dec. 1970): 53–59, 81–97.

———. "Negro Images in American Writing." *Freedom Way* 7 (Spring 1967): 152–63.

Kent, George. "Ralph Ellison and the Afro-American Folk and Cultural Tradition." *CLA Journal* 13, no. 3 (Mar. 1970): 265–76.

Killens, John O. "Review of *Invisible Man*." *Freedom* (June 1952): 10–13.

Kostelanetz, Richard. "The Politics of Ellison's Booker: *Invisible Man* as Symbolic History." *Chicago Review* 19, no. 2 (1967): 5–26.

Lee, Kun-Jong. "Ellison's *Invisible Man*: Emersonianism Revisited." *PMLA* 107, no. 2 (Mar. 1992): 331–44.

————. "Racial Variations on American Themes." *African-American Review* 30, no. 3 (Fall 1996): 421–40.

Lewis, R. W. B. "The Ceremonial Imagination of Ralph Ellison." *Carleton Miscellany* 18, no. 3 (Winter 1980): 34–38.

————. "Review of *Invisible Man*." *Hudson Review* 6, no. 1 (Spring 1953): 148–49.

Lieberman, Marcia R. "Moral Innocents: Ellison's *Invisible Man* and *Candide*." *CLA Journal* 15 (Sept. 1971): 64–79.

Locke, Alain. "From *Native Son* to *Invisible Man*: A Review of the Literature of the Negro for 1952." *Phylon* 14 (Spring 1953): 34–35.

Lyne, William. "The Signifying Modernist: Ralph Ellison and the Limits of the Double Consciousness." *PMLA* 107, no. 2 (Mar. 1992): 319–30.

Marvin, Thomas F. "Children of Legba: Musicians at the Crossroads in Ellison's *Invisible Man*." *American Literature* 68, no. 3 (Sept. 1996): 587–608.

McPherson, James Alan. "Indivisible Man." *Atlantic* 226, no. 6 (Dec. 1970): 45–60.

Menand, Louis. "Unfinished Business." *New York Times Book Review*, 20 June 1999, 4, 6.

Mengeling, Marvin. "Walt Whitman and Ellison: Older Symbols in a Modern Mainstream." *Walt Whitman Review* 12 (Sept. 1966): 67–70.

Neal, Larry. "Ellison's Zoot Suit." *Black World* 20, no. 2 (Dec. 1970): 31–50.

O'Meally, Robert G.. "How Can the Light Deny the Dark?" *Atlantic Monthly* (July 1999): 89–94.

————. "The Rules of Magic: Hemingway as Ellison's 'Ancestor.'" *Southern Review* 21 (1985): 751–69.

Ostendorf, Berndt. "Ralph Ellison's 'Flying Home': From Folk Tale to Short Story." *Journal of the Folklore Institute* 13, no. 2 (1976): 185–99.

Parrish, Timothy. "Ralph Ellison, Kenneth Burke, and the Form of Democracy." *Arizona Quarterly* 51, no. 3 (Autumn 1995): 117–48.

Pinckney, Darryl. "The Drama of Ralph Ellison." *New York Review of Books* 44, no. 8 (15 May 1997): 52–60.

Reed, Brian. "The Iron and the Flesh: History as Machine in Ellison's *Invisible Man*." *CLA Journal* 37, no. 3 (Mar. 1994): 261–73.

Rovit, Earl H. "Ralph Ellison and the American Comic Tradition."
 Wisconsin Studies in Contemporary Literature 1 (1960): 34–42.

Sale, Roger. "The Career of Ralph Ellison." *Hudson Review* 19 (Spring
 1965): 124–28.

Sanders, Archie. "Odysseus in Black: An Analysis of the Structure of
 Invisible Man." *CLA Journal* 13 (Mar. 1970): 217–28.

Schafer, William J. "Ralph Ellison and the Birth of the Anti-Hero."
 Critique: Studies in Modern Fiction 10 (1968): 81–93.

Schultz, Elizabeth A. "The Illumination of Darkness: Affinities
 between *Moby-Dick* and *Invisible Man.*" *CLA Journal* 32 (Dec.
 1988): 170–200.

Scruggs, Charles. "Ralph Ellison's Use of *The Aeneid* in *Invisible
 Man.*" *CLA Journal* 17 (Mar. 1974): 368–78.

Sisney, Mary F. "The Power and Horror of Whiteness: Wright and
 Ellison Respond to Poe." *CLA Journal* 29 (Sept. 1985): 82–90.

Skerrett, Joseph T., Jr. "The Wright Interpretation: Ralph Ellison and
 the Anxiety of Influence." *Massachusetts Review* 21 (1980):
 196–212.

Staples, Brent. "In His Own Good Time." *New York Times Book
 Review,* 3 Aug. 1986, 15.

Stepto, Robert. "Literacy and Hibernation: Ralph Ellison's *Invisible
 Man.*" *Carleton Miscellany* 18, no. 3 (Winter 1980): 112–41.

Tracy, Steven. "The Devil's Son-in-Law and *Invisible Man.*" *MELUS*
 15, no. 3 (1988): 47–64.

Trimmer, Joseph. "Ralph Ellison's 'Flying Home.'" *Studies in Short
 Fiction* 9 (Spring 1972): 175–82.

Tuttleton, James W. "The Achievement of Ralph Ellison." *New Criterion* 14, no. 4 (Dec. 1995): 5–10.

Vogler, Thomas. "Somebody's Protest Novel." *Iowa Review* 1 (Spring
 1970): 64–82.

Walling, William. "'Art' and 'Protest': Ralph Ellison's *Invisible Man*
 Twenty Years After." *Phylon* 34 (June 1973): 120–34.

Walsh, Mary Ellen Williams. "*Invisible Man*: Ralph Ellison's Wasteland." *CLA Journal* 28 (1984): 150–58.

Wilner, Elenor R. "The Invisible Black Thread: Identity and Nonen-
 tity in *Invisible Man.*" *CLA Journal* 13 (1970): 242–57.

Wright, John. "Dedicated Dreamer, Consecrated Acts: Shadowing
 Ellison." *Carleton Miscellany* 18, no. 3 (Winter 1980): 142–99.

Interviews

Carson, David L. "Ralph Ellison: Twenty Years After." *Studies in American Fiction* 1 (Spring 1973): 1–23.

Cohen, Ted, and N. A. Samstag. "An Interview with Ralph Ellison." *Phoenix* 22 (Fall 1961): 4–10.

Garrett, George, ed. *The Writer's Voice: Conversations with Contemporary Writers*. New York: Morrow, 1973.

Geller, Allen. "An Interview with Ralph Ellison." In *The Black American Writer*. Vol. 1: *Fiction*, edited by C. W. E. Bigsby. Baltimore, Md.: Penguin, 1969.

Graham, Maryemma, and Amritjit Singh. *Conversations with Ralph Ellison*. Jackson: University Press of Mississippi, 1995.

Hersey, John. "'A Completion of Personality': A Talk with Ralph Ellison." In *Speaking for You*, edited by Kimberly W. Benston, 285–307 (Washington, D.C.: Howard University Press, 1987).

O'Brien, John. *Interviews with Black Writers*. New York: Liveright, 1973.

Reed, Ishmael, Quincy Troupe, and Steve Cannon. "The Essential Ellison." *Y'Bird Reader* 1 (1978): 126–59.

Remnick, David. "Visible Man." *New Yorker*, 14 Mar. 1994, 34–38.

Stepto, Robert B., and Michael S. Harper. "Study and Experience: An Interview with Ralph Ellison." In *Chant of Saints*, edited by Michael S. Harper and Robert B. Stepto, 451–69 (Urbana: University of Illinois Press, 1979).

Welburn, Ron. "Ralph Ellison's Territorial Vantage." *Grackle* 4 (1977–1978): 5–15.

Contributors

ROBERT J. BUTLER is professor of English and director of the College Honors program at Canisius College and editor of *The Critical Response to Ralph Ellison* (2000). He is author or editor of five books dealing with African-American literature, including *Richard Wright's Native Son: The Emergence of a New Black Hero* (1991) and *Making a Way out of No Way: The Open Journey in Contemporary African-American Literature* (1998). He has also published extensively on American and African-American writers in journals such as the *Centennial Review, African-American Review, American Studies, CLA Journal,* and *MELUS.* Professor Butler is currently engaged with writing about Ellison's posthumously published stories and *Juneteenth,* and has served as advisory editor for *African-American Review* since 1995.

MARYEMMA GRAHAM, professor of English at the University of Kansas, is co-editor of *Conversations with Ralph Ellison.* Founder and director of the Project on the History of Black Writing, Graham has taught at the University of Mississippi, Northeastern University, and Harvard, where she was also a Du Bois fellow. Recipient of fellowships from the American Committee of Learned Societies, the Schomburg Center for Research in Black Culture, and the Ford Foundation, she has received numerous grants and awards from the National Endowment for the Humanities and other public and private foundations. Her most recent books include the *Cambridge Companion to the African-American Novel* (2004), *Conversations with Margaret Walker* (2002), and *Fields Water with Blood: Critical Essays on Margaret Walker* (2001). Currently she is completing *The House Where Soul Lives: The Life of Margaret Walker*.

LAWRENCE P. JACKSON is assistant professor of English and African-American studies at Emory University, where he specializes in African-American literature and literary history. He is the author of the critically acclaimed biography *Ralph Ellison: Emergence of Genius* (2002). Professor Jackson has published articles in *American Literature*, *African-American Review*, and *Massachusetts Review*. He holds a Ph.D. in English and American literature from Stanford University. He is a recipient of grants and fellowship awards from the National Endowment for the Humanities and the Ford Foundation, and he has been a resident fellow at Harvard University's W. E. B. Du Bois Institute.

JEFFERY DWAYNE MACK is currently a Ph.D. student at the University of Kansas studying African-American literature, with an emphasis on the construction of black masculinity. Prior to coming to the University of Kansas, Mack taught at York College, Winthrop University, and at Floyd College, where he is currently an associate professor of English. He has received numerous fellowships and scholarships, such as the Lyman T. Johnson Fellowship and the University System of Georgia Summer Institute Award, and has published numerous poems and short stories.

WILLIAM J. MAXWELL is associate professor of English and Interpretive Theory and director of English graduate studies at the University of Illinois, Urbana-Champaign, where he teaches modern American and African-American literature. He is the author of the award-winning book *New Negro, Old Left: African-American Writing and Communism between the Wars* (1999) and the editor of Claude McKay's *Complete Poems* (2004).

ALAN NADEL is professor of literature and film at Rensselaer Polytechnic Institute. Nadel is the author of *Invisible Criticism: Ralph Ellison and the American Canon* (1988), *Containment Culture: American Narratives, Postmodernism, and the Atomic Age* (1996), and *Flatlining on the Field of Dreams: Cultural Narratives in the Films of President Reagan's America* (1997), and editor of *May All Your Fences Have Gates: Essays on the Drama of August Wilson* (1995). He has won prizes for the best essay in *Modern Fiction Studies* and *PMLA*.

JAMES SMETHURST is an assistant professor in the W. E. B. Du Bois Department of Afro-American Studies at the University of Massachusetts, Amherst. He is the author of *The New Red Negro: The Literary Left and African-American Poetry, 1930–1946* (1999). His most recent project is *The Rise of the Black Arts Movement and Literary Nationalism in the 1960s and 1970s* (forthcoming). He is also the co-editor of *Left of the Color Line: Race, Radicalism, and Twentieth-Century Literature of the United States* (2003).

STEVEN C. TRACY is professor of Afro-American studies at the University of Massachusetts, Amherst, and a blues singer and harmonica player. He is the author of *Langston Hughes and the Blues* (1988), *Going to Cincinnati: A History of the Blues in the Queen City* (1993), and *A Brush with the Blues* (1997); general co-editor of *The Collected Works of Langston Hughes* (2001–); and editor of *Write Me a Few of Your Lines: A Blues Reader* (2001), *Work for Children and Young Adults*, volume 12 in *The Collected Works of Langston Hughes* (2001), and *A Historical Guide to Langston Hughes* (2003). He has recorded with Steve Tracy and the Crawling Kingsnakes, Big Joe Duskin, Pigmeat Jarrett, Albert Washington, and the Cincinnati Symphony Orchestra, and opened for such artists as B. B. King, Muddy Waters, Sonny Terry and Brownie McGhee, Bo Diddley, and others.

Index

265

LaVergne, TN USA
01 March 2010
174582LV00003B/21/A